THE MUSIC ROOM

The Music Room

A STORY OF ART, FRIENDSHIP, AND GATHERING IN BETTY FREEMAN'S BEVERLY HILLS HOME

Jake Johnson

OXFORD
UNIVERSITY PRESS

OXFORD
UNIVERSITY PRESS

Oxford University Press is a department of the University of Oxford.
It furthers the University's objective of excellence in research, scholarship,
and education by publishing worldwide. Oxford is a registered trade mark of
Oxford University Press in the UK and in certain other countries.

Published in the United States of America by Oxford University Press
198 Madison Avenue, New York, NY 10016, United States of America.

CIP data is on file at the Library of Congress

ISBN 9780197775721 (pbk.)
ISBN 9780197775714 (hbk.)

DOI: 10.1093/9780197775752.001.0001

For Betty and Alan

Contents

Note to Readers

THIS BOOK HAS had a long, hard journey to meet you where you are. It almost didn't happen. And in ways that I'll soon explain, it was a failure before it almost didn't happen.

The Los Angeles Philharmonic Archive holds reader reports that were commissioned by the University of Illinois Press in 2005. Betty Freeman and Alan Rich had, some years before, put together a manuscript about their salon series, and I was looking through letters between the two of them and Judith McCullough, then editor-in-chief of the University of Illinois Press and, judging by her effusive praise of the manuscript, an enthused supporter of the project. Betty had made clear that she would finance the production of the book and guarantee that every music library in the country owned a copy. They wanted the imprimatur of a university press. Alan had once been a graduate student in musicology and likely inherited the belief that this project would require a stamp of institutional approval if it ever were to be taken seriously. Besides, they already had an inside track from some powerful figures within musicology, including champion of American music and celebrated scholar H. Wiley Hitchcock.

The reader reports, even by today's standards, were quite positive. No one doubted the impressive character list, the fantastic setting, and the intriguing blend of oral history and informal gatherings at the base of their story. The book had significance. The book felt weighty.

The fatal wound must have been light criticisms that suggested some further editing and pruning were needed. Print, it seemed, was a difficult medium to capture what was most valuable about these salons. This was unfortunately becoming a familiar problem for Betty and Alan—years before, they had tried to get National Public Radio (NPR) to broadcast tape recordings of their salons; the material was great, NPR responded, but the quality of the recordings was too poor to capture that great material. Now readers, like NPR before, found the presentation of the material unconvincing.

Betty found the criticisms and suggestions for improvement too deflating to continue the project. Perhaps to her mind there simply were no other options. The salons were haunted by material obsolescence. The tapes, the microphone, the DAT recordings, and now print had all in some way failed the project. She dropped it, and in her dropping, so ended a decades-long attempt to capture, describe, and distribute the good of their salons. So also ended Betty and Alan's relationship; he embittered by the sudden abandonment of what, for him, was thankless transcription work and she now directing her attention to new methods of patronage, such as festivals. She and Alan rarely spoke after.

Three years later, over lunch of enchiladas, at the outer edge of the neighborhood both Alan and I would, at different times in our lives, call home, I was handed yet another material version of the salons: two discs of Alan's transcriptions and introductions. The files were kind of a book. They also needed a good deal of help.

These few transcriptions, selected and edited from over one hundred cassette tapes, largely speak for themselves. Alan Rich transcribed much of this himself. After his death, I verified his transcriptions against the original tapes (then held between UCLA Special Collections and Stanford University) and transcribed others to include here. An appendix at the back of the book shows for reference the full program of salons. I had to be selective and so chose these few from among the many to represent the best I could what kind of people and what kind of music were featured. I edited only lightly, almost always to clarify what was intended or to provide brief context. Which means I have left intact most of the spirit of the moment: the wanderings of thought, the sometimes awkward phrasing, and the quirks of speech that at times verge on the unidiomatic, the mundane, and the inelegant. This, I feel, is part of their charm and part of their significance. I have also annotated each transcription, providing additional information in the footnotes.

Any book with a gestation period as long as this one accumulates debts and gratitude for existing in the first place. In my first year of a PhD program at UCLA, Mitchell Morris helped me see how to honor this inherited project while also seeing where and how I should step in to help it. Since then, numerous reviewers, most of them anonymous, made suggestions and corrected mistakes that had held on from earlier drafts. Ryan Dohoney became an especially loyal friend to this book right at the time when it (and I) most needed a champion, and Tracy Floreani helped me see the value in it long after I had been frazzled with indecision and rejection. Dozens of students along the way likewise weighed in with intrigue and creativity for my suspicion about where and how salons continued to live in America. For their particular insights, I thank Chris Benham, Jorge Calaf, Sharri Hall, Nathaniel Harrell, Bren Lunday, Kayla Marshall, Kate Morton, Matthew Newsome, Brianna Sadofsky, Sophia Scholch, Jacob Waymon, Adam White, Annie Youngs, and Zac Zubia. And for all their help and trust and permission to include their own or their loved one's work in these pages, I thank Gabriela Boguslawska, Léandre Boulez, Antonio Bovoso, Anthony Braxton, Shelley Butler, Chris Chafe, John Chowning, Jody Diamond, Betty Ann Duggan, Barbara Monk Feldman, Monica Germino, Philip Glass, Laura Kuhn, Elizabeth LaHorgue, Brooke Larimer, Libby Larsen, Lukas Ligeti, Steve Reich, Esa-Pekka Salonen, Eva Soltes, David Macoto Nancarrow Sugiura, Jennifer Wisdom, and Heidy Zimmerman.

In 2022, I was fortunate to receive a Presidential Faculty and Student Research/ Creative Activity Fellowship from Oklahoma City University. Not only did this fellowship inject some resources and boost my morale but also it brought my student assistant, Caroline Morath, into the project. Caroline was an invaluable collaborator and research assistant and gave me the much-needed thought partnering to close out this book. Additional financial support for publication was provided from the Office of the Vice President for Research and Partnerships and the Office of the Provost, University of Oklahoma, which helped cover costs associated with reproducing the images featured in the book.

I thank the staff, past and present, at the Los Angeles Philharmonic Archive, the UCLA Special Collections, the Judith Rosen Collection in Stanford University's Archive of Recorded Sound, and at the University of California, San Diego, Mandeville Special Collections for assisting me in navigating the immense amount of materials Betty Freeman left. A special thank-you to Steve Lacoste for his willingness to help me navigate the collections at the LA Phil Archive with such grace and positivity when I was a young graduate student. And for permission to include his caricature of Betty in this book, my gratitude to the brilliant Ken Fallin.

Finally, this book is dedicated to Betty Freeman and Alan Rich. I knew both of them only briefly at the tail end of their lives, but they continue to shape the world I travel through. They were each generous and kind to me, and their often-selfless work on behalf of vulnerable artists and their listeners reminds me of the quiet way people care for one another. But most of all, I am grateful that they entrusted me with their story and that it is now in your hands and heart, too.

Betty Freeman, November 13, 1994. Courtesy of Shelley Butler.

An Evening at Betty Freeman's
(1/12/86—or why I would rather hear music there than anywhere)
By Melinda Wortz

I arrive late—5:30
Morton Feldman's "metaphorical fugue" performed on the piano
by Robert Krupnick
has already begun
I make not a sound, and sit in the foyer, on a bench
beside the Dan Flavin.
Feldman's piece is subtle but not severe
reverberations massing in layers
(later Clayton Eshleman tells me
he associates the sound with Monet's *Water Lilies*)
Not seeing the composer, the instrument, the performer, or the guests,
I experience simultaneously the music itself
and the art works surrounding me.
I see the white front door, when opened
bordered with green—
Flavin's green, of course, hidden from the viewer
but reverberating wavelengths of light to a space
at a distance from their origin
I suddenly suspect why Betty has such an affinity for Flavin—
his vibrational process is analogous to music's—
finds kinship with sound—
Tone patterns, both.
Like Feldman's music, Betty's house presents itself as a layering of tonality and pattern—
all of a piece.
Did she buy the Flavins because their yellows
correspond to the edge of Lichtenstein's mirror?
or vice versa?
Was/is the correspondence unconscious?
Like music's reverberations, the dots in Lichtenstein's
mirror
float away from their surface
and Flavin's red seeks Lichtenstein's oval to run
with pink.
I hear Feldman's alternation of consonance with

dissonance
And become aware of Betty's oppositions—black and white
Black velvet walls behind Sam Francis
bring his monumental gesture to life!
White fabric walls in the foyer
rhythmically positioned against black and white stripes . . .
black and white checks of dining room chairs—
black and white daisy patterns which add yellow
in the bar
in tempo with Flavin's Tubes—
an uncanny confrontation.
To Feldman's more spaced and spare sequences—
Doug Wheeler's greyish light responds.
From the kitchen—the Cageian sounds
of Franco's deep toned swearings
and finely tuned seasonings
bring anticipations of oral delectations
to enrich the already sensuous fare
a synaesthetic mix that knows no simile.

Preface

Click—scratch—zoom—thud—click—whirl.

I need to hear again what Philip Glass said at that moment, when he shifted weight or turned his head or took a drink of water or whatever it was that for those three syllables took his voice out of reach of the microphone. I must *press*—not push—a sequence of levers on the tape deck to go back in time. Tampering with outmoded technology can make evident that there is a labor to listening. That labor is also disquieting. The placid rhythm of UCLA's Special Collections Library where I am seated among maybe seven other scholars and students this day is being disrupted by my lever pressing.

I'm just as flustered by the work as they are. With three cartons the size of donut boxes full of cassette tapes on my table, each tape capable of holding 120 minutes of fuzzy sound or fuzzy silence, I have long days cut out for me. I have been issued a tape deck the dimensions of a cereal box that, surprising to me, weighs as much as a classroom encyclopedia. The student worker guarding the front desk of the collections hands it and a set of earphones to me like she might handle either a delicate artifact or maybe a detonator—"do I cut the green wire or the red wire?!" her look panics. The awkward handoff is touching, really. Outmoded technology in our grasp feels repulsive. We ought to know. For as much as we handle technology and feel it an extension of our bodies, its own product development has by now earned a familiarity bordering on the biological. Older models, rarely seen

Cassette tape holding Philip Glass's salon and descriptive insert. From the Alan Rich Papers at UCLA Special Collections. Photo by the author.

nowadays outside trash heaps, once touched, trigger a repulsion similar, I guess, to the startled animal when smelling of death or dying. What we are holding, our genetics whisper, has stopped living.

Even with the rate of speed turned to 1:5 I can't make out Glass's word here. It's fuzzy, I'm tired, and context is not helpful in this situation. I start fiddling with things around me as I strategize. After a while I begin noticing there is a queer pleasure in opening and closing a cassette tape box. The clear plastic is scuffed along the hinges from the times it was opened, and its contents pulled out to be heard. Betty and Alan hired an assistant to scrub the recordings so they could be used for radio broadcasts. NPR might be able to use them, they thought. NPR thought they would love to use them, that the material was of tremendous value, but the microphones, unfortunately, simply were not positioned close enough or the cassettes, you know, were not the right material for professional broadcasting in the first place. These tapes I was handling in the air-controlled basement of a research library were evidence of failure. Had they done their job you would have heard them by now. As it were, the tape's medium could not deliver on their message. Their very existence screamed with an apologetic thud with every press of the buttons.

> Click—scratch—zoom—thud—click—whirl—thud.
> *Dances*, I startle. He said "*dances*."
> Click—whirl.

In preparing this book, I have been reminded of James Agee's charged introduction to *Let Us Now Praise Famous Men*: "If I could do it, I'd do no writing at all here."

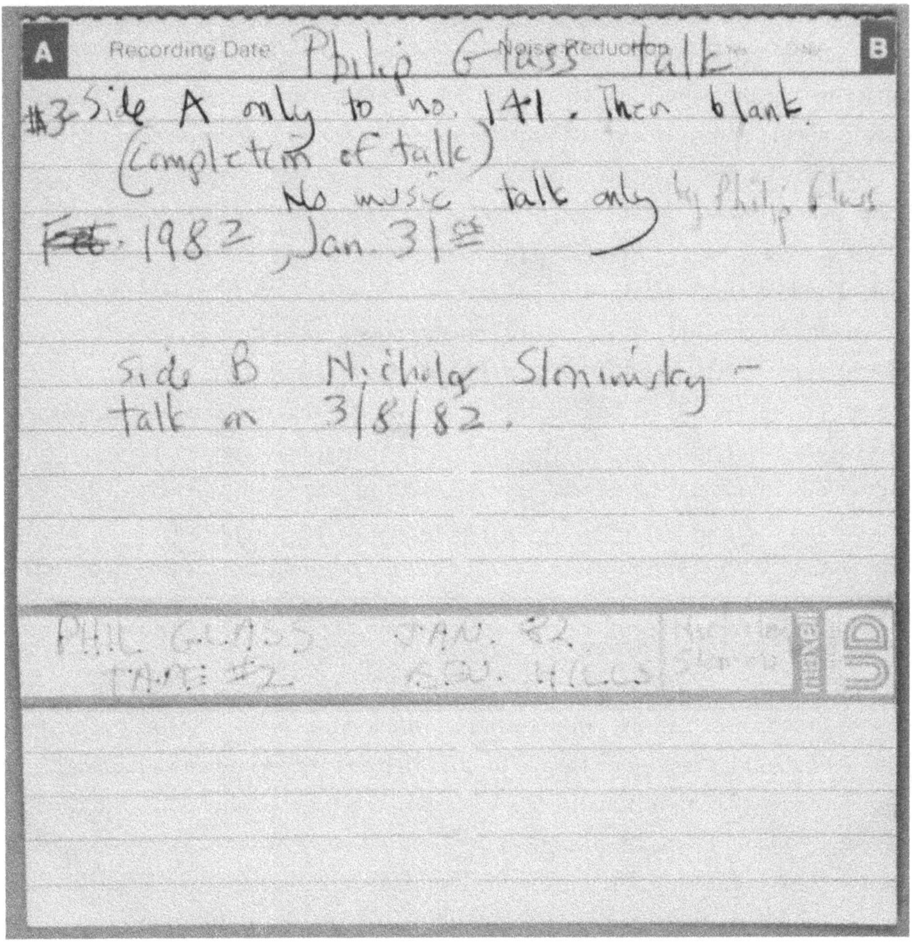

Cassette tape holding Philip Glass's salon and descriptive insert. From the Alan Rich Papers at UCLA Special Collections. Photo by the author.

> It would be photographs; the rest would be fragments of cloth, bits of cotton, lumps of earth, records of speech, pieces of wood and iron, phials of odors, plates of food and of excrement. . . . A piece of the body torn out by the roots might be more to the point. As it is, though, I'll do what little I can in writing.[1]

While writing is its own form of materiality, I take Agee's point here about the truth and immediacy of material evidence in telling stories. The limitations of even the warmest written words are made all the more evident when held

1 James Agee, *Let Us Now Praise Famous Men: Three Tenant Families* (Boston: Houghton Mifflin, 1941; 2001 reprint), 10.

against the cold edges of photographs, books, letters, and sticky notes. Agee's journalistic ethnography and these transcriptions of salons may seem miles apart in comparison, but the instinct for totality is tempered by limitations in our modes of communication. Lacking a definitive method for recreating history in its truest sense, I accept the odd comfort Agee puts forth. I'll do what little I can in writing.

I nonetheless cringe that elements from the recordings can't make their way to you. The idle chatter before and after (and sometimes during) the lectures, the frequent interjections of this story's protagonists Alan Rich, Judith Rosen, and Betty Freeman, the rapid-fire speech of Philip Glass, and the thick but boisterous accent of György Ligeti. And, as the interlocutor, I also feel the pain of *almost*—through the veil of recordings, the hours spent listening to cassette tapes of these salons has frequently toyed with my imagination, almost to the extent that I feel I too was sitting in the Music Room watching and listening to the major musical innovators of the last half of the twentieth century. *Almost*. Agee was right in that to dwell on the shortfalls of the written word can anguish the soul when in one's mind lives a truer, more complete version of how events took place.

And yet, writing also represents the best we can do when it takes seriously the entangled nature of ideas, the material world, and our particular form of writerly communication. Ideas need things to hold them together, much as archaeologist Ian Hodder argues that humans need things in order to become human in the first place.[2] By focusing on the thingness of these salons, I believe the collection contained here invites an opportunity of historiographical meditation on the past, how we chronicle that past, and the significance of place and things in making that past real to us today.

Part of what makes this collection powerful is its witness to the dynamic relationships the Music Room initiated. For thirteen years, established composers from around the world were united with aspiring composers—mostly students or young faculty in music programs around southern California—but also musicologists, critics, patrons, performers, and arts administrators. Over bountiful bowls of pasta prepared by Betty Freeman's husband, Italian sculptor and inventor Franco Assetto, social networks (or "art worlds" to use the phrase sociologist Howard S. Becker would coin in 1982 amid the very art worlds these salons were modeling) were established, challenged, and discarded, and new ones erected.[3] I'm aware that the scene in this story may feature exceptional figures (though not

2 Ian Hodder, *Entangled: An Archaeology of the Relationship between Humans and Things* (Hoboken, NJ: John Wiley and Sons, 2012), 12–13.
3 Howard S. Becker, *Art Worlds* (Berkeley: University of California Press, 1982).

always), but it otherwise borders on pedestrian. Food and music shared among a group of like-minded people is so apparently everyday that its banality almost topples from the weight of this historical glance.

One of the more compelling aspects to this story for me has been the space it carves between the everyday and the exceptional. Who is to say that the small details of any everyday moment are insignificant, that they are inconsequential, that they aren't depended on or afforded dynamism simply—or even precisely—because of their familiarity? As Alan Rich put it, "The best that comes out of these gatherings is the putting into circulation of new ideas, the chance for artists, including musicians, to find out what's happening in the arts world that can easily become compartmentalized."[4] Performance artist Yen Lu Wong eloquently underscored Alan's point in a letter to Betty and Franco thanking them "for providing a nurturing time and place for working artists."

> Every fall, I look forward to the first Musicale, to start the year, a ritual which assures me that all is well in the creative arts—Betty is back, artists are working, creating, struggling, stimulating, controversy-ing, and people are caring.
>
> To come to a Musicale is to enter a world—a very rare one, that of supportive colleagues, an ambience of good cheer, good food, good art, and for me, to enter into an inner dialogue of imagery, and kinaesthetic movement induced by the music. This was particularly true of the last one—with Pauline Oliveros and Steven Mosko. In those brief few hours, there was order amidst chaos, and I was privileged to see how other human beings sort out the "beans" in their lives and made sense for them, thus offering us another possibility to deal with reality.[5]

Betty and Alan hoped to continue this circulation of new ideas and support first by broadcasting these recordings over radio and, when that project proved impossible, by publishing transcriptions of these salons in book form. Neither lived to see the projects completed. I met and interviewed Alan a short time before his death. Over the course of lunch, many ideas and materials were shared. The moment he handed me two discs with his transcriptions—rough but loosely arranged in book form—I knew this was a story that needed telling and felt the import of what these salons did for new music then and, quite frankly, what they are

4 Alan Rich, KUSC Music Commentary, August 2, 1985, Betty Freeman Papers, University of California, San Diego Mandeville Special Collections.

5 Letter from Yen Lu Wong to Betty Freeman, November 21, 1986, Los Angeles Philharmonic Archive.

continuing to do today. It would turn out to be a story whose telling has transfixed me for over a decade.

I have chosen in the end to represent Betty's life through a series of vignettes concentrated on her salon series. My introduction foregrounds the material world Betty created for herself and for others and imagines the entanglements of such a world with the ideas generated within it. A traditional biography this may not be. But nonetheless this is a work that insists what one makes of the world can be as important as who one is in it. If, as sociologist Randall Collins suggests, ideas remain in circulation both because of their perceived greatness and their equally flagrant shortcomings, then I hope this incompleteness encourages other scholarship on Betty and West Coast patronage in general.[6] If there are errors, please use them as a source for good. We all do what little we can in writing.

6 Randall Collins, *The Sociology of Philosophies: A Global Theory of Intellectual Change* (Cambridge, MA: Harvard University Press, 1998), 32.

An Invitation

BETTY DECIDED TO send me the check herself. It arrived in the mail like an invitation to a party, more than covering the plane fare and a rental car to get me to and around Los Angeles. It was 2008 and I was writing my master's thesis on Betty Freeman's support of the avant-garde. I remember holding that thin check, feeling relief as palpable as that piece of paper in my hands for not having to dig into my little family's pitiable savings to pay for the cross-country trip. I also felt some pangs of panic that in opening her letter and finding the unsolicited check I was already a compromised scholar, bought and sold from the start.

A few months later, my wife, BrieAnn, dropped me off curbside at 703 Hillcrest Road in Beverly Hills. A petite housekeeper named Bertha ushered me into the same foyer where salon guests once mingled with pasta bowls clenched in grateful hands. A small, fragile woman appeared on the landing above my head and, with the help of Bertha, gingerly descended the stairs. She was wearing a sling from a recent shoulder injury, I was told. She was smiling, warm, but also distant. Five months later I learned, along with the rest of the world, that Betty had been living with pancreatic cancer.

I sat with Betty for a few hours that afternoon. The tulip table where we perched was covered with Betty's photographs of iconoclast composer Harry Partch and tiny handwritten Post-It Notes with memories or scribblings to herself about which photos should be placed where. She was preparing a book about her life with Partch and was racing to get it finished. We chatted about him, but also about her life in music while friends and family zipped in and out of the house, depositing containers of food in the fridge—a clear token of caregiving whose significance I failed to recognize at the time. We promised to stay in touch. I walked out the door on my own.

The Music Room. Jake Johnson, Oxford University Press. © Oxford University Press 2025.
DOI: 10.1093/9780197775752.003.0001

music room

SIXTH YEAR - GRAND OVERTURE
SUNDAY, NOVEMBER 9, 1986
5 - 8 P.M.

PAULINE OLIVEROS: Tuning Meditation
and Roots of the Moment

STEPHEN MOSKO: Indigenous Music II
Dorothy Stone, Flute, and
Atu of Tahuti, tape

with ALAN RICH
BETTY FREEMAN • 703 HILLCREST ROAD • BEVERLY HILLS • 271-3993

FIGURE I.1 A 3×5-inch mailed invitation, November 9, 1986. Photo by the author.

That was September 2008. Betty died January 3, 2009, at the age of eighty-six. The Partch book lay unfinished.

I'm an unlikely narrator. The afternoon I just described is all the time I had with Betty. I never even stepped foot in the living area she dubbed the "music room," where her salons took place. It remains as much a mystery to me now as ever. And that's part of my story.

This book balances the equation between *what* is true and *how it comes to be* true. It is at once a collection of primary sources, a biography of place, a memoir of history making, a meditation on historiography. The story spans thirteen years but almost all scenes take place in one room. I take to heart Gaston Bachelard's phenomenological treatise on architecture *The Poetics of Space*, in which he suggests that the value of an idea literally resonates louder when remembered within walls, floor, ceiling, texture of place. "Memories are motionless," he writes, "and the more securely they are fixed in space, the *sounder* they are."[1]

Sound thus paved my ontological path through these historical documents. I place center the material evidence of a once-vibrant series of events that filled this space—objects such as index-card sized invitations (like the one pictured above), artwork that hung on the walls of the music room, the cassette tapes that so often mediated audience and composer during them, plates of pasta dutifully

1 Gaston Bachelard, *The Poetics of Space: The Classic Look at How We Experience Intimate Places* (Boston: Beacon Press, 1958), 9. Emphasis mine.

accompanying conversations here and there, and even the room itself. Art historian Melinda Wortz's poem, printed as an epigraph to this book and originally penned in the music room ledger, speaks to these same material experiences of the salons. In Wortz's words, Betty's home and decor take on the values of sound, the house practically resonating with bellows of its own.

> Like Feldman's music, Betty's house presents itself as a layering of tonality
> and pattern—
> all of a piece.
> Did she buy the Flavins because their yellows
> correspond to the edge of Lichtenstein's mirror?
> or vice versa?
> Was/is the correspondence unconscious?
> Like music's reverberations, the dots in Lichtenstein's
> mirror
> float away from their surface
> and Flavin's red seeks Lichtenstein's oval to run
> with pink.

Her poem captured my imagination. *How does the material world sound? In what ways do the objects around us enable a sonic memory? How might sound enable a deeper memory of the past? What of those memories surround us, in the air and in our touch?*

To answer these questions, I needed to fashion the story in a way that began, not ended, with the primary source material in mind. The materiality of those transcriptions became my focus, made malleable by the warm turning of them in my mind. Allow me in these pages to touch and feel our way through these material leftovers of the salons, to guide through Betty's home, to stop and show what the salons were like then and there, to consider these and other objects that give texture to the ideas floating through the room, and finally to tilt an ear to the words and sounds of Betty and her guests. While this book at times flits with whimsy, what is important to me is that what you come to glean from the transcriptions can be put in technicolor by the way you come to arrive there. Truth asks more than whether or not something is real.

ORIGINS

Born Betty Wishnick in Chicago in 1921, Betty spent her formative years in Brooklyn. She inherited wealth from her father, Robert Wishnick, who emigrated from Russia as a small child and, despite losing most of his right arm in an accident, worked his way through college—and later law school—to become a chemical engineer and founder of the manufacturing company Witco. He was a giant to his daughter and instilled in Betty a love for philanthropy.

Betty only reluctantly began patronizing composers in the 1960s, after a longer tenure promoting and advancing modern and contemporary visual art. She adored contemporary art and artists, and two unpublished monographs on American painters Sam Francis and Clyfford Still sit in her archive. When she finally decided to host these salons, her home was becoming a de facto art museum. In this regard, music and paintings were coequal furbelows—Betty in a sense decorated her home with pieces of sound as much as with pieces of cloth and glue.

In fact, the first composer she ever supported was LaMonte Young—a composer likewise who received his warmest receptions within art museums—whom she helped bail out of a Connecticut prison on a drug possession charge. Young had heard tell of Betty's art patronage and wrote her a lengthy letter asking for whatever financial help she could offer in exchange for some of his records. Though she had never met Young she sent the money anyway: "So I sent a hundred dollars and didn't get anything in return," she told a reporter in 2006. "When he got out, he sent me a collection of his records which I listened to and was fascinated. He's somebody who can play one note for four hours, but it's what he does with this one note, with the overtones and the undertones and how he combines it. I became a fan and I'm still a fan [after] all these years."[2] An auspicious beginning.

Betty's salons were held monthly for about nine months out of the year. Betty and her second husband, Franco, traveled to Turino, Italy, during the summer, so this was her Los Angeles project. Each salon typically profiled two composers, one local or emerging and another with often a much more established career. The idea was to help foster development in the new music scene. The audience was a mixed group, invited by Betty and strictly curated. Arts administrators, scholars, composers, and of course other patrons were among the elite group invited and included in her salons. Invitations were mailed out on iconic letterhead, notifying of the next Music Room event, which were usually held on Sunday afternoons or evenings.

Alan Rich helped organize these gatherings and served as master of ceremonies. Originally from Boston, Alan studied music first at Harvard and then

2 Betty Freeman, interview by Vicki Curry, *Life and Times*, Segment 3: A Patron of Composers, July 14, 2006. Betty tells more of her background, framed within a larger narrative on women patrons and salon culture, in Cyrilla Barr and Ralph P. Locke, *Cultivating Music in America: Women Patrons and Activists since 1860* (Berkeley: University of California Press, 1997), 59–64.

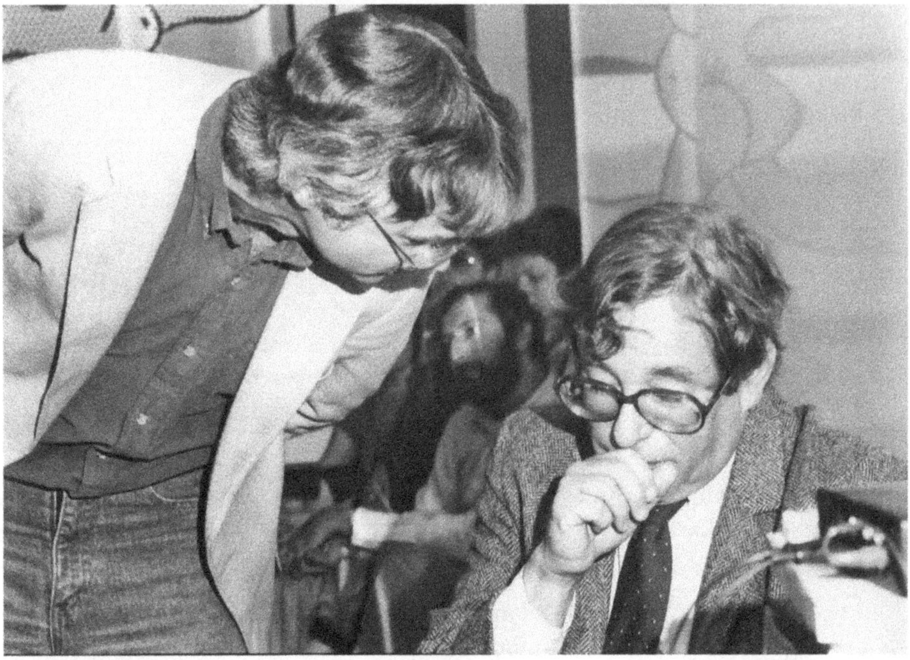

FIGURE I.2 Alan Rich and John Adams, November 3, 1985. Photo by Betty Freeman, courtesy of the Los Angeles Philharmonic Archives.

entered graduate study in musicology at the University of California, Berkeley. While there, Alan served as music director for KPFA, a radio station legendary both for using the public airwaves to oppose American military action abroad and for the fervent support and subsequent broadcasting of contemporary art music.[3] He worked as a music critic for a host of publications, including the *New York Times*, *Newsweek*, *Boston Herald*, and *LA Weekly*—the latter a post he maintained for sixteen years, parting ways just two years before his death in 2010. Alan's background and position within Betty's orbit made him the point man between her and many in the professional music world. He often interjected questions or comments during the salons, led the Q&A afterward, and introduced each speaker. Betty of course frequently added her two cents, introducing the event and welcoming everyone and occasionally asking a question. Although she left the more professional courtesies to Alan, Betty's genuflection was not for lack of musical knowledge. Betty was a trained pianist and attended Wellesley College as a music and English major. She later continued her

3 For more on the history of KPFA, including how the station's pacifist ideology aligned with its adventurous music programming, see Michael Lasar, *Pacifica Radio: The Rise of an Alternative Network* (Philadelphia, PA: Temple University Press, 2000).

FIGURE I.3 Spine of the leather-bound scrapbook for Betty's salons, dubbed *Il Salotto Musicale*. From the Los Angeles Philharmonic Archives. Photo by the author.

studies with teachers at Juilliard and New England Conservatory, and seriously considered a career in performance before marrying her first husband, Robert Freeman.

Betty's Beverly Hills home was large, but not palatial. The interior was covered in a stunning collection—paintings, sculpture, light installations, and textiles from some of the foremost artists in the contemporary art world. The dining room where we sat and chatted was engulfed by a large double-canvas David Hockney painting of her posing in her backyard, auspiciously titled *Beverly Hills Housewife*.[4] She loved taking pictures (something Harry Partch's assistant Danlee Mitchell claims to have introduced her to during filming of the 1972 documentary *The Dreamer That Remains*), and studied with Ansel Adams for a period of time.[5] Even after Franco died and she stopped hosting the salons in her home, she continued to be a part of the series and often photo-documented them. The Los Angeles Philharmonic Archive contains over 7,000 photographs she took over the years, many of them taken at her salons.

The Los Angeles Philharmonic Archive also houses a large leather-bound book that served as a ledger of sorts for the salons. Inside are registers from each event, sometimes signed elaborately with notated musical gifts from composer to Betty. Poems in honor of the event are also included, as is one about Morton Feldman. As I flip through the book, the historical weight of these events becomes heavier, and

4 Betty may be more implicated in the piece's title. Barbara Jepson reveals that although "Freeman did not commission [*Beverly Hills Housewife*] . . . she claims to have suggested the impish title." See Jepson, "A Cultivated Ear: Betty Freeman's Living Room Is the West Coast's Center for New Music," *Connoisseur* (February 1987).

5 See Jake Johnson, "Two Studies of Harry Partch: Conversations with Danlee Mitchell and Betty Freeman," *Echo: A Music-Centered Journal* 12, no. 1 (2014): http://www.echo.ucla.edu/two-studies-harry-partch-conversations-danlee-mitchell-betty-freeman-jake-johnson/.

more apparent, for the signee. Guests seem to understand how important these gatherings were, and were becoming, and not just for Southern California communities. The avant-garde and new music communities internationally were drawing focus on Los Angeles, not without some sense of amazement to Alan Rich, or Betty herself for that matter. He attests that Los Angeles was a cultural wasteland when he arrived in 1979 and, as she recounts in a letter to Brian Ferneyhough, Betty held similar frustrations with the city's lack of available resources: "Somehow Los Angeles is still in the provinces and doesn't have enough exposure to newer ideas taking place in Europe," adding that, "your music was extremely helpful in correcting that imbalance."[6]

Betty and Alan were not alone in their characterization of that nascent desert city, although things had been improving in that regard for some time.[7] Salons and music gatherings intended to support new music were a hallmark of Los Angeles culture long before Betty. She stood on the shoulders of those who had come before, including most famously the Evenings on the Roof series that began in 1939, literally on the roof of the small bungalow of Peter Yates and his wife, concert pianist Frances Mullen. Modernist architect Rudolf Schindler was contracted to build a music studio, which was erected as a second floor, and thus held commanding views of Los Angeles and the Pacific Ocean. The expansion took place during an ongoing financial struggle and personal crisis as Yates sought spiritual solidarity in contemporary music. After returning from a "long trek in a Theosophists' cooperative community," a vision for what would become his music series opened before him. He envisioned a space open,

> once a week or month to all comers, free or at local movie prices, to give an informal recital without bows, entrances, or exits, performing not only unusual music but also such things as the Bartók children's pieces and often repeating a big work in an evening or in successive evenings . . . until both audience and performer have digested it. . . . Outside artists should be invited to perform works not ordinarily allowed them in recital, their fee being the evening's take. In every case it should be impressed on the mind of each player that the primary reason for his performance is his own pleasure in it, that if the audience be small or absent that is no reason for

6 Letter from Betty Freeman to Brian Ferneyhough, April 24, 1987.

7 See Catherine Parsons Smith, *Making Music in Los Angeles: Transforming the Popular* (Berkeley: University of California Press, 2007), and Mina Yang, *California Polyphony: Ethnic Voices, Musical Crossroads* (Urbana: University of Illinois Press, 2008) for broader histories of music-making in Los Angeles and California more broadly.

> personal disappointment or loss of pleasure. . . . Such is the community idea.[8]

Initially those early salons were more desperate, trying to keep up with trends elsewhere in cities with a much longer-earned reputation for fostering radical ideas (for Yates, radical ideas manifest as spirituality), most notably New York City and Paris. This was also the time when art galleries and studio lofts were more frequently spaces where new musical works were premiered. Homes or rooftop spaces in Los Angeles, therefore, sprouted up in the mid-century and helped encourage a hunger for the kind of salons Betty hosted in the 1980s.

WOMEN, MUSIC, AND SALON CULTURE

Betty's career in the arts raises questions about the nature of patronage, and how new musical ideas gain traction and earn the requisite money needed to produce and record new works in a climate where patronage has largely become institutionalized.[9] Betty Freeman's work to host and advocate for new music in her home is not a departure from previous attempts to develop new music, particularly in Los Angeles, but the scope and purpose of her patronage does invite renewed attention to her and these events. It is telling, for instance, that Betty more than once referred to herself deferentially as "just a Beverly Hills housewife" in demur toward the (mostly) male composers she championed and no doubt in reference to the Hockney piece hanging in her dining room. Her statement could be taken at face value, a reflection of her self-awareness of where she stood in relation to the work she most admired and a modest admission of her class and social status that enabled such a relationship. But that would be an admission not in keeping with how Betty otherwise communicated her commitment to these composers and their works. Her letters to John Adams were among the most voluminous and honest. They convey an intense attachment she had to the creative process—she herself was a musician and an intelligent patron, unlike the stigmatized models

---

8 Quoted in Dorothy L. Crawford, *Evenings on and off the Roof: Pioneering Concerts in Los Angeles, 1939–1971* (Berkeley: University of California Press, 1995), 21.

9 For recent scholarship on the institutionalization of arts patronage, particularly in America, see Michael Uy, *Ask the Experts: How Ford, Rockefeller, and the NEA Changed American Music* (New York: Oxford University Press, 2020) and William Robin, *Industry: Bang on a Can and New Music in the Marketplace* (New York: Oxford University Press, 2021). Martin Brody's edited volume on the Rome Prize in musical composition, *Music and Musical Composition at the American Academy in Rome* (Rochester, NY: University of Rochester Press, 2014), tells another story of patronage in American musical culture, and Tia DeNora's *Beethoven and the Construction of Genius: Musical Politics in Vienna, 1792–1803* (Berkeley: University of California Press, 1997) models the payoff when patrons are analyzed at the center of, rather than periphery to, the lives of composers.

of female patron buffoonery and vacuous socialite antics pockmarking literature and popular culture. Betty doted on Adams in her letters, referring to him as her "golden boy" and relishing in learning of his children's births and extramusical life events. When he dedicated his opera *Nixon in China* to her, she responded maternally by writing that she was "filled with grandmotherly pride" and felt to be "a proud mama."

This kind of gendered, maternal sentiment frequently characterized Betty's feelings toward the works she commissioned and were not out of character with patrons of another time. In her remarkably progressive 1948 book *Music and Women*, amateur musician Sophie Drinkler noted that the term "patron" itself was unnecessarily gendered and therefore limited in capturing this quality of women and their investment in culture, government, and institutions. "The very word 'patroness,'" she writes, "has something spurious about it. It is made by the lacy addition of 'ess' to the word 'patron,' whose root means father. An honest word for an honest woman saint of music would be founded on a word whose root meant mother, as the word 'matron' does."[10] Not all allusions to maternal guidance are created equal, of course. Literary scholar Marjorie Garber relates that Charlotte van der Veer Quick Mason, the wealthy white patron of literature from the Harlem Renaissance, preferred to be called "Godmother" by those Black writers she supported.[11]

Betty's framing of her patronage as maternal support led to a sincere interest in the comings and goings of those she financed—the "music people" as she called them.[12] Institutions dedicated to funding the arts such as the NEA, the Rockefeller and Ford Foundations, and the Fromm Music Foundation outspent Betty by magnitudes, and some of the same figures she gave to also benefited from organizations like them. But it was the spirit and personal value she placed on her relationships with those she supported that made what Betty did of such significance in their lives and of supreme importance to the music world.

The way she supported also felt personal, tailored even, to that person's needs. John Cage received an annual stipend from Betty for years ("living grants"), money not tied to any piece or project, but just money to be used at his discretion. But that was a rare strategy. She instead regularly gave money specifically for simple, but pricey, parts of a premiere like engraving and copying the orchestral parts. One of her earliest and most influential engagements as a patron was her relationship with Harry Partch, a self-described maverick and notoriously difficult man

10 Sophie Drinkler, *Music and Women: The Story of Women in Their Relation to Music* (New York: The Feminist Press at The City University of New York, 1948; 1995 reprint).

11 Marjorie Garber, *Patronizing the Arts* (Princeton, NJ: Princeton University Press, 2008), 12.

12 Betty in fact published several books of her photographs, titled *Music People*.

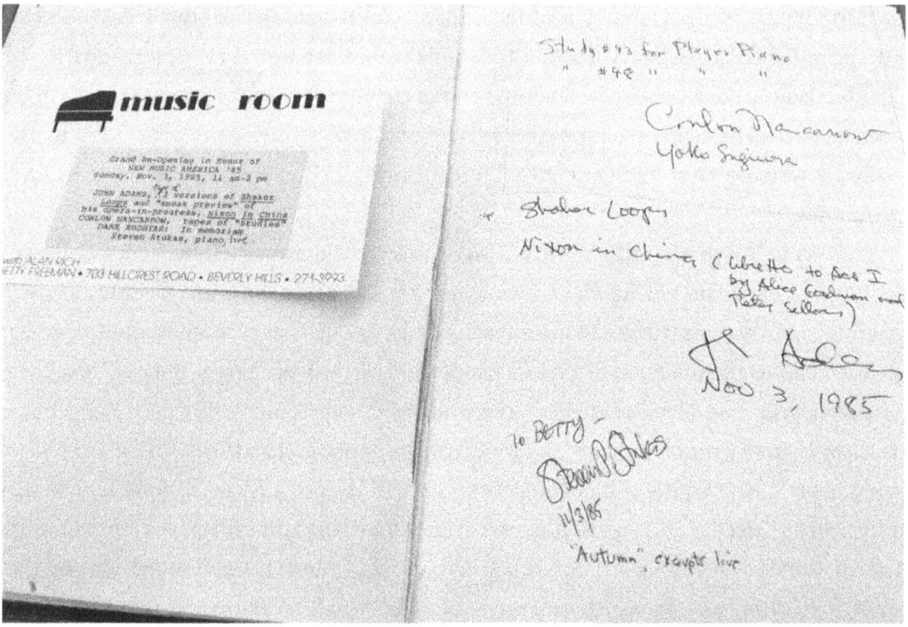

FIGURE I.4 A glance at the records kept inside the leather-bound scrapbook for Betty's salons. From the Los Angeles Philharmonic Archives. Photo by the author.

to tolerate even among his most adoring disciples. After meeting at the Pasadena Art Museum in 1964 and discovering over tea that Partch had just that day given away his car, Betty offered to drive him home "and for the next ten years I drove Harry and that's the way I learned the L.A. freeways. I would never have gone on them if it hadn't been that he directed me onto them wherever we went."[13] Betty bought Partch a home near San Diego and made sure he had food and shelter at critical times of his career, caring for him from that quirky first meeting over tea up to his death in 1974. He didn't always know how to respond or react to her generosity given his mercurial temperament and predilection to be unattached both emotionally and physically from the rest of the world, but he knew he needed her. She probably needed him, too. In many ways, that earliest relationship thickened Betty's skin in working with subsequent composers and in turn forced Partch, especially in his older years, to accept sorely needed help and soften his demeanor toward those lending hands, if only provisionally.

Partch had been dead for several years by the time Betty was first impressed to begin her salon series, but in many ways his presence haunted the space. She was standing in her living room one afternoon, she once wrote, near the Steinway

13 Johnson, "Two Studies of Harry Partch."

FIGURE I.5 Betty Freeman as depicted in *The Wall Street Journal*, January 14, 2009. Drawing by Ken Fallin. Used with permission.

piano, when it dawned on her that she could begin *in that very room* a new form of patronage that invested more acutely in the future of the art to which she was most loyal. It was in that very same room, in fact, where Betty had once hosted Alan Rich and filmmaker Stephen Pouliot as they strategized making Partch's documentary, *The Dreamer That Remains*. Alan later used a set of chimes tuned to Partch's idiosyncratic tuning ratios to herd guests away from food and toward the salon happenings. Funny that anything of Partch's would be used for such pleasantries as shepherding order and timeliness. And yet in this and other tender ways explored in this book Partch the dreamer did, for Betty, remain.

Rather than stick to the conventional patronage playbook and give small amounts of money to single commissions or recording projects (which she also did, of course), Betty envisioned giving roots, not just fruits, to the new music community. To her, it wasn't the individual works she commissioned that were important, but rather the spirit of creativity that her giving provided. "As for me, I don't think that many of the pieces I've commissioned or aided have been particularly outstanding," Betty told a shocked audience at the Kyoto City University of Art and Music in 1990. "However, I'm glad to have put my energy into keeping alive the flame of music—and I always have the hope that the next work might just be a universal masterpiece."[14] To that end, she worked with Alan to build a salon series that would foster relationships among established and rising figures in the new music community, providing simultaneously a platform that could project the highest levels of achievement in that art world (at least as defined by her taste) and provide a foundation for young composers and performers to hone their craft among the veterans. It was in this spirit that the Music Room was born.

The Music Room builds on a historically underserved performance of female patronage known as salon culture.[15] Some scholars have argued, in fact, that the Enlightenment and its accompanying revolutions might never have ignited were it not for the salons of intellectuals, writers, and prominent thinkers hosted by women in their homes.[16] Innovative ideas need protection and safe spaces to develop roots. Trace a paradigmatic shift in society or culture back to its origins and you are likely to find its genesis in the drawing room of a woman's home. Yet these women have rarely been honored for the significance of their contributions, neither in their time nor in ours. Rousseau, for example, bemoaned those "arbiters of public opinion" put in place merely by virtue of having wealth—women who "in society . . . do not know anything, although they judge everything."[17] Representations of women patrons and salon culture never quite rise beyond this trite concern. Consider this depiction from music critic W. J. Henderson's 1912 satirical novel, *The Soul of a Tenor*:

> Mrs. Harley Manners, just stepping from her car in front of the Waldorf-Astoria, was a vision of radiant expectancy. She was hastening to one of those perfectly delightful Monday morning musicales at which, for an inconsiderable price, you could sit and rub shoulders with people right in the

---

14 Taken from a transcription of Betty's speech at the Kyoto City University of Art and Music on January 19, 1990.

15 While studies of music salons themselves have mostly been limited to a few studies of notable salonnières—including Cyrilla Barr, *Elizabeth Sprague Coolidge: American Patron of Music* (New York: Schirmer, 1998); Jeanice Brooks, "Nadia Boulanger and the Salon of the Princess de Polignac," *Journal of the American Musicological Society* 46, no. 3 (Autumn 1993): 415–468; and Christoph Wolff, "A Bach Cult in Late Eighteenth-Century Berlin: Sara Levy's Musical Salon," *Bulletin of the American Academy of Arts and Sciences* 58, no. 3 (Spring 2005): 26–31—the very concept of salon culture has in recent years developed to now include revisions of older thinking and expansions into other musical genres and spaces as with Rebecca Cypess's *Women and Musical Salons in the Enlightenment* (Chicago: University of Chicago Press, 2022), Anja Bunzel and Natasha Loges's edited collection *Musical Salon Culture in the Long Nineteenth Century* (Rochester, NY: Boydell Press, 2019), and Michael C. Heller's *Loft Jazz: Improvising New York in the 1970s* (Berkeley: University of California Press, 2016).

16 See Dena Goodman, *The Republic of Letters: A Cultural History of the French Enlightenment* (Ithaca, NY: Cornell University Press, 1994).

17 Jean-Jacques Rousseau, *Politics and the Arts: Letter to M.d'Alembert on the Theatre*, ed. and trans. Allan Bloom (Ithaca, NY: Cornell University Press, 1968), 49.

> heart of the smart set. Mrs. Harley Manners was not in that set. She knew many people in it, and purred audibly when they spoke to her. When they did not, which was the more usual occurrence, she retained her composure and waited. She knew that all of them would have to speak to her from time to time, for she was a cheerful and insistent laborer on all sorts of committees for charitable entertainments, benefits, and what not. She was always ready to do most of the work, all of the talking, and to sign a really handsome check.[18]

A few paragraphs later, Mrs. Harley Manners arrives at the musicale and "step[s] from her olive limousine just as if she were one of the elect." Described as "prattling vivaciously and saying all sorts of priceless nothings," her character is so obtusely constructed that her attendance at "those perfectly delightful Monday morning musicales" obviously smacks of authorial derision. Mrs. Harley Manners's social life at these musicales is frequently thwarted by the dashing music critic Philip Studley, whose exaggerated perspicuity and forthright presence set up the joke Henderson perpetuates throughout the story with a wink and a nod.

Yet *The Soul of a Tenor* is more than just a tongue-in-cheek autobiographical jest. The character names themselves hint of an allegory. If Henderson, like Proust with his similarly single-minded salonnière Madame Verdurin, could satirize the dynamics between vacuous high society women and the all-knowing music critic, the satire only succeeds because audiences knew they were in on the joke.

THE INVITATION

One might be forgiven for side-eyeing this book as yet another tired tome honoring (perhaps mocking) a scenario similar to those constructed by Henderson or Proust, where salons merely appear to sponsor fledgling artists but in practice serve mostly as an echo chamber of self-congratulatory antics of the host and her wealthy, philistine friends. That is not the case for this book, as this was not the case with Betty. She understood well the kind of work she was doing—"Helping composers is not a socially upscale activity today," she once told a reporter. "You don't get your name on a plaque"—and was uncompromising in her expectations for those she invited.[19] Whoever attended joined a small but energetic group, willing to be tightly packed in small quarters and sit on hard folding chairs to listen

18 W. J. Henderson, *The Soul of a Tenor: A Romance* (New York: Henry Holt, 1912), 1–2.

19 Jepson, "A Cultivated Ear."

to what could charitably be called some of the most demanding music ever written. Photographs from her salons show sweat-stained but grinning audience members, some faces familiar and recognizable, others lost from memory. Attendees knew this was not a free concert; Betty intended to "pass the plate" at each event, prodding those with deep pockets to donate *or else*. During the welcome to one salon, Betty explained the absence of a disinvited regular at the Music Room by accusing her of freeloading, coming for Franco's pasta but never contributing.[20] Betty found ways to give composers a self-sufficient platform, inviting composers to bring cassette tapes and scores to sell at a small merchandise table, for instance. Although Betty didn't pay the composers to appear (other than almost always hosting them in one of her spare bedrooms and paying all transportation costs), she did offer to pay honorariums to a small number of local musicians who might be called on to perform at the salon.

Those attending the Music Room moseyed around the home before and after the salon, plates of pasta prepared by Franco in hand, admiring the artwork and the company she held close to her heart. The cozy Music Room appeared even smaller because of the dark velvet walls, though the large white canvas by Sam Francis and oversized crafted rug gave the space an openness and vitality.

If the walls in that small space could talk, I imagine they would pass the mic to the art that they so diligently shouldered. What could we glean from listening closely to those echoing sounds? What sounds still resonate throughout those canvases? What vibrations from countless music people who paused before the works and spoke with garlic and rosemary on their tongues are bouncing still, trapped yet within the paints and acrylics?

The sounder they are.

I could tell you some of what was said during these salons because Alan thought recording them on tape would somehow profit the enterprise if he could sell them to local classical music stations (they didn't and he couldn't). But the story of Betty's salons is richer than what was recorded—an ethnographer of sound's inevitable dilemma. How could I convey, as James Agee lamented, the real essence of these events?

This book speaks to such an impossibility as much as it speaks to the development of new music. The best I know to do to make these transcriptions come alive is take your eye-hands and lead you through Betty's salon as if we were there together, invited guests to gatherings that married the commonplace with the

20 In Betty's words: "I made an announcement at one concert that there would be a collection for the festival [New Music America] and that people who didn't contribute would be dropped from the Music Room mailing list." See Jepson, "A Cultivated Ear."

exceptional. *The Music Room* speaks *of* but also *in* these events themselves. As chapters unfold, I pace through the room and eavesdrop on what was said. The art, the food, the room itself whisper back what we today crane our ears to hear—that which falls between the thoughts of John Cage or Libby Larsen, or the fast-paced chatter of a young Philip Glass and a tight-lipped, world-weary Conlon Nancarrow. The materiality of the Music Room gave place to Betty's story; it only seems fitting that through those materials Betty's story gets told.

Because Betty's home was her most closely associated identifier and primary source of so much of her perceived value, I have chosen this venue to glimpse portions of this self-described housewife's life from the space that at once granted and maintained her position in the world of new music. It is in fact from the attention of a housewife, Bachelard writes, that we may derive this pleasure of invitation in the first place: "From one object in a room to another, housewifely care weaves the ties that unite a very ancient past to the new epoch. The housewife," as he puts it, "awakens furniture that was asleep."[21]

The Beverly Hills Housewife is no longer here to demand your attention, to side-eye how deep you dig into your wallet, to snap your picture poring over Franco's latest pasta experiment. But what lingers in these pages is the force that animated

FIGURE I.6 Audience gathered at Betty's salon, January 10, 1988. Photo by Betty Freeman, courtesy of the Los Angeles Philharmonic Archives.

---

21 Bachelard, *The Poetics of Space*, 68.

such giving and attention and care in the first place. Betty's salons were much more than the sum of these pages, and ink on synthetic paper can only ever capture the impossibility of its own task. The Music Room is still here, though, in echoes and shadow, in love and adoration, in story and in imagination. As are Betty, Alan, Franco, and her darling John. The date has been set and the guests are seating themselves. Furniture is awakening. Consider yourself invited.

Chapter 1

American Shadows

Conlon Nancarrow
Elliott Carter
Milton Babbitt

IF YOU CONTINUE your glance past the Hockney painting in the den to the hallway off the side of the living area, you will come to a room covered in black velvet. The Steinway piano gives away that this must be the Music Room. The room is relatively small, given its importance—thirty-three feet by twenty-eight feet, almost square. It seems an afterthought to its neighboring and much larger den off the back, where Betty posed for Hockney's camera. Folding chairs in the Music Room cover much of the available floor space, in preparation for the afternoon's salon.

Like much of the rest of the house, the walls of the Music Room are fitted with contemporary art. The eye is immediately drawn to Roy Lichtenstein's stoic 1976 painting titled *Still Life with Cash Box*. It's somewhat amusing that an empty cash box would line the room where one of the more significant acts of patronage of the last century took place. In fact, I wonder if the piece's title was in this setting more than just descriptive, but actually a statement in itself—an empty cash box representing the fullness of the giver: the giving of art, the giving of life. Empty pockets and so forth.

An inside-out pocket is certainly one way to think about why these three composers are bundled together. As a trio, Elliott Carter, Milton Babbitt, and Conlon Nancarrow cast a funny shadow. All three composed in a formalist manner, but that's largely where the aesthetic similarities and shared legacies end. Babbitt was

The Music Room. Jake Johnson, Oxford University Press.
DOI: 10.1093/9780197775752.003.0002

gregarious, Carter charming, and Nancarrow awkward. Nancarrow wrote almost exclusively for the player piano, while Carter's and Babbitt's output spills into immense large-scale works as well as intimate pieces firmly in the chamber music repertoire.

Perhaps for this reason alone Babbitt and Carter enjoyed a much more stable and recognizable place in American music than Nancarrow did or does today. Babbitt held a prominent position at Princeton University for much of his career, and Carter was independently wealthy. Nancarrow, on the other hand, lived out his radical politics in such a way that he struggled to have a physical home in America let alone a place at the table. He lived modestly and tinkered with his player piano rolls most of his life in Mexico City, far from the energy and atmosphere and influence of the American music scene.

And yet Nancarrow belongs to the stories of Babbitt and Carter, and they to his, in compelling ways. Composer and historian of the experimental music tradition Kyle Gann has argued that Nancarrow and Babbitt were of a generation of composers, shaped indelibly by John Cage, "for whom music was simply a pattern of sounds, incapable of expressing or eliciting emotion except by some willing self-delusion on the part of the listener."[1] Both Babbitt and Nancarrow gravitated (although at differing magnitudes) toward machinery, technology, and mediated forms of music-making and both located within their musical expression a number of formalist strategies and techniques. They are supreme examples of what Gann calls "composer-scientists."[2] Carter, on the other hand, fingered Nancarrow as one of three primary influences on his development of rhythm (the other two were Charles Ives and Henry Cowell), which became a principle organizational and aesthetic value for much of his career.[3] Carter was a devoted friend and champion of Nancarrow and his work but found often intense emotional expressiveness in his music because of, and not despite, his shared technical ferocity toward rhythm in particular. Betty Freeman sensed Nancarrow's outsized place in American experimental music, along with his underresourced career, and, much as she did for

---

1 Kyle Gann, "No Escape from Heaven: John Cage as Father Figure," in *The Cambridge Companion to John Cage*, ed. David Nicholls (Cambridge: Cambridge University Press, 2002), 243. Babbitt is perhaps most closely associated with the detached listener and privileged expertise of the composer from his now infamous essay "Who Cares If You Listen?," published in *High Fidelity Magazine* in February 1958.

2 Kyle Gann, "Outside the Feedback Loop: A Nancarrow Keynote Address," *Music Theory Online* 20, no. 1 (March 2014).

3 See Elliott Carter, "The Rhythmic Basis of American Music," originally published in 1955, in *The Writings of Elliott Carter*, ed. Else Stone and Kurt Stone (Bloomington: Indiana University Press, 1977), 160–165. For more on Carter and Nancarrow's relationship, see Dragana Stojanovi-Novicic, "The Carter–Nancarrow Correspondence," *American Music* 29, no. 1 (Spring 2011): 64–84.

Harry Partch toward the end of his career, became a steady and important patron in the last fifteen years of his life.[4]

At the Music Room, some composers were loquacious, others allowed their music to do most of the talking for them. Conlon Nancarrow fills a separate space entirely, though one not altogether separate from the persona he carried as stymied outsider. Nancarrow's personality was subdued, and his reckoning of the context for his music highly nuanced. His long-time assistant Eva Soltes accompanied Nancarrow and his wife from Mexico City to Los Angeles especially for this salon, where she introduced the composer and, on his behalf, consequently did most of the talking. Nancarrow's subtlety and the gregarious extraversion of his former teacher Nicolas Slonimsky comically united while Alan tried somewhat halfheartedly to pull information from Nancarrow, who otherwise seemed happily befuddled to be there.[5] In companion to Elliott Carter's and Milton Babbitt's seemingly self-assured place as fixtures in American music, Nancarrow's inclusion here frames Betty's salons as a space where legacies were not determined but *positioned*—an intergenerational space mediated less by establishment of influence than by the power of the music itself.

CONLON NANCARROW

January 29, 1984

Eva Soltes has worked closely with Nancarrow over the years, *Alan speaks over the din of the crowd.* If I have the story correct, she sort of sought him out more or less as a groupie for his music in the beginning. She's been his faithful interpreter and companion as he's traveled around the world and as his music has become more and more known.[6] Eva is here and she's going to introduce the music

---

4 Among the ways Betty supported Nancarrow's work, she commissioned *Study no. 42* and *Piece no. 2*; commissioned a transcription of Studies for chamber ensemble for the Los Angeles Philharmonic New Music group; and gave three grants in 1991 for *Study for Orchestra*, which was rescored in 1999 for a performance led by Thomas Adès.

5 Nancarrow's quietude and humorously brief remarks in front of this crowd seem to be a lasting quality of his, as he was equally terse when interviewed by classical music radio programmers Cole Gagne and Tracy Caras in 1975 as part of their book *Soundpieces: Interviews with American Composers* (Metuchen, NJ: Scarecrow Press, 1982), 281–302.

6 According to Kyle Gann, Eva Soltes met Nancarrow in 1981, when she was a concert director. It was her tireless efforts that secured Nancarrow a five-year visa, which allowed him to travel to Los Angeles, among other places in the country, promoting his music and speaking for his music in public for the first time in his life. See Kyle Gann, *The Music of Conlon Nancarrow* (Cambridge: Cambridge University Press, 1995), 48.

FIGURE 1.1 John Adams, Betty Freeman, and Conlon Nancarrow, November 14, 1985, taken on the back patio of Betty's home, as captured in David Hockney's painting *Beverly Hills Housewife*. Courtesy of the Los Angeles Philharmonic Archives.

FIGURE 1.2 Nicolas Slonimsky and Conlon Nancarrow on the back patio, January 29, 1984. Photo by Betty Freeman, courtesy of the Los Angeles Philharmonic Archives.

of Nancarrow, which is on tape for reasons that she will explain. This is the tape of a concert of his music which was presented at no less prestigious a place than IRCAM [Institute for Research and Coordination in Acoustics/Music] in Paris.[7] Here is Eva to tell you the rest.

I didn't really come prepared with extensive comments, *Eva begins*. I guess I'll speak for Conlon, since I have in the past. These pieces that are on tape, as Alan explained, were done by Bob Schumaker, recorded in Conlon's studio in Mexico City. In a sense, Conlon considers himself a tape music composer, so that what you're hearing really is the real thing, even though if you hear them in his studio, well, then you have the ambience, you know, slightly different ambience of the room. But Conlon feels very proud of these pieces as they were recorded on tape. So, we always tell people that it's the way they're intended to be heard. Some of Conlon's compositions, although you won't hear any of those particular ones today, are actually only listenable on tape because they're done on the same piano (they're two tracks that are put together). In any case, sometimes people feel cheated because they think they're not really seeing the pianos, but I just want to let you know that it's the way it was intended.

We are going to hear most of a concert that was done, as Alan mentioned, at IRCAM in the fall of '82 during a tour that we did sort of celebrating Conlon's seventieth birthday. We're going to start with *Study no. 25*, which is 5'40." After each piece, I'll remind you of the lengths and so forth.

[Recording played of *Study no. 25*]

Next, we're going to hear *Study no. 12*, which is about 4'15."

[Recording played of *Study no. 12*]

Next, we're going to hear *Study no. 36*. I'm just realizing—something special about hearing this music in this room, is that this room is just about the size of Conlon's studio. It feels right in here. So, we'll hear now 36, which is 4 minutes.

[Recording played of *Study no. 36*]

No. 10.

---

7 IRCAM, opened in 1977 by Pierre Boulez, is a French research center dedicated to developing new and experimental music and music software. A number of prominent composers have found support through the auspices of IRCAM, including Luciano Berio, Tristan Murail, and Kaija Saariaho, and the center's resident ensemble, Ensemble InterContemporain, played a decisive role in promoting, recording, and distributing music originating from IRCAM.

[Recording played of *Study no. 10*]

We're going to end this musical segment with a piece that's called *40B*. This particular work is for two pianos. So, you'll hear a little more density of sound. Then, we're going to ask everybody to sort of turn around in their seats and face the Sam Francis [*Japan Line*], which will serve as the screen for the slideshow. It'll give you a little bit of an idea of how it's all made. So, *40B*, and then we'll ask you all to turn around.

[Recording played of *40B*]

Alan interjects here to introduce another musical dignitary in the room, conductor, composer, and musicologist Nicolas Slonimsky:

We have tonight a most momentous meeting of bodies and minds. Conlon Nancarrow in the 1930s studied in Boston with a rising young man of music with a funny accent by the name of Nicolas Slonimsky.[8] Tonight, for the first time in how many years?

Thirty-three, *Slonimsky says*.

Thirty-three years, *Alan continues*, teacher and student came together again to compare notes on what they've been up to in the years intervening. What do you remember about your classes together?

Back to Slonimsky:

There was no class. I wasn't even classified, and I didn't belong to any class. I was, strictly speaking, a proletarian because I couldn't make money in Boston. Well, anyway there was no class. Just Conlon came to me, and he was just Conlon Nancarrow. So, who was he? I mean, he was able to pay me $2.50 for a lesson, which was the foundation of my prosperity. I guess later on I collected $3 a lesson, an hour. There's one thing I do remember: I was extremely generous with my time. I didn't look at the clock, very much to the detriment of my students, because they wanted to get out. But not Conlon, because Conlon was always very serious. That's what I remember.

Now, I read an interview with Conlon in which Conlon was asked obvious questions of being connected with a person like me, who was famous, or rather infamous, for conducting and playing compositions by composers who were absolutely black-listed, black-balled by every respectable conductor, composers by the names of Charles Ives, Edgard Varèse, or Henry Cowell, or Carl Ruggles, or

8 Nancarrow studied in Boston in 1934 and 1935 with Slonimsky, but also Roger Sessions and Walter Piston. Gann, *The Music of Conlon Nancarrow*, 38.

Wallingford Riegger. They were not accepted fifty years ago, when I started looking at them and playing them. So, I had a very bad reputation. The question asked of Conlon by an interviewer was whether I imparted any of my knowledge and intimacy with the aforementioned people. He said no, that I just taught him things. It's probably right, because what would I have accomplished by giving him Ives and Varèse without any preparation? I taught him, I believe, strictly Rimsky-Korsakov. Well, Rimsky-Korsakov occasionally wrote modern music. In [Rimsky-Korsakov's 1909 opera] *The Golden Cockerel*, for instance, he has funny scales, supposedly Oriental scales.[9] Of course, the Orient was strictly manufactured in St. Petersburg. Rimsky-Korsakov never went anywhere near the Orient. But I understand that in Persia—I mean before that bearded guy who took power when Persia was a civilized country—Persian composers actually imitated Rimsky-Korsakov's Arabian scales, which was a very curious development. Well, anyway, this is my memory.

Then, all of a sudden Conlon said that he had to travel. He always liked to see Spain. Well, Spain was a very unhealthy place to go at that time. It was 1936. Because there was a guy named Franco.[10] It's not like Franco [Assetto, who] we love and revere here. I mean, it was a different kind of Franco. He had to be fought against. Now, obviously, I said I sympathize with this idea. I said, what could you do? You have to fight him. I wish I could fight him, but I couldn't, because I never even learned how to manipulate a revolver. Murder or even self-defense is not in my character.

Well, in the meantime I really became convinced that Conlon had something very real. I sent some of his piano pieces to Henry Cowell, who was editing *New Music* [*Quarterly*] at that time. I was an advisor and a member of the editorial board, as a matter of fact. So, I sent those pieces to him. I said, "I guarantee that they are ultramodern pieces." Because you see Henry Cowell only wanted to publish ultramodern pieces. When I tried to submit to him a trio by Roy Harris, he said, "This is not modern. I can't publish it." I had to persuade him to publish it. That was the first publication in *New Music* of a piece by Roy Harris.[11] Perhaps it's not modern, but anyway, he was Roy Harris. This is the story. Then, I remember

9 What Slonimsky refers to as Oriental scales are, more accurately and in today's parlance, both octatonic and whole-tone scales.

10 Francisco Franco, the military dictator of Spain, who began ruling in 1939, after three years of civil war sparked by a coup attempt following the 1936 elections.

11 Harris's piano trio appeared in a 1936 issue of *New Music Quarterly*. Cowell's trial and imprisonment in San Francisco on morality charges beginning in May of that year brought his editorship to a close. See Michael Hicks, "The Imprisonment of Henry Cowell," *Journal of the American Musicological Society* 44, no. 1 (Spring 1991): 92–119, for further insights into this period of Cowell's life. For more on Cowell's understanding of Harris, see Beth Levy, "'The White Hope of American Music'; or, How Roy Harris Became Western," *American Music* 19, no. 2 (Summer 2001): 131–167.

that Aaron Copland wrote something very poignant after reviewing those pieces that were published in *New Music*. He said, "Conlon Nancarrow is obviously a composer of imagination and individuality and originality. It would be a terrible loss to American music if he were to be killed in Spain." And certainly, it was. Well, fortunately he wasn't killed in Spain. But, instead, finally Franco was toppled over and now he sleeps quietly or unquietly in a mausoleum some place.[12]

Now, the rest should be told by my partner, guest, and strangely enough, former pupil. You see, here it says, "Nicolas Slonimsky, first teacher of Conlon." Now, this is my claim to fame. I always say, "Slimsky, Splinsky, Plopsky? Nevermind, I'm the first teacher of Conlon." So, anyway, I feel proud of myself. I can face the musical community with this wonderful introduction. Here, of course I knew that he was doing something extraordinary and in the meantime, he was in Mexico because the Republican government in Washington didn't care to accept him in the United States because he was a *Red*. As a matter of fact, he wasn't. He's just a nightmare of a person.[13]

To us it was a Democratic government at that time, *Rich adds*.

No, that's right, *Slonimsky offers*. After the World War. After Roosevelt. And then Truman, but—well, let's not go into that. Anyway, he'll tell you about it. Then, I learned that he was doing this extraordinary work by perforating ribbons and inserting them into player pianos. Now, I love new techniques. As a matter of fact, I have a profound theory that a technique, if it's new, well-developed, and self-consistent, will generate interesting compositions, provided the composer has brains and talent. Now, in this case both brains and talent were available. So, in 1951 I visited Mexico. And there was Conlon Nancarrow working on all his pianos. Not only pianos. This may not be so well known, but he had other instruments: clarinets, and horns, and trumpets.

No, no. *Nancarrow finally stirs*.

What? *Slonimsky asks*.

No.

No horns?

No, just the drums.

Yes, but you had clarinets, *Slonimsky insists*.

No.

12 Nancarrow joined the Communist Party in the 1930s and, after the Spanish Civil War embroiled, he went to Spain as part of the Abraham Lincoln Brigade to fight against Franco. In 1939, he was captured by the French and held in the Gurs internment camp.

13 Nancarrow moved to Mexico in 1940 to avoid US government censorship based on his Communist affiliations, becoming a Mexican citizen in 1956. Aside from these rare ventures outside of the country, he spent the rest of his life in Mexico.

Slonimsky again:

Well, didn't you have an idea of doing something similar with other instruments?

No, only the percussion instruments, which never worked anyhow.

Well, I sit corrected, *Slonimsky sits back*. I don't know where I got it. I'm afraid I put it in my article![14]

Oh, I think you did! That's right.

Slonimsky:

I did because there was your picture. Well, the picture could be unearthed and perhaps we could find out.

Well, I had my picture with all those instruments. They are all drums! *Nancarrow laughs.*

All drums? *Slonimsky still can't believe it.*

All of them.

Well, you see at that time I was not familiar with clarinets and trumpets, so I thought they were clarinets and trumpets. *Slonimsky and the audience laugh.*

That's true, *he continues*. I'm not trying to be funny. I really thought that you tried to do something similar with other instruments. Drums, of course, but I thought there were other instruments for a future orchestra that would be completely computerized. Whatever it was, there I heard those things. Now, correct me if I'm wrong, but I thought that you said that it took you half an hour to write a single bar.

More or less, *Nancarrow concedes*.

Slonimsky continues:

Well, anyway, so I figured out how long it would take him to compose Mahler's 9th Symphony or [Schoenberg's] *Gurrelieder*.

Alan steps in:

Conlon, we've had a report of your musical evolution from a close observer. Can you fill in with anything that you'd like to say about your own stylistic evolvement? You told me before when we were talking out in the yard that during your time before you went to Spain, Stravinsky played an important part in your career. Can you imply things that you've taken from Stravinsky into your own music?

Not really, *Nancarrow shrugs*. As a matter of fact, I think the main influence of Stravinsky on me was his mind—I mean this really brilliant musical mind—because my music doesn't resemble Stravinsky's at all.

Someone in the audience stirs:

Do you interact with the musical community in Mexico City at all?

---

14 See Nicolas Slonimsky, "Complicated Problem—Drastic Solution," *Christian Science Monitor*, November 10, 1951.

Almost none.

He continues:

Do you go to concerts over there? There is a big musical community.

Well, there are many mafias there, but I'm not in any of them. *Nancarrow gives a slight laugh.*

The audience member keeps prodding:

Is your music ever performed there?

No.

Do you derive any kind of inspiration from living in Mexico City? *Another asks.*

Possibly, *he adds*, but I'm sure it's all for me unconscious. I'm not aware of it.

A somewhat exasperated audience member chuckles:

Do you *like* living there?

Well, I used to. Not so much anymore. No, it's really getting bad.

Alan pipes up again:

Have you ever been tempted to find out what tape might do for something that you might have on your mind musically?

You mean electronics? *Nancarrow asks.*

Yes, *Alan answers*. Do you use all the devices that electronics allow you?

Nancarrow shifts in his seat:

No, it's too late for me now to start learning a new technique. Well, before I started the player piano thing, I vaguely felt that it had sort of started, and that that would be a solution, but it was so primitive at that time that I didn't, and I got into player pianos and stayed there.

Have you had the desire to work in just intonation? *Someone asks from the back corner of the room.*

I'm not too interested in different forms of tuning, *he responds*. Because what I'm doing really is mainly temporal and rhythmical things. It could be even non-pitched instruments to do what I'm doing. In other words, drums of some sort.

Another guest speaks up:

What happens if you accidentally punch the wrong hole?

Nancarrow again:

If it's just one wrong note, you put a little scotch tape over it and punch it right. If it's a big section, it's very deadly. You have to cut it out and redo that section, and splice the piece in. So, it's a little difficult.

Did you doctor your player pianos, *another asks*, or is it a normal player piano?

Well, they're hardened hammers, *he responds*. One of them, I took a leather strip and put a little metallic thing in the strip, and then glued it over the felt on each hammer. On the other one, I had some wooden hammers made, purely wood, and covered them with a strip of steel. That's the very metallic-sounding piano.

Alan:

Can you get maintenance for your player pianos in Mexico?

Nancarrow:

Up until now. As a matter of fact, the man who was the expert at that just died a couple of weeks ago. So, I don't know what I'm going to do. As a matter of fact, most piano tuners can't tune that piano. Well, I have someone now who is very good. Before, after two or three times someone would come in and tune the piano, leave, and it was worse than when he came.

Eva Soltes enters the conversation again:

We're going to play *Study no. 37*, which is an extensive work of ten and a half minutes. If anybody's interested, we could ask Conlon about that particular piece. It's one of the most complicated ones.

Nancarrow corrects her:

Well, no, it's a little complicated in one sense. It's a piece that has twelve different tempi. Of course, during the progress of the piece there are a few times when all twelve are going at once, but not very frequently. Usually there are several going along and then several others. It's sort of a continuous thing. But as I say those twelve very seldom are playing at the same time.

You make it sound so easy, *Alan snorts.*

How do you strap your microphone to record that sound? *Someone asks from the audience.* Did you set the microphone in any special way?

Nancarrow, gesturing to Bob Schumaker:

Ask the engineer.

Schumaker sits up:

It's actually rather simple because the sound in the room is magnificent. We're just using good stereo recording techniques and good equipment. You just find what's the loudest point and leave it alone from there on. You just start the tape when the piano roll starts. It's very, very simple.

Alan marvels:

A recording of that room is the artwork.

Eva again tries to move the evening along:

So, let's turn our chairs back around.

[Recording played of *Study no. 37*]

I just wanted to say a couple of things, *Eva adds.* One is that Peter Garland published a score to that last piece—Betty has it on sale; it's in the boutique.[15] And

15 Peter Garland published the score to Nancarrow's *Study no. 37* in the 1976 issue of his periodical *Soundings*, a publication that introduced Nancarrow to a wider public. Some salons featured a kind of merchandise table where composers could sell recordings of their music or, as in this case, sell scores.

it's a wonderful thing to listen to and look at the score at the same time. The second thing I wanted to say, tomorrow night there are a few special things happening at the concert at the Japan America Theater.[16] One is that Bill Kraft will be conducting the world premiere of three orchestrations that Dorrance Stalvey has done of three of the studies.[17] For the first time three of the studies will be heard as instrumental pieces. Then, the world premiere of a work that Betty Freeman commissioned for tomorrow night's concert.[18] And, a piano four-hands version of a sonatina that will be played on acoustic piano that Conlon's never heard: he wrote it forty years ago! So, that's tomorrow night.

Betty stands to signal the evening's end:

I would like to thank Conlon and [his wife] Yoko and [son] Mako for coming all the way from Mexico City to bring us this joy. And I would like to invite everybody for Franco Assetto's composition: pasta marinara!

ELLIOTT CARTER

January 12, 1994

I think that I should talk about this *Piano Sonata* a little bit, *Carter begins*.

It was actually something I wrote at the end of the war in 1945. At that time, most composers that I knew were writing music for piano that was very restricted. It was the kind of thing that Hindemith and Milhaud and even Stravinsky were writing—pieces that were really music of the type of Bach in which the range of the piano was very limited and it was rather linear. I decided that I would like to write a piece and use the entire sonority of the piano at that time. In that particular period, this was a rather unusual thing to do. I don't know, I've always gotten stuck on ideas of this sort.

So, I started thinking about how the piano sounded and how you could make a grand piano ring and you will hear all sorts of different things that happen. However, the music itself began to be a transition from the music which I had been writing before, which was rather neoclassic and sort of Americanizing. This actually has a second movement fugue that is somewhat like jazz. I was getting away from what I had been doing before, which was more popular, more jazz-like music,

16 The Aratani Theatre is held within the Japanese American Cultural and Community Center.

17 Stalvey orchestrated *Studies nos. 14, 26*, and *32*.

18 *Study no. 45* was commissioned by Betty and renamed the *Betty Freeman Suite*. It premiered January 30, 1984.

and writing something that was on a grander and larger scale. This was a big step away from what I had been writing, which was, as I said, a rather limited neoclassic style and leading toward the music of the type that you will hear later. This is one of the first steps that I took. It's rather, for instance, [as if] the tonality of the piece is indefinite. It's constantly wavering between two keys a semitone apart—B-flat and B—so that one is never sure which key the piece will be in. And, in fact, I've made it so that this is quite blurred in many, many places. This was an attempt to get away from the traditional harmonic scheme—well, not so traditional, but the kind of harmonic scheme I had been using prior to this period.

I was asked to write this piece by a pianist, John Kirkpatrick, who played the *Concord Sonata* of Charles Ives for the first time. He disliked this piece because he thought it was too brilliant and too showy—I think that's why. In any case, he didn't play it. We had a very nervous performance by Webster Aitken, who was a pianist who was well-known at that time, who nearly died of excitement and distress when he played it. Then, finally the man who started to play it more frequently was Beveridge Webster, who recorded it and played it and even then, it was a piece that was very hard on many pianists at that time. Now, there are lots of people. I think there are five or six recordings of this. There's even somebody who sent me a recording from Australia. So, this seems to have gotten around.

Alan interjects:
Scott Dunn will add himself to the list of people who play this sonata. A young resident of this area, retired ophthalmologist and extraordinary pianist who is a name to conjure with.

[Performance of *Piano Sonata*]

I don't know see how he remembers it! *Carter congratulates Dunn.* How can you play that without notes? I think it's extraordinary. And so well, too! Thank you very much.

Are we ready to move on [to the next piece]? *Alan asks.*

Carter again:
Anyhow, let me say about this particular piece that there was a festival, and it was a very odd festival, I must say, in Avignon.[19] The French Radio organized two weeks of poor people that had to deal with my music. They gave courses. Charles Rosen came and taught people to play the *Piano Sonata*. The Arditti Quartet came and taught

---

19 This Festival of Avignon took place in July 1991, in a series of concerts devoted to Carter's music.

FIGURE 1.3 Elliott Carter and Mel Powell in the home of Judith and Ron Rosen, January 12, 1994. Photo by Betty Freeman, courtesy of the Los Angeles Philharmonic Archives.

quartets to play my quartets. There was a timpani player [Sylvio Gualda] who came, it seemed to me, with all the timpanists in the world and they were all banging away. For two weeks, all I could hear was my timpani pieces being played in this enormous Cistercian monastery that this school uses in the summer. Not only that, but there were lectures. I had to lecture. When I lectured in French the Americans in the audience complained; when I lectured in English the French complained. They also brought a number of different people who were experts on my music, and they lectured about it. It was really hard to take, but everybody liked it. It was hard for me.

In any case, I was asked by the flutist, Robert Aitken, a flutist from Toronto, to write a piece that they could give as a first performance. I remembered that Avignon is of course the place where the popes went after they had problems in Rome and lived there for a while. They brought with them a poet, Petrarch, who lived and wrote a vast number of poems about his girlfriend. We don't even know whether he saw her or not, but anyhow I looked for a title for this piece and finally found this poem of Petrarch in which this is one line. If she gets it, it's an amusing poem. But what happened was: then we drove around the countryside. There is an extraordinary place—La Fontaine de Vaucluse, not far from there—where there is a cliff with an enormous cave and out of it a river comes, a huge river that runs into the Rhône. Petrarch, when the popes forsook him, went and lived in this place, and we visited it. Then we played the piece. We found that on that day it was played it was something like the 500th-and-something birthday of Petrarch by chance. I'll read you about it—I think maybe I should read it in English:

> Blessed in my dreams and satisfied to languish,
> embrace shadows and chase a summer breeze,
> I swim in a sea that knows no depths or shore,
> plow waves and build on sand and *write in wind*[20]

. . . which is the [translated] title of this piece. Later on, he complains about his Laura—Laura who didn't pay attention to him.

[Performance of *Scrivo in Vento*]

Riconoscenza per Goffredo Petrassi—who is and was one of the leading Italian composers of the twentieth century—when my first string quartet was played in Rome in 1953 when I was at the American Academy, he was one of the few people that thought that this was a very good piece. He came up and said to me something that no one has ever said to me before, and that is we talked French and decided we should address each other as *tu*, which, as you know, is the familiar form. I was very touched by that because no one had ever said that to me before. Now, we always say *tu* to each other. We've remained friends ever since 1953. I've followed his music and he followed mine. When he became eighty in 1984, I was asked by a festival in Italy, the Pontino Festival, to write a piece for his eightieth birthday. This is the piece. I thought of it actually as a piece in which the violin is playing a sort of continuous line, like a line of life. In it, there are interruptions. The violin plays rather rapidly and angrily and at other times rather quietly, but somehow this line continues on no matter what the interruptions are.

[Performance of *Riconoscenza per Goffredo Petrassi*]

Let me say that this Pontino Festival occurs in a very wonderful place, where Circe had her cave that Odysseus went to. They have this festival there every year. One year was devoted to me. These people have become very good friends of mine. The man who runs it [Raffaele Pozzi] decided to start an institute of musicology in

20 This is Petrarch's Canzone 212.

the nearby town of Latina and asked me to write a piece. They give annual prizes for the best musicological essay. They asked me to write a piece for the opening thing. They said to me, you know we have a new idea about musicology. It's really represented by Italo Calvino. Well, Italo Calvino at that time had written a series of essays that he was going to give at Harvard University called "Six Memos for the Next Millennium." In Italian, it was *Lezioni Americane*. He died before he gave the lectures. But I read the book (the book was published).[21] I took the title from this. I will read what he said about this. Each chapter in the book is about a quality of writing. There was one chapter on lightness, *leggerezza*:

> Above all, I hope to have shown there was such a thing as a lightness of thoughtfulness just as we all know that there's a lightness of frivolity. In fact, thoughtful lightness can make frivolity seem dull and heavy.

[Performance of *Con Leggerezza Pensosa*]

Well, finally, the last piece is a piece that was actually commissioned for a lady named Ann Santen, commissioned for an X-birthday—I don't know, maybe we shouldn't say! Anyway, she was fifty. Her husband asked me to write a piece for her birthday. Ann Santen has been quite a remarkable person in the field of modern music. She has run the National Public Radio station in Cincinnati for many years and has emphasized American music and has had it performed over the radio. She also encouraged the Cincinnati Symphony to play a lot of contemporary music. Actually, when Michael Gielen did my Piano Concerto with the symphony, she raised the money to have it recorded. So, I felt that I owed her something at the time of her birthday. So, this is what I wrote.[22] The title is taken from a poem of Wallace Stevens. It's part of a very long poem. It's a poem called "The Pure Good of Theory." This is the little bit that I quote with this piece:

> Time is the hooded enemy,
The inimical music, the enchantered space
In which the enchanted preludes have their place.

[Performance of *Enchanted Preludes*]

---

21 These essays were gathered as part of Harvard's Charles Eliot Norton Lectures, given in 1985. Italo Calvino, *Six Memos for the Next Millennium* (New York: Vintage, 1988).

22 Santen writes about this commission as well as her first meeting Carter in Cincinnati in a tribute on ElliottCarter.com, https://www.elliottcarter.com/tributes/ann-santen/.

Now Alan speaks up:

In 1978 you did a radio interview on WKCR, a Columbia University station. You were asked the question at that time, which you answered quite eloquently: "How much does it matter that when I listen to your pieces, I don't hear the processes that you write about in the program notes?"

Carter again:

Well, let me put it the other way around. When a student goes to a conservatory and spends two years learning how to write a harmony in great detail, he doesn't expect the audience to hear that when a Beethoven symphony is played, or does he? I mean, it's quite a difficult thing and a very elaborate thing to write harmony and counterpoint. It's a very intellectual thing, let us say, on certain levels. What does the audience hear when works use the common practice of music when it's being played?

I want them to get a message out of the music. The reasons that all these things are that way is because there is an expressive intention which isolates one group of instruments from another and makes them contrasting. I'm talking about the things like red, yellow, and green and so forth when I'm talking that way. When you read [the program notes] as you did, it gives the impression that this is a mechanical thing, but it isn't a mechanical thing at all. A major seventh is very different from a minor seventh, for instance, just as red is different from green.

Now Betty:

In Europe, the composer is treated with great respect, the music is given great interest, and it's a major thing in Europe when a new composition is performed. Here it just seems to pass over. There isn't the same level of enthusiasm or regard for classical music as there is in Europe. Could you speak a little bit about that?

I can't explain that really, honestly, *Carter says*. I think that there is a very simple way of talking about [it] that may be an explanation, I'm not sure. One of the simplest ones is that there has been in Europe, as you know, a very elaborate state subsidy of performances. In England, for instance, the British broadcasting system was for many years run by a man who loved contemporary music, Sir William Glock. He insisted on having very large amounts of it played over the radio and gradually a public was formed. When my music is played, but mine isn't the only one (there would be many contemporary composers that would be played) and the audiences are familiar with this and know it. This man was able over all those years to play a great deal, to commission works, to get them played in concerts. The general support of music is deteriorating somewhat now, but it was for a long time. This is a similar thing in Paris. Boulez first started with small concerts and then finally the IRCAM and the Ensemble InterContemporain [see Chapter 4]. They give a regular subscription series of contemporary music and it's played very well. They've made a great deal of effort to publicize this and to draw in a public. They get big publics. My concerts are sold out in Paris. I'm always rather surprised at it myself.

There was a pianist named Jacob Lateiner whom the Ford Foundation was going to support. They gave him the possibility of choosing a composer to write a piano concerto. He came up to me and said, "Would you write a piano concerto?" I said, "Well, do you know my music?" I wanted to be sure he knew what he was going to get before I wrote one note. After we had gotten an agreement within two weeks, we got a telephone call from the Ford Foundation saying, "How much are the parts going to cost to copy?" I said, "I haven't written a note! I don't know." Then they kept checking up on me every week. Finally, I said I won't write the piece unless you shut up. That went on for a long time. It took me a long time to write the piece. So, many different things happened. I finally went to Berlin as a composer-in-residence and wrote most of it there.

Then, the other part of the story was the Ford Foundation wanted it played by several local orchestras, the Atlanta Orchestra and the Denver Orchestra and some other small orchestra. And Jacob Lateiner who wanted to be a well-known pianist, didn't feel that would help his career very much. So, he quietly talked to Mr. [Erich] Leinsdorf and Leinsdorf agreed to do it with the Boston Symphony. The Ford Foundation was furious! They wouldn't put up any money for the rehearsals with the Boston Symphony. If it would have been done in Atlanta, they would have paid for it all, but they were so angry that they didn't follow this out. Then Leinsdorf raised money to have it recorded and that was also nice. I later dedicated it to Stravinsky. He wrote me a very charming letter. I don't remember what it said, but it was very sweet.

MILTON BABBITT

March 2, 1986

I remember when Betty brought me out here many, many, many years ago and put me up at the Chateau Marmont, *Babbitt starts*. That was before John Belushi got there.[23] It's a great joy to be here. I look at so many old friends and young composers like Morty [Feldman] and Mel [Powell] and Mort Subotnick back there, who played my *Composition for Four Instruments* so beautifully on the clarinet many years ago. I could go on and on about this. And Leonard Stein,[24] who is surely one of my oldest friends and colleagues in the world.

23 Babbitt is referring here to actor John Belushi's overdosing in Hollywood's Chateau Marmont Hotel in 1982.

24 A frequent guest at Betty's salons, Leonard Stein was a highly influential musicologist and educator at the University of Southern California.

FIGURE 1.4 Milton Babbitt, March 2, 1986. Photo by Betty Freeman, courtesy of the Los Angeles Philharmonic Archives.

And, therefore, I think I'll start with Leonard because I remember one of the last times when I was with Leonard, though we've been together many, many, many times, it was out at the Schoenberg Institute when there was a convention of the Society for Music Theorists.[25] I addressed the Society for Music Theorists and thanked them profusely and profoundly for having finally come into being and for having provided us with a group for which I have real affection and real admiration: professional music theorists. Because, I said, that made it possible for me to stop passing as a part-time theorist and to go back to my full-time vocation as a part-time composer. I say that only because having to speak at all about my music rather undermines my absolutely final farewell appearance as I thought that would be at that time.

And I, again, realizing the conditions under which I find myself here, wonder if I'm here as some sort of an anachronism, you know. Alan could have referred to me as some sort of an anachronism, you know, an unreconstructed, old fashioned, academic serialist. This is a role that I'm perfectly willing to assume. I'm not being paranoid about this, but I find that lately, and this will have to do something with one of the pieces that's being played here today, the unaccompanied violin piece which was written for Paul Zukofsky. But, when I talk about that piece, I'm not even going to talk about *detachables*. There'll be no technical conversation tonight because remember, right down the road I told the Society for Music Theorists that

25 This meeting took place October 29 through November 1, 1981. Babbitt's invited lecture, titled "The Music Theoretician's Dilemmas," was given October 30.

I stopped being a music theorist, and that applies to my own music as well as to anybody else's.

I'm going to have a lot of music played here later in the week.[26] It's going to cover about forty years of my compositional effort. I've suddenly realized that lately I've been placed in a position of—given that kind of a compositional, chronological span—of justifying my compositional constants, or if you wish, my inspirational invariance, or more or less trying to, again, trace the path of my progress, or my reluctance to retrogress. The point of all of this really is, is that in speaking about my music now, I realize that there's some of you probably out here right now who wonder when I'm going to stop beating a dead set.

The audience laughs.

I shan't continue in this vein very long. You know, one man's evidence of compositional probity is another man's evidence of sheer intransigence and stubbornness.

The two works that you're going to hear tonight are relatively recent works. And, therefore in a certain sense it's not particularly relevant that I speak of forty years of compositional activity and talk in Leonard's presence as I have before of being—and again I shall be slightly paranoid—of, you know, being a legitimate (if abandoned) child of the Schoenbergian Revolution. But the two pieces that you are going to hear tonight are quite recent. One is '82 and the other is '84. We're going to play them in the order of the unaccompanied violin piece and the guitar piece. Now, I'm not going to say any naughty words about them. It reached my ears one time—and indeed it so happens by coincidence when I was appearing on a program of one Pierre Boulez, on one of his Encounter series[27]—and it reached my ears at that point, in fact he mentioned, I think, putting me on or putting me off, that somehow there are people out there who suggest that we write our music with at least one ear directed toward its susceptibility to public exegesis. In other words, we write our music so that [we] can talk about it. Now, actually, nothing can be farther from that truth because there's nothing more difficult of course than talking about one's own music.

Now, tonight you're going to hear two pieces which one of them I'm sure you've never heard before. It's been played only once before and that's the *Melismata*, the violin piece, which you'll hear first. The second piece, the guitar piece, perhaps some of you have heard the record. Write for guitarists and you get recorded and you get played.

---

26 Babbitt was in Los Angeles as part of a birthday tribute (his seventieth) at CalArts March 7–8, 1986.

27 Boulez organized the "Prospective Encounters" concert series of contemporary music in New York during the 1970s.

But I think I'll talk about the first piece first. The first piece is called *Melismata*. It's a piece for solo violin. It was written for Paul Zukofsky. The occasion for writing it I think is all I'm really going to tell you about. The problem for me, and I'm being very serious about this, is how to provide any kind of information about a first performance that might provide some of the valuable aspects of a later performance without dulling that very special effect of that first aural encounter. I really don't know what to do about this unless we went into demonstrations, and we're certainly not going to do that. Other than that, I'd rather just tell you a little bit about the piece and warn you about its length.

When I was asked to write this piece, it was because Paul Zukofsky was putting on a series of showcases for composers at Kennedy Center. And, I had written a piece for him before called *Sextets for Violin and Piano*. He played it many times, but every time with a different pianist because no pianist satisfied Paul Zukofsky. So, the question became what would he play on this program at Kennedy Center? He had hired Robert Taub, whom you'll be hearing later in the week, to play my piano music—Bethany Beardslee, whom many of you certainly have heard do my vocal music—but I thought that Paul Zukofsky should be brought back into, not the mainstream, certainly, but some side stream. And I would like him to play on the program, too, even though he was the presenter. Well, he didn't want to do *Sextets* because no pianist would do it right. So, he asked me to write an unaccompanied violin piece for him. I should have known better because a few years before, the clarinetist Anand Devendra—who some of you may remember as Allen Blustine—asked me to write an unaccompanied clarinet piece.[28]

Some laughter erupts from the room.

Well, it's true! I mean, I liked him in both forms. And if he wishes to change his name, why not? I mean, after all, there are other people who have changed their names, too. When Allen Blustine (and then he became Anand Devendra) asked me to write an unaccompanied clarinet piece, he said, "Look, write me a six-minute unaccompanied clarinet piece. Write it unaccompanied, or with tape. I don't want anything that requires a pianist. They never want to practice." Who wants an accompanist? It's too much of a trouble. I didn't write the tape piece because as you know, and Charles [Dodge] knows better than anyone, as Morty knows, because it takes too long. So, I decided to write an unaccompanied six-minute piece. It became sixteen minutes. Well, it's been played a lot because if you write a piece for solo clarinet,

---

28 Blustine told me he used the name Anand Devendra between 1976 and 1980 when commuting between New York and Poona, India. According to Blustine, he didn't commission the piece, but rather Babbitt "approached me and asked if I'd like him to write a piece for me." Email correspondence with the author, September 13, 2018.

a clarinetist will play anything.[29] So, the same thing happens with the unaccompanied violin piece. Paul said, "All right, I'll play an unaccompanied violin piece, but I'm really not playing that much these days. Write me a five- or six- or seven-minute piece." So, I wrote a piece that lasts thirteen, fourteen, fifteen minutes.

Now, I don't want to presume to say anything more about it than this. I was delighted when Yoko [Matsuda], who played it for me for the first time, that I heard her play it. She's only the second violinist to play it. Paul feels that he owns the piece, is protecting the piece, but was perfectly happy to have Yoko play it. When Yoko played today, after it was over—this is not prepared, and Yoko will attest to this—rather spontaneously after we played it and talked about a few little details, she said, you know, she feels it should be played very lyrically. Well, that's the whole point of the title. *Melismata* is supposed to imply that it's melismatic on the surface. It's rather figurative, it's rather florid, and it's also melismatic beneath the surface as it rather elaborates a few rather basic kinds of succession of tones. You notice that I'm being very discreet and I'm not saying the naughty word.

But it's a one-movement work. I don't want to presume anything about your reaction to it, your awareness of it, but it's a very demanding work on the violinist. I don't say this, I assure you, with any sense of accomplishment. You know, to say that a work is difficult, we don't revel in the difficulties of our works. The performance of the works are not revels if they are. It's rather, this is a demanding work. I thought of it as such as I wrote it. It was for Paul Zukofsky, who's an exceptional violinist, as is Yoko. I'm not warning you about anything except that I'm extremely grateful to Yoko for having learned it and for playing it tonight, and why don't you just ask me about it after you've heard it?

[Yoko Matsuda performs *Melismata*]

Thank you. I really can't tell you how grateful I am to Yoko for learning this piece. I hope nobody's going to leave here tonight saying, "*Sixty Minutes* would have seemed shorter." It *is* Sunday night.

One of the few advantages of being a senior citizen composer is that you're permitted to indulge in nostalgia, and I know that nostalgia ain't what it used to be. But the fact is that I do feel that I've omitted certain things that I would have liked to say tonight. For example, apropos of younger composers, Nicolas Slonimsky is certainly the youngest composer here tonight, if he's still here. I wanted to also say something about [film composer] David Raksin, with whom I played clarinet back

29 The piece referred to here is *My Ends Are My Beginnings* (1978).

in the University of Pennsylvania band. This may not seem relevant to you, but it seems terribly relevant to me. In the words of a great American thinker Yogi Berra, "It's déjà vu all over again."

The next piece that you're going to hear is a much shorter and in some respects—I don't wish to indulge in this kind of self-appreciation—it's not as heavy a piece, if you will. The piece is unfortunately entitled what I did not wish to entitle it. David Starobin, the guitarist, asked me to write a piece for him. I like to have titles that say something about the piece in a very specific and individuated way. I have a piece called *All Set*, a title that I was very proud of, because it meant so many things to the piece. When I was asked to write a tango in a collection of tangos, I wrote a piece called *It Takes Twelve to Tango*. These are titles that have something to do with the piece.

Well, when David Starobin asked me to write this piece—and I must tell Leonard [Stein] this right now in case I forget to tell it to him privately, I want to see what his reaction is going to be—I'm writing a piece now for the Philadelphia Orchestra, believe it or not. It's for the strings of the Philadelphia Orchestra, only the strings. I was trying to come up with a title. I was having great difficulty with this. I just wrote a piano concerto and I had to call it *Concerto for Piano and Orchestra*. I've been working very hard on a title for the Philadelphia Orchestra, for the strings of the Philadelphia Orchestra, and I'm going to call it *Transfigured Notes*. Is that all right? Is that all right, Leonard? May I have that? May I have that, Leonard? Well, I think I'm really going to use it. So, when David asked me for a piece for guitar, I wanted to call it—after thinking about it a great deal, and I hope there's nobody in my generation here who will understand the title because David didn't—I wanted to call it *Sheer Pluck*. But it seems this is a very poor title if it only refers to the guitar. But that's a very famous Horatio Alger novel. Does anybody remember that? It was one of the celebrated Horatio Alger novels, and I thought it was rather relevant from many points of view.[30] He didn't. So, I went back to the roots of my rubrics and called it *Composition for Guitar*. And David was very happy with that because it made the piece seem so very, very serious. And so it became *Composition for Guitar*. He's recorded it.

Once a wise man said, "Look, write for people who care about your music. Write for your friends." And I've been doing that more and more lately for people who ask you for pieces, not because they know what they're going to get—because they don't know what they're going to get. And I wrote this piece, the violin piece you've just heard, for Paul Zukofsky. And I've written a number of pieces for Bethany Beardslee. And I've just written a piece for Robert Taub, *Canonical Form*, which he's

30 Alger's book is titled *Luck and Pluck*, which was serialized between 1869 and 1875.

going to be playing here. And I've just written a piece for the phonograph record which Robert has made of my piano works. The people responsible for that are present here today, too, so I won't mention their names and embarrass them. But I've written a piece for the record called *Lagniappe*. Those of you who grew up in my part of the world will know what a lagniappe is. How many of you here know what a lagniappe is? It's a gratuitous little offering. When I was a little boy and I'd go into a grocery store and my mother would buy something, she'd say, "Here's a lagniappe for the little boy." So, it's a *lagniappe*. That's where it comes from. That's a Creole word, actually.

About *Composition for Guitar*: I'm not going to say any more, except it's one of those rare occasions where you have the opportunity to hear a piece played for the first time along with you. I've not heard Mr. [Stuart] Fox play this piece. I like this. I've had this experience on only very rare occasions, not rehearsed or anything. But I know guitarists these days and I know this is going to be a sensational performance.

[Stuart Fox performs *Composition for Guitar*]

Alan steps in:

I have a question for both of tonight's composers. You [Babbitt] have written a piece, a pretty good piece, if I do say so, called *Philomel*, which is an aria for soprano and tape. You [Charles Dodge] have played us a piece tonight in which you use the voice of Caruso, synthesized, or read by a synthesizer which became an instrument on which you could compose. Is technology at its present state capable of creating a Caruso performance of *Philomel*?

Babbitt again:

I'm going to leave that to Charles because Charles is working with a computer. I've never worked with a computer. I wish I had been young enough to, and really it's the computer where it's at. What about this Charles?

Charles Dodge stirs:

I think there are probably people working who can come close enough.

Yeah, I think so, too, *adds Babbitt*.

Alan again:

Is this what you live for, to hear *Philomel*?

Oh, no, *Babbitt laughs*. Bethany's going to be doing it again next month, and as a matter of fact, Judith Bettina, who's going to be singing here at the end of the week, also does a wonderful *Philomel*. I must confess, and I know Charles agrees with this, we were never interested in supplanting human performers. We were interested in supplementing the materials of music. And when performers came and asked me for a work, you know, for voice and piano—I know Charles has had the same thing. We've all had it. Morty certainly has. I know that Morty's had it. I was just on a program with one of Morty's pieces with our dear friend [cellist] Joel Krosnick.

Performers love, love the idea of having electronic works written for them. It does so many things for them. When I wrote *Philomel*, it was never with any question except writing it for a live soprano. The only reason I haven't done more is because of the logistics for saxophone and tape. Performers love this, Alan. You know, they love the idea of having a work which they don't have to rely on that dreadful accompanist who will not want to rehearse as much as they do. They can stick that tape under their arms, go out on the road, get as much rehearsal time as they want, do it at home when they wish, and also have the challenge of this unyielding accompanist.

An audience member raises a hand:

Have you ever been picketed by Local 802 [The New York local of the Musicians Union]?

Babbitt:

You know, that happened. That happened in Canada. There was a time in Canada when you were not permitted to put electronic works on. And I was in Toronto once when there was a great problem about playing my piece for piano and tape because of exactly that. The CBC musicians didn't want it on. I think those days are gone because they know we're no challenge.

Alan again:

I'm also interested in your writing for guitar. I mean, the first reaction when you think of classical guitar is the [Andrés] Segovia repertory, the strumming, one to flat two, and the whole repertory of classic guitar works. And yet, there's almost none of the old-fashioned guitar sound in your piece.

Babbitt:

Alan, look, you know, I don't want to seem to be playing in your hands because you know I wouldn't, but the fact is that was one of the things I really was going to say. When David Starobin asked me to write this piece, and I've known David as a performer around New York for years, I told him about my difficult life with the guitar. Many, many years ago, oh boy, many, many, over forty years ago, I wrote a piece called *Composition for Twelve Instruments* which strangely enough is going to be played at the end of this week. It's one of my earliest pieces. When I originally wrote that piece, it had a guitar in the ensemble. Starting in 1948, when it was written, it was canceled. Four performances were canceled by people you all know, conductors whom you all know, because every time we tried to find a guitarist who could just read it—it's a very simple part, I mean, the ensemble is difficult, the individual parts are extremely simple—that we couldn't find a guitarist who could read music or could follow a conductor.

The first guitarist who came out of the West to play the guitar seriously was someone named Stanley Silverman. When Stanley turned up in New York, by this time I had thrown in the towel. I had completely given up. I had completely rewritten the piece and substituted a harp for the guitar. That was my life with the guitar. So, when David called me, I said, you know, this was my life, and now I know there are guitarists everywhere. They're a breed unto themselves, and a remarkable breed. So, when he asked me to write this piece, we talked a lot on the phone, we never got together. I just didn't want one of these things of "show me what the guitar can do," you know, knocking on wood and drumming on the keys and so forth. The fact is that I didn't want that, but I did talk with him. When I finally sent him the piece, and David was by that time an old friend, he called me and says, "I'm working on your piece and I'm going to give the first performance far from you in London and then in Paris. You won't hear it until I get back." But, he says, "You realize you didn't use the upper few highest notes on the guitar." I said, "No, I didn't use the upper few highest notes!" Then he said, "You know, the guitar really only has a great deal of volume when you play all six strings." I said, "I don't want to write a flamenco piece."

So, when we got together and he played it for the first time and that was after he had already been playing it, the only thing I had to change was to give him a sense that this was a sort of a single line and very delicate piece in which I thought of the guitar, and I shouldn't have said it, and I apologize for this now, even again, I said to him, "I thought of the guitar as a kind of harpsichord which one could do a great deal more with the life of the individual sound." And he said, "Oh, it's a much more flexible instrument than the harpsichord."

Alan senses the evening has worn out:

Soup's on. Let me remind you in case those of you who are new here haven't discovered, we do have a boutique with all kinds of goodies available for sale. We do have the Robert Taub record[31] of Milton's [music] available, and the distributors are here so we can have the records autographed not only by the composer, but by the creators. I can guarantee you that the record will give you a Harmonious Monday, *he winks*.

Oh, you may say that! *Babbitt smiles as he walks toward the kitchen.*

31 Robert Taub, *Milton Babbitt: Piano Works* (Arles, France: Harmonia Mundi, 1992).

Chapter 2

Musical Phases

Philip Glass
Steve Reich

ANOTHER PAINTING IS mounted on the other side of the door frame. Another Lichtenstein, this one the colorful 1977 *Frolic*, which captures a Picasso-inspired nude blonde woman bouncing a Pepsi Globe–inspired volleyball along a beach. This is a vivacious blonde, her strong movement a striking contrast to the other blonde woman more somber in Hockney's painting around the corner. What's most captivating right now is how her singular eye seems to catch my own. This woman, like me, is at the moment more interested in casting her glance toward the Music Room than volleying the ball toward her beach companion. A dialogue balloon opens above her head but remains out of view among the clouds billowing in rhyme with her body's curvature. What is she trying to say? What sound has distracted her from her labor? The work is breathless and energized like a piece of music. The bodies, clouds, and shadow hurry in playful rhythms held in abeyance by the serious maritime emblems of structure, which forms a bar line next to an anchor, itself gifting gravity as if to keep the painting from floating away altogether.

Lichtenstein's blonde repeatedly defies expectation, resists categorization. Likewise, composers featured in this chapter cannot always be justified by the titles forced on them. The aloofness with which the term "minimalist" has been used is a case in point. Michael Nyman's original use of the word referred to characteristics that united the music of composers LaMonte Young, Terry Riley, Steve Reich, and

The Music Room. Jake Johnson, Oxford University Press. © Oxford University Press 2025.
DOI: 10.1093/9780197775752.003.0003

Philip Glass.[1] The degree to which each of these composers attempted to distance himself from minimalism as a label seems to parallel the gradual deflation in audience appreciation (or patience) for minimalism as a practice. During one of Philip Glass's appearances at the Music Room, for example, one audience member, like a disinterested student, passed this note to a neighbor: "he is *triad-ing* my patience."

Yet Betty's attachment to these composers was renowned and her contributions to them legendary. The appreciation ran both ways. John Adams dedicated *Nixon in China* to her, as Reich did his *Vermont Counterpoint* and *Different Trains*. Likewise, those at the Music Room seemed not to forget that minimalism had reinvigorated American concert music at a time when more cerebral, professorial composers were still experimenting with music that, in polite terms, alienated many listeners. Instead of allowing minimalism to run its course, Betty's cohort of composers found ways to use the more favorable qualities of minimalism while also experimenting with its further development. As John Adams wrote in one of his letters to Betty, "Simply put, I am looking for an expression which is capable of a greater emotional and psychological richness."

> In its heyday [minimalism] seemed to pour forth from its masters. . . . But lately all of our work seems to show signs of a kind of stagnation.
>
> . . . Who knows? Maybe the early stages of any great revolution in style goes through such levels of naiveté? If I can deal with my present self-doubt and if I can find the courage to break through, perhaps I will be able to find something worth listening to.[2]

This chapter offers a window into two composers' agonizing search for that *something*. That window takes the shape of a blonde volleyballer whose visage, like all of Lichtenstein's work, was once declared a "magnificently blank thing[]."[3] The clouds rhyme her body the way her magnificent thingness rhymes the music's repetitive void—both threaten to float away into its ether. Now, on second thought, perhaps she only appears to be watching because she has tilted her ear toward the room. She isn't *watching*. She is *listening*. Perhaps it is she who has been waiting *to be*, who was after all and above all created *to be*, an arbiter of sounds. Sound is her

1 Michael Nyman and Wim Mertens, *American Minimal Music* (London: Kahn & Averill, 1983). See also Kerry O'Brien and William Robin's updated and more holistic overview of minimalism's roots in American music in their introduction to *On Minimalism: Documenting a Musical Movement* (Berkeley: University of California Press, 2023).

2 John Adams to Betty Freeman, February 25, 1983, University of California, San Diego, Mandeville Special Collections.

3 As quoted in James Rondeau and Sheena Wagstaff, *Roy Lichtenstein: A Retrospective* (Chicago: Art Institute of Chicago, 2012), 22.

FIGURE 2.1 Philip Glass (at piano), October 22, 1989, surrounded by Sam Francis and Roy Lichtenstein paintings. Photo by Betty Freeman, courtesy of the Los Angeles Philharmonic Archives.

domain, a woman who so effortlessly holds command over the room like a territory of the mind. This must be her room; this must be Betty's room.

Philip Glass offers rare candid and emotional insights into the struggles he faced in mounting his opera *Satyagraha* in Europe. And Steve Reich demonstrates representational challenges of another kind—that of representing his Jewish heritage in *Tehillim* and trying to at once claim his minimalist roots while at the same time distancing himself from its all-encompassing features.

While neither of these composers attended the salons at the same time, they were united by the spirit of Betty's support and interest. Minimalism was coming to be defined and then redefined by the world; this chapter reveals how much of that reckoning took place within the walls of Betty's home. The Music Room thus lived up to its reputation as a laboratory where minimalist music could be appropriated and built upon by other composers.

PHILIP GLASS

January 31, 1982

What I brought with me today was some music from the opera *Satyagraha*. I'd like to play one scene of it. I'd thought it would be better to play one complete scene than to do excerpts from different things. Then, I have some pictures from the production in Holland so we can see what it looked like. And then I thought maybe we could talk about it together, if anybody has anything to say about it.

To start with, I guess I could say something about how I came to write this piece, how the commission came about. It was commissioned by the city of Rotterdam and was produced by the Netherlands Opera. I had been in Holland in '76 with *Einstein on the Beach*, a work that traveled around Europe a lot in '76. We had played in Amsterdam, Rotterdam, and different places. There was a lot of interest in the piece, but very little from the opera community in Europe.

Most of the people that were coming were people involved with theater, or new music, or whatever. I met actually very few opera producers at that time, with the exception of Hans de Roo, the director of this Netherlands Opera. He came to America about two or three months after we had closed that show. That would be January '77. We met and he said, "Of course I was very interested in *Einstein*, but it wasn't an opera. How would you like to write a real opera?" I said, "Well, what do you have in mind?" He said, "I have this opera company, singers, and a chorus, and whatever you want to do. But it has to be for these people." Then, at that point, a man named Willi Hoffman who was in charge of the theaters in Rotterdam had suggested that the city of Rotterdam would commission the work. I had been thinking about Gandhi for a long time. In fact, I had suggested that as the subject of the collaboration that I was going to do with [stage director Robert] Wilson, but he didn't want to do Gandhi, he wanted to do Hitler. So, we compromised on *Einstein*! Actually, that's how *Einstein* got done. [*laughter*]

So, I had this idea about a Gandhi opera, and I had picked this period of Gandhi's life when he was in South Africa. When I talked to Hans about it, I said I would like to do that. At first, he said, "It will be for my orchestra," and so forth. Then later on, he said, "Well, I don't think my orchestra wants to do it. Why don't you do it with your ensemble?" I said, "No, I don't think that's a good idea. I think we should do it with your orchestra because that's what's interesting for me to do. I can always do operas with my ensemble. What is interesting for me is to try [to] write for your people and to see how that's going to turn out." Then he said, "Well, why don't you send part of the score?" Then I said, "Wait a second. I thought you were going to do this opera, and now you want to look at the score." And he said, "Well, we want to make sure we can play it." It got kind of comical. I said, "Okay, I'll show you the score, but [you've] got to promise that you'll do it." So, Hans said, "Okay, we'll do it, but let's see the music."

So, I sent him the music. I don't know what they did with it. I think they gave it around to orchestras, and they tried playing parts, or whatever they did. I don't know. And they said, "Okay, we'll do it." The kind of music I do, as you know, is demanding in a way that they were not used to. They had done lots of new work in Holland. It's one of the places that takes a great pride in doing new opera. They had been involved with commissioning the Ligeti opera [*Le Grand Macabre*]. There's a whole history of doing new opera there. Hans de Roo is actually a wonderful guy. He's totally involved. He believes that it's part of his mission in life as an opera director to help bring new pieces into the world. They do about two or three new operas every year. And about half of them are Dutch, and the other half could be anything.

But, at any rate, I finished the score, and I went there about six weeks before the opening. We began rehearsing it in the summer of 1980. The other thing is that we got to audition the singers in New York in '79. Hans suggested that we pick mainly American singers. They don't really have a resident company in the way that a German opera company might have. They hire people to come in to do shows. They'll audition for whatever opera they're doing, and they can be from anywhere. In fact, there are five or six Dutch orchestras, and they really don't have one orchestra for the opera. I got the worst orchestra, by the way. You'll hear it in a minute, but I don't know why they did that. At any rate, they're just building an opera house. What they do in Holland is that when they're doing any new work, they'll take it around for five or six cities. So, everything has to travel. That's all part of the calculations of doing a piece there. So, we auditioned the singers in New York, as Hans suggested, so I could work with them before we went there, though actually we did very little work together. So, five or six of the soloists were American.

Then, they got the chorus from the Rotterdam Conservatory, who turned out to be terrific, actually. They were very enthusiastic about the piece. But the trouble with conservatory choruses is that they're very shy of tenors and the basses aren't real low. So, everything sounded higher than I thought it would because there just weren't any low voices there. They just weren't old enough to have low voices. By the way, we did this opera later in Germany and I got to hear all those voices. They had plenty of them in Germany. I should mention that the opera was restaged in Germany about a year later, at Stuttgart, whose opera director is Dennis Russell Davies, who you all know from out here.[4] Dennis is commissioning new works, not only from me, but from other people. Apparently, they love him there, and he'll be there till '85, in case you have any operas. You can send it to Dennis. He's really interested!

From someone in the audience:

What was the reaction?

4 Before moving to Germany in 1980, Davies served as music director of the Saint Paul Chamber Orchestra and later was music director of the Brooklyn Philharmonic.

Well, we had very different representations of the piece, and I'm sorry I don't have the slides from Germany. The Dutch designer was Bob Israel and the Dutch director was an English guy named David Pountney, who you may know because he's done some directing in San Francisco and Houston. He's a really traditional opera director. He does [Mozart's] *Così Fan Tutte*. You know, that's what he does. He had a little trouble figuring out how to deal with this opera. But he actually did pretty well, all in all. The guy in Germany was a man named Achim Freyer from East Berlin, who was also a designer and a director, a similar situation that I had with [Robert] Wilson, in a way, though Bob was really a coauthor of *Einstein*. Though in the end, the way Achim dealt with the work, I began to wonder whether he wasn't a coauthor, too. He interpreted it so differently than we had done.

He came and saw the Dutch production. When we talked about the German production, he said, "My production isn't going to look like that. It won't be the same." I said, "Well, of course. I don't expect it to be." And he said, "No. It'll be more different than that. My Gandhi is different from your Gandhi." I said, "Oh. What do you have in mind?" He said, "Well, he's much more active and more political." Actually, I thought this was pretty political. And, I said, "What do you want to do?" He said, "You have to understand that we have to interpret this for the German public."

When they premiered it in Germany a year later big riots were going on in Berlin. Many of the kinds of things that go on in this opera were happening in the streets of Germany at that time. Achim is very politicized, and he really wanted to bring Gandhi into a contemporary setting, and that's the position he took. At the time we were talking, I said, "Look, you can do what you want, but you have to use the settings I set, and you have to use the characters." I have these three people who are upstage and looking at the action. One is Tolstoy in the first act. That represented Gandhi's past. In the second act, I had [Rabindranath] Tagore, who was his contemporary. In the third act, I had [Martin Luther] King; Gandhi was his teacher. I felt that was very important. It was especially important for me, as an American, that this historical stretch was represented. He said, "Oh yes. We'll do that." I said, "Do you think your interpretation can be supported by the music?" He said, "Absolutely." I said, "Well, when do you want me to come?" He said, "Come to the dress rehearsal." [*laughter*]

They didn't want me around. In fact, I found that I don't know how opera companies work. I only know what I've done. I was told by other people that, in fact, the first production the composer can often be involved with and have a lot of input. After that, I was told that you're often not there at all. It's basically a question of the opera company dealing with the publisher. The composer may be invited, and he may not, but they don't feel that obligation to work with you in that way anymore. I was busy anyway. I thought, "What was I going to do? Just go there and worry about it?" He probably would have done what he wanted to anyway. He's that kind of guy. It was interesting. It was pretty shocking in a way. But I got used to it.

The other thing that was interesting about this opera was, in the Dutch production they had cut about half an hour of the opera. The reason that was done was that the director said, "Look. I just don't know what to do with this material. This act cannot go on for an hour and ten minutes. We have to cut." I said, "Well, there's nothing wrong with the music." He said, "Well, then you direct it." I wasn't ready to do that. It got kind of heavy. We compromised, and we cut this and trimmed that. Then, they began conducting it faster. The opera ended up being about an hour longer in Stuttgart.

Well, what happened was Dennis [Russell Davies] came to see the Dutch production. He said, "Why did they cut the music?" I said, "Well, they couldn't do it." I didn't know what to tell him. I didn't know how to stage it myself. I said, "Dennis, this is totally shocking that they didn't even try before they began cutting." He said, "We're going to put all the music back in." And they did. He reopened the cuts. I thought that was an interesting expression—they *reopened the cuts*. Well, I went to see it in Germany. One thing I found was that I heard it the way I wrote it. I was right. I had done it right the first time, or at least Dennis, the way he did it, he convinced me that I was right. Achim, perhaps because I wasn't there and he had his own ideas about it, he had no trouble with the staging, given the way he wanted to stage it. Now, if you didn't like the way he staged it, you might say that the whole four hours were wrong. In fact, he said it could be longer.

So, that's how I learned very quickly why there are so many versions of operas. I found out that before I even got started, I had two versions of this opera. Now, I've got a Dutch version, I've got a German version. If someone wants to do the opera, I have to say, "Well, which version do you want to do?" There's a couple of people who want to do it now. I'm sending them the complete score, and I'm going to mention that there have been cuts and these are the specific ones that have been made. Though they're not encouraged, they can be tolerated, but none other. That's it. Or, that anything else has to be discussed with me. I don't know. If you don't go, who knows what they'll do. I usually play the music myself. I'm never in this situation unless a singer decides to do something else. One of the people I've worked for a long time is here, Joan LaBarbara, who I'm sure you know. But that was different. I was working with people and collaborating with people. They were helping and involved with the music. Those kinds of changes are things you grow with. But this is a different thing.

I'm going to play the opening of the second act. This is a scene in which Gandhi appears on stage, but he doesn't sing. One of the things about writing an opera about a main character is that he can't sing the whole evening. So, I had to work out ways that he would sing in various places, but still kind of cover the material that I wanted him to. In this scene, unfortunately we don't hear the singer, Douglas Perry. He doesn't sing in this scene. He appears on the stage. It's a scene where Gandhi has returned from a visit to India. He's met at the docks by a crowd of thugs. They kind of beat him up and roughhouse him a bit. By the way, this is a historical incident. I found this in a newspaper clipping. I was in India, and I was looking through newspaper clippings. He saved everything. There are ninety volumes of stuff that he saved. I found this newspaper column of this event, and I set the event in the opera. The wife of the police commissioner, Mrs. Alexander, was walking by and she saw this going on. She walked over and she opened her umbrella—she actually did this. He got underneath the umbrella, and she led him away. That is in fact all the action we'll hear. Gandhi appears coming upstage. You hear a very small chorus of twelve men and they're kind of laughing at him. Then, there's a little orchestra interlude. You might even hear some of the noises on the stage. They're kind of grabbing him and throwing him on the ground. Then they begin singing again. The next time there's an orchestra interlude we hear Mrs. Alexander. Then there's another little encounter and then it's over. It's about fifteen minutes.

[Recording played of *Satyagraha*]

I wrote music for the scene changes. I like to work with the designer and the director right from the beginning. When we were doing this piece, I was talking with [set designer] Bob Israel about this scene. I asked, "How much time do you need to get this stuff off the stage?" We figured out how much time and where the singers had to be. So, I wrote music for that to happen. What happens is that the scene changes and the people start applauding. That almost always happens. Sometimes you actually have to stop anyway. The idea was that the first two acts would have three scenes each so that it would just run all together as one continuous piece. The music had been arranged so that there was time for people to rest, to change the set, and everything.

Glass and Rich begin fidgeting with the technology as they set up the projector, shining upon the Sam Francis painting slides of recent production stills. Discussion spills between explaining these slides and explaining the action of the opera.

Act one, Scene one, *Glass again*, begins in the mythological setting of the *Bhagavad Gita*. You may have noticed that people were not singing English, Italian, or German. They're singing Sanskrit. The text of the opera is from the *Bhagavad*

Gita, which is the book that Gandhi had memorized. He measured his actions against it. It was a kind of moral guide for him. The action of the opera is very clear. For example, there's a scene where registration cards are burned. It's not necessary for the singers to say what they're doing because we can see what they're doing. So, then I was free to choose a text that could run parallel and in a way comment on the opera. So, I chose the *Gita*. I asked the writer I was working with to find passages in the *Gita* that appear as commentary to what we were looking at. Then I had the problem of whether to translate the Sanskrit to Dutch. I decided that it sounded so much better in the original that if I provided the translations in the program then people could understand.

This is the last scene of the second act. It begins with a prayer scene. There are three big choral numbers in the opera. This is one of them. This is going to be a scene in which they burn the registration cards, which actually was another event that happened. A lot of these events were things that I read about in the newspapers. I just set them in the opera.

[Recording played of the very end of the opera]

And that's that. That's the end of the opera. By the way, what we're hearing is from *Einstein on the Beach*. I took the same material, and I just rewrote it so it would sound different. So, I connected those two operas. In the new opera I'm doing, I'm going to build another bridge. I don't know how I'm going to do it yet. I might use the same thing again.[5]

Alan again:

Isn't this a sort of strange time for you to be making a strong commitment to opera?

I'm doing other things, too, *Glass responds*. I've worked a lot in the theater. I associate a lot with theater people. When I began working in opera it never occurred to me to take a play and set it to music, because that wasn't my experience in the theater. My experience in the theater was you start with a subject, and you built it around the subject, and that's how I've worked. So, in a certain way that's also been part of the problem. Not everybody wants to think about opera that way. What I'm doing in my own immodest way is trying to reinvent a musical theater that makes sense for my music and for myself, and I'm finding other people are interested in it.

5 Glass was writing at the time a third opera, *Akhnaten* (1983), rounding out what has been called his "portrait trilogy."

STEVE REICH

January 16, 1983

I thought to play one piece on tape today, *Tehillim*, which is a setting of some of the psalms in the original Hebrew. I'm sure some of you have heard it, and some of you have not. After a bit of that, Ransom Wilson, a flutist I'm sure you all know, is here today. I thought he would play *Vermont Counterpoint* together with a tape that Ransom has made. After that, you might have some questions for Ransom or myself. Then, if we could keep that down to a minimum, maybe he could play it again. So, that's the overall plan.

I thought I'd do one thing: since *Tehillim* is in the Hebrew language, I thought I'd just quickly run over the text. There are four parts of four psalms. I didn't set entire psalms, the reason being is that I wanted to choose texts that I felt that I could really say wholeheartedly from beginning to end. Consequently, I made these selections.

The first is from the 19th Psalm [*reads first in Hebrew, then*]: "The heavens declare the glory of God. The sky tells of his handiwork. Day to day pours forth speech. Night to night reveals knowledge. Without speech and without words, nevertheless their voice is heard. Their sound goes out to all the earth and their words to the ends of the world." Then, without any interruption in the music, there's a brief percussion interlude which just carries the music forward but gives you a sense of a stop. The second text begins in the same tempo: "Where's the man who loves life, loves many days to see good? Guard your tongue from evil and your lips from speaking deceit. Turn from evil and do good. Seek peace and pursuit it." Stop. Turn over the cassette. Musicians stop and turn their pages. Conductor mops his brow.

Then there's a slow movement which is a lesser-known text for those of you who know these kinds of text. It's from the 18th Psalm: "With the merciful, You are merciful. With the upright, You are upright. With the pure, You are pure. With the perverse, You are subtle." The last text is the last four verses of the 150th Psalm: "Praise Him with drum and dance. Praise Him with strings and winds. Praise Him with sounding cymbals. Praise Him with clanging cymbals. With all that breathes, praise the eternal, Hallelujah!"

[Recording played of *Tehillim*]

Everyone who is interested in what I've been doing has heard that I've been interested in my own background as a Jew, and in the cantillations, the chanting of the Hebrew scriptures. There's no question about it that *Tehillim* would never have been written if it were not for that interest. But, there is no chanting of any sort in this piece. As a matter of fact, as I rather laboriously spell out in the program notes, I chose to set the psalms because the tradition for singing psalms in synagogues here in Los Angeles, in New York, in Europe, has been lost. It's been lost to the Western communities. When we sing songs in the synagogues, as some of you know, the tunes are probably stolen from the churches in the nineteenth century.

I chose to set psalms for two reasons. The first was that it's obviously the most musical text in the Hebrew scripture. The second is that in contrast to the Torah, the five books of Moses, and in contrast to the prophets—where there is an oral tradition, where there most definitely is some kind of continuity between the time of Ezra, five hundred years before Jesus, and the present, with all kinds of influences—the tradition for singing psalms has been lost. Actually, for those of you [who] know anything about the little markings, they're called *tamin*. They're accent marks. The word *tamin* means "taste." The tastes of the writing are different little signs in the Psalms, the Book of Job, and the Book of Proverbs than they are from the rest of the Hebrew scripture. Scholars write what they might have, what they should have, what they could have, but nobody knows. The Yemenite Jews and the Sephardic Oriental Jews do have a living tradition of chanting the psalms in their oral tradition, that is from father to son, from mother to daughter. We don't have that. So, I felt free to Compose, with a capital "c," without a musical superego looking over my shoulder.

Earlier on in my life when I was studying African music, I didn't want to use an African bell, which although it's tuned in rough octaves or sixths, is in no way related to that or any other piano or keyboard, except by accident. To use one in the music would mean scraping it with a metal file or something like that. It's fine. I'm sure that people are going to write a great gong-gong part. I know I wish I did. It's not for me, and I didn't want to use Balinese instruments. Since I was brought up reformed, i.e., Unitarian, with a lip-sync bar-mitzvah, I didn't know what it was that I was doing. I didn't really learn Hebrew until I was thirty-seven. I volunteered at that late age to finally get that information. The chanting was not in my ear, it was not something I grew up with. It wasn't something in the guts. I ended up feeling most comfortable taking the text and the accentuation of the text. All the rhythms come out of the words and many of the notes come out of the words. But there's no chant.

Alan:

It seems to be fair game among newspaper critics on both coasts these days to take this word "minimalist," which is a journalistic catch-all, and throw it back at several composers as though it was just the worst swear word in the vocabulary.

How do you react to that, and how do you react to the term "minimalist" as it applies to your kind of music?

Reich:

I feel like a broken record because I really have been asked this question a lot, and I keep trying to make fresh replies. As far as I know the history of it and I may be wrong, but I believe that Michael Nyman, the English musician, composer, and sometimes journalist, coined the word in about 1970 or 1971 to describe the music of myself, Terry Riley, Philip Glass, and LaMonte Young.[6] He, or whoever it was, definitely took the term from the visual arts, where it would refer to people like Frank Stella or Sol LeWitt or Donald Judd, who were working in geometric and sometimes repetitive structures. There was a kind of analogy. At the time the word was coined in 1970 or 1971, I was getting into a piece like *Drumming*. Certainly, there are some analogies: there's obviously a tremendous amount of repetition, it does work with a limited harmonic compass (there aren't too many notes in the piece), and the focus is on rhythm in a kind of single-minded way. Many other aspects of traditional Western music (changes of harmony, modulation) were simply forgotten about in quest of something that I was concerned with.

Later on, as time passed, I became interested to go forward and perhaps go backward vis-à-vis our own musical history and to reinvolve myself with just the traditional questions that Western composers have always involved themselves with, namely harmony and orchestration. I believe that what I was doing rhythmically sort of took care of the counterpoint, and still does, but that's something we can discuss separately. And consequently, I think the term "minimal" became less applicable to the music. I'm thinking of pieces like *Music for Mallet Instruments, Voices, and Keyboard*, [and] certainly a piece like *Music for 18 Musicians* is less minimal, less harmonically static than a piece like *Drumming*.

By the time you get to a piece like *Tehillim*, I think the "minimal" tag doesn't fit very well. There are some da capos, as Bill Kraft [composer, percussionist] will vouch for, but basically, it's a big fat score and you go from the beginning to the end. The kinds of repeats that are in it are basically the kinds that you can find in a Minuet and Trio in Haydn. I don't think the kind of repetition that's in *Drumming* really is applicable, although there are other things that are very clearly a continuous thread. So, my answer is, sure, if you want to call it "minimal." We refer to Debussy and Ravel and sometimes Satie as Impressionistic. It's easier to say

6 It is unsure where exactly the term "minimal music" originated, but Nyman played a key role in naming John Adams, Terry Riley, Philip Glass, LaMonte Young, and Steve Reich as its key developers, if not original creators. See O'Brien and Robin, *On Minimalism*.

one word than to say six words for three different names. In that sense if you want minimal music to refer to me, Glass, Riley, and perhaps now John Adams—although I think that's a very poor description of his marvelous music—sure. It's like picking up a teacup: you don't want to burn your hand picking up a cup, [so] you use a handle. So, it's a handle.

I think music creates very different states of physical and, consequently, emotional reactions in people. Thank God for it. I wouldn't do it if it didn't. You know, there's no telling. I mean, not in our society. Perhaps in India or in another society where they really got into a science—which I've never been involved in—of creating very precise emotional reactions which can be calculated according to scale degrees and things like that. I hope it will move all of you to tears or something like that, but I don't have any devices for turning them on or off. Perhaps I should take lessons.

Well, maybe we could prevail upon Ransom Wilson to come downstairs here and play *Vermont Counterpoint*. The piece *Vermont Counterpoint* is dedicated to Betty Freeman. It's a commission from Ransom Wilson. When Ransom and I first talked about the piece, we discussed the possibility of writing a flute solo, and Ransom seemed to be interested in the possibility of having a piece for multiple flutes where most of them would be on tape, prerecorded by himself, and he would play the live part. That's precisely what the piece is. It actually ends up being for three alto flutes, three flutes, three piccolos, and two solo parts, which Ransom plays one live, or he would be playing all of those instruments. All of the other flutes that you will hear prerecorded were recorded by Ransom here in Los Angeles at Angel Records. Maybe that's enough said.

[Performance of *Vermont Counterpoint*]

Someone from the audience speaks out:

Your music is so joyful. Are you an optimist?

I've generally been described as a pessimist by those who know me best.

People sometimes wonder what relationship this style is to Western music, and I've often said if you look at the immediate past, particularly to Schoenberg and his school and those at Darmstadt, it doesn't bear [a clear] continuation. But if you look at earlier Western music, certainly before 1750, the Medieval, Renaissance, and Baroque periods, and more recently at the music of Debussy, Stravinsky, and Bartók, I think there are many similarities. But, if you're focusing in on the orchestral repertory from Haydn to Schoenberg, it's a rather tenuous connection at best. But, *Tehillim* has some little connection there with those kinds of works.

FIGURE 2.2 Steve Reich signing the Music Room ledger book, December 7, 1986. Photo by Betty Freeman, courtesy of the Los Angeles Philharmonic Archives.

December 7, 1986

[Live performance of *Clapping Music, New York Counterpoint*, and *Music for Pieces of Wood*]

What an honor to have this room and that music in our lifetime, *Alan Rich proclaims. Betty takes her cue*:

How much is written in the score of this one?

Of this one, *Pieces of Wood*? Everything is written, and the number of repeats has got flexible limits. Everybody's memorized their parts. Glen [Velez] and I memorized it first. The number of repeats—we just did it. I've always relied on Russell [Hartenberger], Bob [Becker], and Jim [Price], and then later Glen and later Mort [Silver], to make musical decisions about things like numbers of repeats, assuming that good musicianship will simply answer that question in performance. Faced with a score to write it with, which the publication was done after we had done it for a number of years, I put something like "X 3–7"—repeat it three to seven times—giving you wide limits, because I didn't want the players to have their heads full of counting the number of repeats. I'd rather have their hands full of trying to get a good rhythmic unison. And that's a different kind of concern. So, it was just a way of less clutter in the brain for this particular kind of piece.

Betty again:

Who was the leader?

Well, there's no leader. Glen sets the tempo. Whoever plays the pulse part sets the tempo. I play the ostinato of the patterns, and then one after the other, first Russell and then Bob and then Jim, on ascending notes come in playing the same pattern as I start, but in another rhythmic position. They have as many repeats as they need to do each adding of the note. It's as if you had a glass of water and you pour in a little bit, you check that out, and pour in some more. After a while, it's filled up. You drink it and have another glass.

The audience has piqued attention:

What's the pulse of *Pieces of Wood*? Is it not to change, or do you feel it should change according to the performer? Once you set the pulse in *Pieces of Wood*, is your aim to keep it exactly at that rate?

One of the performers, Glen Velez, speaks up:

Yeah, I think so. Just keep it more or less the same. It probably has a tendency to get a little bit faster as the piece goes on.

Another audience member to Velez:

When you feel it going faster, do you feel yourself drawing back to try to control it, or do you just let it go?

Yeah, sometimes I try to control it. It depends on how much you feel, you know, that it's moving. Try to keep it in the same area.

Yet another question:

Were those instruments made for you for *Pieces of Wood* or are those bought?

This time, performer Bob Becker responds:

Well, I play in a percussion ensemble called Nexus and we performed this piece and recorded it for a long time. I was dissatisfied with the sound of the commercial instruments, which is what Steve had to work with when he originally wrote the piece. They still have to be tuned because the piece is written for specific pitches. I was attracted to some of the kinds of wood that my friend Andrew Feldman was using to make snare drumsticks and mallets and four bass drums and things like that. He was using beautiful hard woods from different parts of the world. One kind of wood that he used a lot is called purple heart wood, which I love the look of and feel of. It's a very dense, heavy wood. I asked him to make for me a set of claves out of that wood. Andrew, being the thorough craftsman that he is, got very involved in the project and he turned out about twenty-five different claves, all different kinds of woods, brought them into a rehearsal and then Steve looked at them. I picked out the kinds of things I wanted and tried several ranges of pitches, transposing the piece up, and arrived at some notes that we liked. When I finally got a set that I liked, I brought it to a concert that we did in Long Island. Steve liked them and he ordered this set.

There's time for one last question, this time back to Reich:

Has anybody done movement or dance with any of these pieces?

Laura Dean choreographed *Clapping Music* in 1972. It was called *Circle Dance*. It involved two dancers. Russell and I played, and Laura and another dancer performed it on sort of like a clock face. They would do steps going in, and when we switched, they'd go to the opposing clock side, and they went around. It was a short piece, but I thought it was a very good choreography. *Music for Pieces of Wood* may have been choreographed. I don't know. *New York Counterpoint* is too new, as far as I understand it. It hasn't been commercially released yet, so people don't know that much about it. But, of course, a lot of other pieces have been choreographed.

Chapter 3

European Sirens

Louis Andriessen
György Ligeti
Witold Lutoslawski

THE SAM FRANCIS painting Eva Soltes directed the audience toward was hanging along the wall perpendicular to the cash box piece. Honestly, with its large white swatch against the dark velvet wall, *Japan Line* was hard to miss. Aside from its value aesthetically and personally to Betty (she started but never finished a monograph about Francis, whom she knew personally), its white canvas apparently also served rather usefully as a projector screen during her salons. Up close, it is easy to see better how actually *un*-white it is—plenty of scrapes and imperfections riddle the canvas. The dominant color streak loudly zigs and zags in a fit of rage. Drips of hardened paint draw the eye down their getaway path and below the frame of the canvas. Like how the volleyball player in *Frolic* speaks beyond the scope of the piece, *Japan Line* gestures downward beyond itself. Both works resist capture. Escape seems to be their fancy.

"There are but a handful of creative musicians working today, just as there always have been," Betty once explained. "These special few deserve all the help and attention we can give them. In Europe, especially in Russia and Germany, there are musical giants with even more ambitious aims than in America. By returning to liturgical music as a source they have created a new music of powerful spiritual content."[1]

1 This was taken from a speech Betty gave on January 19, 1990, at the Kyoto City University of Art and Music in Kyoto, Japan, called "A Creative Approach to New Music." University of California, San Diego, Mandeville Special Collections.

The Music Room. Jake Johnson, Oxford University Press. © Oxford University Press 2025.
DOI: 10.1093/9780197775752.003.0004

This speech is telling. It gives focus to a shift in Betty's aesthetic away from American music, where most of her attention and support were invested, and toward European composers. The shift started in the late 1980s, though the reason for this shift is not all that clear. One significant explanation is that Betty had begun living half of the year in Turino, Italy, with Franco. Her proximity to and subsequent involvement with the Salzburg Music Festival each summer, for example, easily placed her within new art worlds and social networks. Also, the European state sponsorship of the arts historically provided far more resources for composers living there than their American counterparts, which is why Betty's patronage was of such a vital necessity to American experimental composition in the first place.

"In the last year, composers have been on the cover of *Time* as well as on *Esquire*'s list of twenty-five up and coming young men. That would have been unheard of five years ago."[2]

It could be that as certain branches of contemporary American music found a foothold within American universities (and some even landing commercial successes), those composers sought out private patronage less than before. Relieved from being a sole support for these composers, perhaps Betty felt free to explore other music, which led her to European fronts. And, as she hinted to Elliott Carter in the previous chapter, the prestige of new music in Europe made pale the rather stunted American response to premieres: "In Europe the composer is treated with great respect, the music is given great interest, and it's a major thing in Europe when a new composition is performed. Here it just seems to pass over."

While the composers in this chapter represent a European origin (though not the only Europeans in this collection), in many ways this is where their similarities end. These are significant musical figures, both then and now. And yet Betty gave money directly to only one of them, Witold Lutoslawski, as part of a co-commission with the Los Angeles Philharmonic for his fourth symphony. Still, this group's presence in the Music Room represents a heightened awareness of the European avant-garde and, partially through events like Betty's salons, important connections between composers on both continents were made.

2 Taken from a transcript from a colloquium at the University of California, San Diego, titled "The Patron and Producer: The Final Word?" on February 19, 1985, University of California, San Diego, Mandeville Special Collections. Moderated by UCSD sociologist Aaron Cicourel, other panelists included UCSD pediatrics professor Robert Hamburger, UCSD music professor Thomas Nee, and Dorrance Stalvey, director of the Monday Evening Concerts. Betty may have been referring to the *Time* magazine cover of January 17, 1983, that featured conductor James Levine or, far less likely, to covers from July 18, 1983, and March 19, 1984, that featured David Bowie and Michael Jackson, respectively. The December 1, 1984, issue of *Esquire* ran a feature on opera director Peter Sellars, which is perhaps what Betty is referring to here.

LOUIS ANDRIESSEN

March 3, 1985

First of all, I would like to say thank you very much for the hospitality of Betty Freeman and Franco, and I think I've heard we will have some *penne carbonara*. For those who were in Italy, Franco's recipes are much better than you get in that country.

I think the piece I want to talk about is called *De Tijd* which means "time"—it has something to do with [time] in a specific way. It's one of the two pieces which will be performed at the CalArts festival by the students.[3] But, I would not like to ask you to listen to the whole piece. It's forty minutes—it's very long, it's all very slow, and it's all mostly very soft.

I think the best thing I can do is a little bit explain a little bit about the piece and have you listen to the second half, which is not really a second half. It's just the moment when the record has to be turned over. I don't like to write music which fits precisely to what the record company directs. It's true that this piece lasts forty-one minutes, more or less. About half way, there are loud chords which means we are half way now. There is a long decay of the sound of these chords and then the whole process is continuous. So, it's not completely ridiculous to have you listen to the second half of it. However, like in movies, when you only look to the second half, sometimes it's not too bad to tell what has happened before. Otherwise, you don't know who is the mistress and who is the husband, of course.

Like all operas, in general, operas have always the same subject. The tenor who wants to go to bed with the soprano and the baritone who tries to hinder this. I won't call this dialectical, but there is a sort of dialectics within this sort of musical structure in the piece *De Tijd*. First of all, I should tell what Frans Van Rossum [head of CalArts's music department] said about writing for specific groups: that's true. It's also true that I did not write for symphony orchestra since 1968, which has something to do with my ideas about symphony orchestras, also. I won't go into this with you now. The commission of the San Francisco Symphony was a sort of surprise for me because I did not do that for a long time.[4] In fact, it was not [Dutch conductor] Edo De Waart who asked me, but it was his artistic advisor John Adams who asked Edo to do it because I'm not sure if Edo liked the piece, in fact. However, that piece doesn't sound really like a symphony orchestra because I divided it into three groups and it was a very in a way aggressive and hectic and

3 Both *De Tijd* and *De Staat* were performed at CalArts on March 16, 1985.

4 The San Francisco Symphony commissioned Andriessen's *De Snelheid* in 1984.

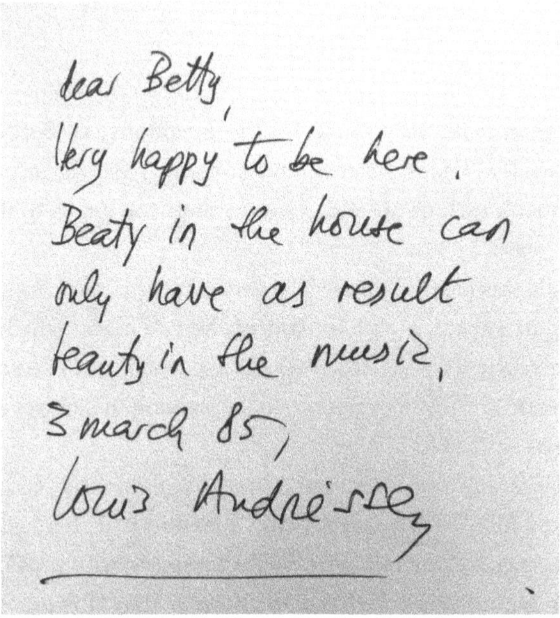

dear Betty,
Very happy to be here.
Beaty in the house can
only have as result
beauty in the music,
3 march 85,
Louis Andriessen

FIGURE 3.1 Note from Louis Andriessen to Betty Freeman, as recorded in the Music Room ledger book. Photo by the author.

closed piece. It was not what you would call an attractive sort of music, seducing music. It's the kind of music that I'm not sure if you should judge for yourself.

It's written specifically for an occasion, namely the new building of the Den Haag Conservatory.[5] There were two halls, and the director asked me to choose a hall to write this piece for, made for the students of the conservatory. That's probably the main reason why the piece has the sound it has. Ideally, I think every composition should have its own sound, its own character, like your children. You can try to educate all your children the same way because you think there's one ideal way to educate your children, but it seems that still, all those children go different ways so there's something strange and particular with all your children. Since I have no children, I have all those compositions [to take their place]. I try to make them all as different as possible. So, when you will listen to *De Tijd* and you decide, "Oh, this is the sort of guy who writes very slow and very soft music," then you are completely mistaken because the slowness, the motionlessness is the subject of the piece. It's not my style, it's not my way of expression.

In fact, I have very little confidence, so in that sense I'm a Stravinskyian, if you want, or classicist, also. I don't trust very much the idea to express your feelings in music. I think the expression of musical feelings then at least (because what else could you express in music apart from musical feelings?) should be the result of

5 The Royal Conservatory in The Hague. By "Den Haag," Andriessen is referring to The Hague.

the music, should not be a goal of the music, I think, for the composer. Of course, you take care of the fact that sort of result can happen. You have your own experiences. Why else listen to beloved composers?

De Tijd is written for the students of the conservatory in Den Haag. The sound, this particular sound of the piece, has to do with the fact that at a conservatory you have, for instance, a lot of flutes, so there are eight flutes in the piece. This gave the people from CalArts gigantic difficulties—to collect together those different strange instruments I had in the piece. For instance, what I thought were typical American percussion instruments were typical European percussion instruments. Problems like that. We had also at the conservatory a very strong bass clarinet department, a lot of students and a very good teacher. They not only have these big bass clarinets, but they also have contrabass clarinets, you call them here, which are quite seldom found. I think we're still trying to find one around, but finally it seemed that in the neighborhood in the valley near Valencia there's a small music school where there's one. They were almost forgotten, but they found one and this one we'll play on. The same story with the cimbalom, which is the Hungarian ancient piano—the piano without keyboard. After a lot of telephone calls and strange adventures I had with the pianist, going down to Hollywood to obscure music shops where behind all the loudspeakers we found a sort of cimbalom, but it was not very good to use. Finally, we found a very beautiful cimbalom, and it seems that all the strange instruments for my piece have now been collected. The reason that I wrote long lines for three bass clarinets and one contrabass clarinet is that the school in Den Haag had these instruments. They weren't so much exotic; they were just around, in the hall at the school.

The main subject of *time*, of the piece, of course, is how to deal with time. That's very clear. It sounds quite stupid because all music does that, but this is in a very particular way. I think the nonmusical reason, I should tell you, why I started to do it the way I did was because a physical—I would say almost, or spiritual, or both—experience which you all will have had in your life and if you did not [have it yet] you will have. I hope, at least. The consciousness of the fact that time stands still. I had this happen for a long time, I would say about four seconds. Now, this is for musicians very interesting, what happens for them in this sort of consciousness. It is a euphoric experience I should say. I decided to write a piece on this feeling, without knowing whether it could be possible. I didn't know. I started to read about time perception. Of course, I started in my own time, but I seemed to get lost in the space-time theories because I'm not very well educated in physics so I got lost in those books. And I also realized what I was dealing with I could not find in the period in physical history where time is something determinatory we all know about, let's say the period between Newton and Einstein. So, I had a lot of time left because I didn't work out very well with the space-time theory which, in fact, I now try to renew my adaptation in dealing with the small "sparks," you call it?

Quarks, *someone in the audience volunteers.*

Quarks. Yes, *Andriessen continues*, because the piece I'm going to write now is about matter, objects, things. When I have written this piece, I have finished with the big things. I will write about smaller subjects.

There was time before Newton, and there I got into a gigantic labyrinth which interested me very much. I think, I'm not sure, but I think I have had some very important things I learned from that which I used in the piece. More and more the studying and reading went into obscure places like France, 1310, writers like Occam or Erasmus—I don't know if those names mean anything to you. In the meantime, more or less as a sort of free work, I read *La Divina Commedia* of Dante which I consider one of the most impressionable books I've ever read which, in fact, is written at the same time, as you know. A friend of mine, a philosopher, said, "Yes, you're on the right direction when you want to talk about this point of time which has to deal with eternity. Scholastic philosophers know a lot about it. But, don't forget [St.] Augustine." And, of course, he was right. For people who probably have read the *Confessions* of Augustine in which the eleventh chapter deals with time and the perception of time. Augustine you should not consider as an old bishop, but as Wittgenstein and [Bertrand] Russell both called him, a founder of Western philosophy, and it's mostly probably because of what he has written about time in the *Confessions*. Now, I'm not going to tell you about all this depth, ways which had no exit in this labyrinth of twelfth, thirteenth, and fourteenth century.

Finally, I decided to use Augustine for the whole text for the whole piece. And, I have used a motto of Dante for the piece. There were a lot of ways I could have done the piece which I'm not going to tell you about because it takes too much time. I decided to try to combine two different musical principles. The text of Augustine is sung by a chorus which doesn't breathe. That means that there are the chorus divided into two groups, one who sings the first part of the words and the other one takes over for the next part. So the whole text of Augustine sounds continuous, almost continually, throughout the whole piece, like incredibly slow singing. That's what I call the *cantus firmus*. And the singing is always in regular values. It's very slow. They start with values of twelve seconds which is very slow. And the chorus is always accompanied in the same values by instruments which can hold their tone, like flutes or violins—there's a Hammond organ in the piece. So, instruments who, when they can sound, can keep their tone as long as you wish. And they have always, as I said, regular values in count two because the piece is very precisely organized. That's one layer, I would say, which is throughout present in the piece and of course the values will be later a little bit faster than those twelve seconds, but they will be still in multiples of two and always regular.

Apart from that, there's the second basic layer which I should call the bells sound. It's about the bells, it's about everything that counts the time. But, strange enough, those values are not regular and they are speeding up very slowly. That means that all the bells are based on the rhythm of the Greek verse, the *iambic*. It starts very slowly and you will not recognize it. Gently, slowly, they get a little bit faster which is of course in divisions of three, as you have seen. However, I remember once a choreographer in Holland who started to rehearse "the waltz" as she called it. She said, "Now, we're going to do the waltz. One-two-three [pause], one-two-three [pause], one-two-three [pause]!" Which, of course, had no waltz because she didn't count the fourth count which is hidden.

The big difference, of course, is that the bells are always in three or otherwise which have to do with three, and the other layer which is always in twos, or longer layers. The biggest difference is also that the bells, as I have said, accelerate very slowly. In the beginning, they are very slow and toward the end they are little bit less slow. That's the way it starts. But, from the moment on, I would like you to listen to it. It's, as I said, halfway. Of course, some more things are happening then. In fact, there are not really more things, but it sounds like there's more happening. But, it can happen, for instance, that the lower sustained chords which have to do of course with the choruses, they play almost the same values as the chorus. But, for instance, slightly out of phase (as you know now it's called since we have composers like Steve Reich). So, they're always a little bit too early. And then it's also possible that there is another layer which is dealing with the same musical subject, but it's just a little shorter. It has, for instance, the value of nineteen against the value of twenty which the chorus has at that moment. But, the whole situation is a continuous measuring of time.

Then also later, which you will hear. I thought of that since I saw this incredible, beautiful Sam Francis [painting], there's a division which is something in between the two because the bells are short sounds. They go away, they die away, and the rest is sustained. But there are a lot of tricks as all composers know, you should make things not too simple and you should make always exceptions to your rules, of course. To hear later, for instance, trumpets playing very staccato, very loud, almost an aggressive chorus. Of course, their timing is another dimension, another clock which we need at the moment to measure time. When I tried to explain to the musicians how it should sound, I tell them, "Imagine that you have a big piece of textile and you take an incredibly sharp knife, and you [makes a cutting gesture and sound] like this."

I thought of that not because I want to do it to the Sam Francis, but the white reminded me, as you certainly will know, of the white paintings of Lucio Fontana.[6] He's particularly the guy who does that with a very sharp knife. I don't think he does it by hand. I think he uses a sort of material to make them very precise. I'm telling you this because I saw the Sam Francis, but also because it's a way to explain to musicians how they should sound, how they should play. In fact, the piece sounds in a way easy and slow and it's about emotionless, and if you want, it's about measuring time. But, it gives incredibly big problems for musicians to have this incredibly slow piece and, go *ahhhh!*, exactly in time with six trumpet players.

I should tell you about other details, and then we'll start the second part of *Time*. What you cannot perceive now is that the last six minutes are a sort of coda. It's the sort of music after the music. I should tell you this because you can only hear that when you hear the whole piece. So that's after about fourteen minutes. You can check your watch. Then the ending is a strange sort of surprise. It's the sound of a wood instrument which you have heard before and which the rhythm is completely new in the piece.

[Recording played of *De Tijd*]

GYÖRGY LIGETI

February 28, 1993

Alan:

Pierre-Laurent Aimard is going to play the *Études* of Ligeti and the sheet that you have gives the order in which they are to appear.

Ladies and gentlemen, *Aimard announces*, I would just like to make a little change in the program of the order and to put "Vertige," the study who is the third on the list—the number nine—almost at the end just between the number two and the

6 The artist Lucio Fontana, who was born in Argentina but spent most of his life in Italy, used knives and other objects to puncture and break the surface of his monochrome canvases. He would often affix black fabric to the back of the canvases so the fissures and breaks would be more visible.

number six. So, the order is *Fém*, *Arc-en-ciel*, then *Fanfares*, then normal list and at the end *Cordes à vide*, *Vertige*, and *Automne à Varsovie*. It seems to me that it works musically better. Thank you.

[Performance of *Nine Études*]

Now Ligeti:

So, ladies and gentlemen, so far I have nine *Études*, which you have heard. I continue them. The number twelve is a beautiful tradition. Chopin had twice twelve and then Debussy had twelve etudes. The day before yesterday, I just finished the last etude, number twelve. I put French titles also because of the tradition. Liszt's *Études* have French titles, then the *Préludes* of Debussy and also the *Études* [have] French titles. The Chopin *Études* have no titles. The title of my last etude, number twelve, is "L'escalier du diable," which will finish the cycle.[7] But number ten and number eleven are still not ready.[8]

Now, first I want to say it's not possible for a composer to speak about music. Why should a composer speak about music? There are music critics—very, very good people—and there are musicologists. They can speak. But a composer has to imagine music and write the notes. Then, several times I'm put in the situation that I'm asked. Now, Alan and Judith Rosen asked me to make some comments and I can make some comments, but nothing about the emotional content of this music because if I would speak about emotional content or some nonrational things, then I better write poems or write essays or philosophy. Music is nonverbal, like visual art is nonverbal. So, in fact, you don't have to speak about it. But, I can give some explanation, some remarks to the technical aspects. These twelve—until now nine—studies are studies in the sense of Chopin and Liszt and Debussy and Rachmaninoff, both technical studies for the pianist and also technical studies in a sense of composition because in each etude I put [onto] myself a certain idea, what I want to realize technically in this piece. So, I can speak about some technical details, but if I stress the technical details you shouldn't forget that, in fact, music—for me and I think for many composers, for almost every composer—is a thing more of intuition and free imagination than something

7 Ligeti completed a cycle of eighteen etudes between 1985 and 2001.

8 According to Judith Rosen, Aimard performed the etudes the following evening at a Green Umbrella concert (the Los Angeles Philharmonic's New Music series), but "in an order that had evolved a few times overnight. We would like to think that the Music Room itself was a laboratory for the development of these wonderful pieces." Rosen, introduction to *Il Salotto Musicale* manuscript, Los Angeles Philharmonic Archives.

calculated and constructed. Still, if you think of the most wonderful musics of Bach they are both imagination, poetry, and construction, and the same applies to Chopin and Schubert, only to mention two very emotive composers.

So, I believe that this dissection—here is construction, there is emotion—is something artificial which is in the mind of many people who had the prejudice that always new music—what is new music today, what people write today, but a hundred years ago there were other composers writing new music, always it was new music and it was very much stressed that new music—has to be something doing with the brain and calculation, and so on. This is not true, simply not true. When Philippe De Vitry in about the year 1320, wrote this wonderful book about a new way of notation, which he called it *Ars Nova* (Ars Nova was not only a musical style, it was a new musical notation, it was a measured notation), it was the first possibility to notate very exactly subdivisions of duration elements, subdivision in three and in two and then dividing the three and two again in three and two and going to very, very complex rhythmic, metrical structures, which then this notation gave the possibility of a fantastic development of European music during the fourteenth century from Machaut until Du Fay during about a hundred years. I mention this because it's always stressed in a very naive way that the new music has to be a thing of brain and calculation.

There are some composers, some very distinguished colleagues, who really use algorithms, use methods, calculating methods. I don't do them. However, I feel very close to the scientific community, to the computer people, to the artificial intelligence people. I'm a bit involved. I'm a member of a secret mafia of fractal geometry, of geometry of chaotic and of dynamic systems and nonlinear equations, but I use them in a very indirect way. For example, one of the etudes has the title *Désordre*—disorder—which is in fact [a] self-repeating, self-similar structure, absolutely fitting the concept of a fractal structure. But, I don't want to stress here the scientific and the mathematical side of what I do. I would more make a couple of remarks about techniques, about pianistic and composition techniques. The two tools which I put for myself when I had the first idea to write these *Études* were a new kind of rhythmic articulation, new concept of rhythm, and also certain new concepts of harmony. First, I make a remark because some of you were there when my violin concerto was played—by the way wonderfully—by Saschko Gawriloff and the Los Angeles Philharmonic.[9] Then I spoke in my introduction more about aspects of tuning and about harmony because I am looking for new paths, new ways in building harmony. In fact, if a composer pretends that he invented anything, then he is a liar. Nobody invented from nothing. Everybody is starting from

9 This was the American premiere of the piece, performed on February 18, 1993.

somebody else. I stress very much that my main influences in the new kind of harmony, the violin concerto, was one side the music of Harry Partch—whom I met twenty-one years ago here, south of Los Angeles in Encinitas—and the other starting point were a lot of different ethnic cultures, especially gamelan in Java and gong in Bali, but also other north Pacific Malaysian cultures, New Guinea cultures, southeast Asian cultures, and cultures in Africa south of the Sahara, using tuning systems which are very different from our twelve-tone temperament.

I mentioned those questions but I only want to speak now about a special case: piano music. I don't want to change the tuning. I'm bored. I don't like more than major because this third [*plays a major third on the piano*] is so bad. The seventh is too high. If you heard one on the synthesizer—tunable synthesizer like a Yamaha DX7-ii or one of the Harry Partch instruments, a real pure intonation dominant seventh chord—then you cannot stand any more the piano. Anyway, the piano is a compromised tuning to allow all modulations, all other keys. This is a pretty good compromise, but it's a bit worn out. So, my starting point was that both total chromaticism—of Schoenberg and post-Schoenberg music, including also Webern and Boulez and my music from the late '50s, early '60s—this kind of thinking, of total chromaticism, became a bit obsolete. On the other hand, to return to tonal diatonic music—many of my colleagues do it—is for me a bit trivial. I don't want to condemn them, but I really look for possibilities which are not more chromaticism and no clear tonality, not functional tonality or modality. Still, as you heard, a lot of moments of this piece, of these *Études* and also in the violin concerto are in fact a kind of tonal music, but not tonal music in the sense of the nineteenth century or the time before.

Now, what I experimented here, what I can do, I have the right temperate piano. I don't want to change the tuning because it's pretty difficult to change the tuning. You have to work with hammers and so on, and then the tuning doesn't stay. It stays for half an hour. The screws have a certain tendency then to go back where they were. They can be out of tune, but mainly they maintain. So, it's no use. It's very, very practical to retune string instruments or harpsichord or harp or guitar because they are soft tunable instruments, but this is a hard tunable instrument. So, my idea was can I do some music which is not more chromatic, but not really diatonic? Then in the first etude, which is called "Disorder," (*désordre* in French) I had the idea why I don't use the white keys which gives diatonic in one hand, the other hand [*plays the black keys from c*<sharp>*4 to c*<sharp>5]—I combined them. I cannot play it as good as Pierre, but he will play it again. So, what you hear here is in fact a total twelve-pitch chromatic scale there, but you don't hear chromaticism because they are sometimes together, sometimes separate. So, it's always a change, a kind of chameleon like, you know, shining between diatonic and pentatonic, and together chromatic, but they never merge to chromaticism. So, it's something in between.

But, in another piece, in the gamelan piece number seven with the title *Galamb borong*—in fact it's a beautiful Indonesian fake word. In Balinese theater, there is a demon person who is maybe a good demon or a bad demon, but in any case, a very big demon which is called *Borong*. It's normally performed by several people being in a huge kind of tiger and dragon mask and so on. Because this is fake gamelan music—you will listen again, concentrate on the *Seventh Étude*, *Galamb borong*—because I make a music which is fake gamelan, from some Indonesian island that doesn't exist. You don't find it on a map. Then I gave it a title, *Galamb borong*. I don't speak Indonesian language. In fact, it's Hungarian! What it means in Hungarian is not important, but it sounds so beautiful [in] Javanese. I have two Hungarian titles. One is *Galamb borong* and the other is *Fém*, which Pierre-Laurent played the first time. *Fém* means metal, but the title "metal" in English or French or German, European languages is just metal, but in Hungarian "fém" has a connotation of something very bright. So, it's a metal which is very, very shining because there is a word for light which is "fén," so "fém" and "fén" are for a Hungarian brain very close. So, it's a combination between metal and light. It should be something very bright. The other titles are French and you can understand them.

Now, in the fake gamelan music, I gave only one example of combination of the keys, of the possibilities of the piano which were not used before, outside of the antagonism of chromatic and diatonic. Debussy used, in wonderful ways, the whole-tone scale. Think of the wonderful gamelan inspired piece *Cloches à travers les feuilles*. So, footnote: gamelan music, both in Java and in Bali, have two basic tuning systems—one is the *pelog*, which I don't want to explain, the other is the *slendro*. Slendro is dividing an octave which are approximate octaves, never exact, in approximately five equal steps. It's something which is not only in Indonesia. It exists in all of southeast Asia and also in the southern half of Africa. This not exact five but approximately five—I cannot play it on the piano. On the piano, we can divide the octave in twelve equal, or in six equal, or in three or in four, but not in five. We don't have it. Then, I make a kind of new *equi-disjunction*, that means dividing in equal parts, which is close to the slendro—it's an allusion of a slendro—but it's not in five. In fact, it's in twelve. What I use, I take in one hand [*plays c, d, e, f<sharp>, g<sharp>, a<sharp>*] and in the other hand the other six notes [*plays c<sharp>, d<sharp>, f, g, a, b*] and when I combine them then I combine them, for instance [*plays minor and major sixths*]. This doesn't sound chromatic and it doesn't sound diatonic. It doesn't sound whole tone.

So, if you concentrate on the *Seventh Étude* you will hear that it's a kind of whole-tone, but two whole-tone scales superimposed. So, it's a kind of diagonal illusion of equidistance. When in this etude the two hands are far enough—so I have six notes in the right hand the other six notes in the left hand, never changing the notes—when they are far enough we hear two whole-tone scales. At the moment. it's very close to the Debussy sound-world, but when they are totally together then it's chromatic, but in between it's neither chromatic nor diatonic. In some new etudes, the tenth etude, for example, I will combine two hexatonic scales which are not whole-tone, combining to a chromatic total, but never giving chromaticism. So, the *First Étude* was the pentatonic plus diatonic and the *Seventh Étude* with the two whole tones gives the example how I can make illusions of nontemperate scales. They are temperate, but nonchromatic, nondiatonic on the piano.

Now, another remark about rhythm. I was very, very much interested—since I wrote in the early '60s—'62, a piece for one hundred metronomes—in the superimposition of different rhythmic patterns. I'm very, very deeply interested in polyrhythmic thinking, therefore a very, very deep love for Charles Ives since the '60s, since Stokowski's Ives fourth symphony recording came out.[10] I was totally, totally impressed by the courage to do something which nobody did before. [I was] very deeply impressed and interested in the music of the fourteenth century in Europe, which is in fact a very complex polymetric music by the possibilities of the measured notation. Much later, in the year 1980, when I first heard the player piano music of Conlon Nancarrow, I was also very much impressed. For me, Nancarrow is the greatest living composer. I tell this always. There are people who believe, but people who give prizes do not always believe in this.

So, I feel myself very, very close to the thinking in rhythmic complexity. What I did here, I used certain techniques of African music. African music [can be] divided in[to] two big cultures. In the north, the Sahara and north of it, which is Islamic. It's melodic and heterophonic, music of highest complexity, richness in melodic and rhythmic conception, but it's not polyphonic music. And then south of the Sahara—the non-Islamic, the animistic part—is highly intricate polyphonic and polyrhythmic music. Of course, they are so different cultures. The distances between Sierra Leone and Malawi are huge, but there is something which is general in Africa, that the thinking in form is very simple. You have cycles, you have periods which never change. So, they don't have the concept of large form. The

10 Leopold Stokowski, conducting the American Symphony Orchestra, released on Columbia Masterworks this premiere recording of Ives's fourth symphony in 1965. Although Ives completed the symphony in the mid-1920s, Stokowski oversaw the first full performance of the piece on April 26, 1965.

concept is always the same, but inside of these cycles there are crazy asymmetric subdivisions. A European period, for instance a minuet of Haydn, is mostly eight stresses divided in four plus four. Then in a very elaborate way [the composer can] change the symmetry of four plus four in making prolongations and developments of the period. But, in the African period, for instance, twelve is not divided in six plus six. It's divided in seven plus five. So, it's always a tendency to asymmetry inside of these equal periods, sometimes because there is a lot of polyphonic music. In Central African Republic there are orchestras, about twenty different musicians, for instance antelope horns, and with an all-horn orchestra each horn can only produce one pitch.

So, there is an orchestral heterophony. For melody, everybody has a different pitch so the instrument is a kind of *hocket* technique like in Machaut's time. Extremely rhythmic, extremely complex, extremely rich, overcomplex polyphonic, polyrhythmic music. Listening in the early '80s to more and more of these records, they made a very deep impression so that I began to study a bit the Third World literature. Ethnomusicologists who made wonderful collections transcribing a lot of scores of complex central African orchestral music. What is important is that these asymmetries in the periods are only possible by a common denominator, which is a very fast pulsation which is not played, but felt. Now, for instance, in Uganda—in the south of Uganda, in the old kingdom of Buganda—there is xylophone music, so-called Konjo with three to six players on the xylophone. Two players who sit opposite—one has a melody, a very fast melody and the other has another very fast melody. The left hand of one corresponds to the right hand of the opposite one. They play a so-called interlocking technique. That means one begins the melody and the other begins his melody between, in the silences, but it's extremely fast. By the way, this technique seems to come from Indonesia, because in Indonesian gamelan you have also the interlocking, but there's no scientific proof that there was some Indonesian influence to Africa except of Madagascar, which is influenced by Indonesia.

As you listen to the piano *Études*, it has nothing to do with Africa. There's no African folklore in it. It has a lot to do with Chopin, Liszt, and Debussy and this tradition, but still they are very new in a certain way. But I used the idea of very fast pulsation [with] two results. One: if you take the last *Étude* you heard, the sixth, *Automne à varsovie*, and if you listen again—because the pieces are so complex rhythmically, one listening gives no real impression, you can't concentrate on what the pianist is doing. He only has two hands and sometimes we have the illusion that he plays in two different speeds, sometimes even in three, sometimes even four different speeds. In fact, he cannot do this. It's only an illusion. It's Maurits Escher–like, like the illusions in Maurits Escher's graphic.[11] What he does, for instance, I have the very fast pulsation which is played but we forget it. Then having for instance five pulsation elements for a duration on it in one hand, in the other hand three. That means that five will be slower and three will be faster. That means I developed in fact in this *Étude*, the *Sixth Étude*, which was played last. I used prime numbers not to make doubling except that two would be too fast and instead of two I used four, which is not a prime number. You see, it's arithmetic but a very simple one. I don't use mathematics or arithmetic as a thing to impress, but making very practical constructions. From this point of view, I feel very close to Maurits Escher, who used certain dramatic constructions, but for making art.

Another, maybe the most complex piece rhythmically is *Désordre*, where you have together accents, melody in both hands, and then you have the impression that the left is behind, shifting, shifting, shifting. In fact, what I do, I have eight pulsations per bar and in one moment—I have to show you how it looks—I leave out one note. For instance, here I have eight units and then I have one bar in the right hand only seven units in the left eight. That means that the accents—the next melodic accent which is an octave in the right hand—will come earlier and the left hand a bit later. It's very difficult to the pianist, but he can do it because he has a coordination with the even pulsation. So, I can produce therefore the title *Désordre*. I dedicated it to Pierre Boulez, to his sixtieth birthday, because he doesn't like disorder! So, starting with order and then shifting it. [It] has very much to do with Terry Riley and Steve Reich and a lot of other people who I like, but still it's a different music. This is not minimal music, it's maximal music. I'm very arrogant.

I have a question to start things off, *Alan charges*. You have mentioned Nancarrow. Have you observed Nancarrow's work [all] along, and does this play an important part in your own thinking?

Ligeti:

No, I even never heard his name. Very few people knew his name before 1980. So there are certain very interesting coincidences between my music and Nancarrow's music before. For instance, my piece for harpsichord *Continuum*, could be a Nancarrow piece, which is '68, but I had no idea of Nancarrow. Also, the piece for one hundred metronomes is the idea polyrhythmic, it's a Nancarrow-ish idea. Also, a Terry Riley-ish idea, having no idea about Terry Riley and it was about the same time. I enjoyed very much listening to *In C* and later Nancarrow. Now, in fact, one of my pieces for two pianos—which is called *Monument*, the first of

11 Maurits Cornelis Escher (or M.C. Escher, as he is more commonly known) was a Dutch artist whose fanciful work derived inspiration from mathematics and, as with his more famous works such as *Ascending and Descending* (1960) and *Waterfall* (1961), often toyed with illusions and improbable scenarios.

FIGURE 3.2 György Ligeti in the home of Judith and Ron Rosen, February 28, 1993. Photo by Betty Freeman, courtesy of the Los Angeles Philharmonic Archives.

the three—I wrote in '76 having no idea about Nancarrow. Then, when I listened first time in the year '80 the two records which came out in the Arch Record series, I was deeply impressed that his *Study no. 20* is absolutely like my piece *Monument*. If we discuss priority questions like Schoenberg and Hauer,[12] I give freely the credit to Nancarrow. He was much before me. In fact, I discovered his music by chance and I became a fan of him. Then, I told everybody and invited him to Europe and so in this way he came first time in '82 to Europe and then some other times.

My music has a lot to do with jazz, but it's not jazz. It's definitely not jazz. You know, we have certain drawers. There is a drawer of so-called classical music and jazz is in a different drawer and pop and rock in a different drawer, but there are still some places where the two drawers mix. So, I have my love for jazz, even [if] I don't play jazz, but my love for jazz is present here.

In fact, I dare to say that the real musical style of the twentieth century, the real big thing that happened was jazz, was this melding of African rhythmic thinking and English, Irish melodies which happened in the beginning of the century in the south of the United States. It's more important, I feel, than many, many of

12 Josef Matthias Hauer claimed to have invented a twelve-tone method prior to Schoenberg. For more on the legacy and historiography of Hauer, see Simon Shaw-Miller, "'Out of Tune': Hauer's Legacy and the Aesthetics of Minimalism in Art and Music," in *Visible Deeds of Music: Art and Music from Wagner to Cage* (New Haven, CT: Yale University Press, 2002), 163–207.

the very deep learned music. But, jazz has its limitations. Playing jazz has a certain stylistic criteria which you have to maintain. Even if you change the style, the range between Louis Armstrong to Ornette Coleman is tremendous. They are totally different, but there is something which is common. You have a basic pulsation, which by the way in the '20s was more two and then became four, and you put what you play in this measure, in this *metre*, in this bar with a very small shifting which is swing. It's very difficult to define what swing is. In fact, it's a very, very, very slight syncopation to be earlier or a bit later. So, you have not a geometric shape but an *approximate* geometric shape. You don't step this way, but you *slender a bit*. This slendering feeling in jazz, and the great jazz musicians—this is the real poetry to develop something which is not fixed, which is just lingering.

So, this feeling of jazz which surely came from Africa—but, in Africa it's not based on the bar. Then the combination of African rhythmic thinking with the bar thinking, the metrical thinking of European, this was jazz. Now, in fact, I am very, very deeply—not only interested in it—I am a deep lover of jazz. Not for everything, just high-level jazz. You feel the influences of jazz in this music, but I would never pretend that this is jazz. Maybe *Arc-en-ciel* is. Really, my ideal would be [the late] Bill Evans, if Bill Evans would play this piece once, in heaven.

Really the African influence came [at] the time when I had already strong influences from Latin America, from both Brazilian samba and then different Caribbean musics. It's a certain combination between Latin American musical thinking, so the 3+3+2 rhythm for instance, or 3+2+3, or to divide eight not in 4+4, but in 3+2+3, which is an African origin, but I didn't know the African music. It has very strong correspondence with certain cultures in the Balkan peninsula, which are so-called Magyar, what Bartók used as Bulgarian rhythm, but it's not only Bulgarian. It's generally in the Balkan, Anatolia, and also North Africa.

As a child, I heard a lot of Romanian folk music, violin music where they used these kind of asymmetries. So, it's no, how to say, *correspondence* between Balkan, Anatolia, and the African cultures because geographic totally different, but interestingly in these asymmetric metric patterns there are some very similar formations. But, I have to say I developed a kind of static music in the late '50s, early '60s. So, the best known piece is the orchestra piece *Atmosphères*, which is completely without rhythm, without melody, without harmony. It's only the sound color and the dynamic change. But, it was more thinking to the end the consequences of serial music, that in serial music you have a so high level of rhythmic complexity that the rhythmic complexity, how to say, changes in rhythmic noncomplexity. Then, why to use complex rhythm? I use no rhythm at all. So, it was a totally different idea. But, then during the '70s I became accustomed with Latin American music, and during the '80s and exactly '83 it was a big shock, a positive shock when I heard from the UNESCO collection a recording of Central African polyrhythmic orchestral music. This is something amazing. So, in fact, I changed from the composer like before with the static music.

I didn't really change my ideas, but I work like somebody in science—when he solves the problem [then] comes a hundred new problems. I solved this static music imagination, I realized them, then the next step I change. You will hear, if you heard my violin concerto and my horn trio and now the *Études*, seemingly different composers, but in fact it's me from different times only going stepwise from one piece to the next piece, not repeating the solved problem. So, I hate the artistic, you know, fashion. Somebody has a trademark and then repeat[s] it. Yves Klein—I have a lot of admiration for him—but Yves Klein developed—it's a certain blue, a certain ultramarine—and then he only used this ultramarine and only blue.[13] I am the opposite. My ideal is Stravinsky. Stravinsky was always himself, but he went from Russian folk music to Pergolesi and to Bach and to Webern finally. Only, I'm much less dependent on this kind of stylistic quotations, but more influences. I have always influences. Also, the question, am I modern musician or a traditional? Both. I don't see an opposition. I develop new ideas, but always very, very deeply rooted in tradition, both European and many non-European traditions.

WITOLD LUTOSLAWSKI

January 6, 1991

Ladies and gentlemen, *Lutoslawski begins*, I understand that I'm supposed to say a few words about the pieces that are to be played now. So, first of all, the String Quartet. I have chosen the order in such a way because String Quartet is longer and requires more concentration and more effort probably. *Partita* is maybe a more accessible piece and shorter. So, it will follow the string quartet.

The String Quartet I wrote in 1964. It was a commission of the Swedish Radio at the tenth anniversary of *Nutida Musik*—which is at the same time a series of concerts and a periodical.[14] The Swedish Radio designated one of the best string quartets at that time, LaSalle String Quartet, to make the premier of the piece in

13 Yves Klein (1928–1962) was a French artist understood to be a key figure in the development of performance art, pop art, and minimalism. What Ligeti is referring to here comes from Klein's so-called Blue Epoch, where several monochrome canvases were displayed with a deep, intense hue of blue—a color now known widely as International Klein Blue (IKB).

14 *Nutida Musik*, or "contemporary music," began in 1957 as a Swedish music journal. It was also the name of a Swedish music association—the largest in Sweden—that hosted concerts and organized a festival every year.

FIGURE 3.3 Witold Lutoslawski, January 6, 1991. Photo by Betty Freeman, courtesy of the Los Angeles Philharmonic Archives.

Stockholm during a festival devoted to that anniversary. I decided to write the string quartet rather hesitatingly. It was only when I found the method of writing a piece, which consists of a series of mobiles in a way, because it's music in which the element of chance plays a great role.

But, if speaking about the element of chance, immediately there is a question: If [there is] the element of chance, so the result is not to be foreseen and the composer can't really control it. This is not my case, because what interests me in using the element of chance in music is not to give the chance the leading role in a piece of music. No, it's just a device to enrich the repertoire of means of expression. It gives the possibilities of rhythms and textures that are impossible to achieve in any other way. Nevertheless, I keep full control over the pitch organization of the piece. That means the harmony, because it wouldn't interest me to leave the harmony to chance, it's still in control. It's, of course, a little mysterious for a listener who hears for the first time such a remark. If I were to explain how it's possible, I'll take the simplest example, which is in fact on the first page of the first piece in which I used the element of chance. The piece is called *Venetian Games* (*Jeux Venétiens* is the original French title). Seven woodwinds play the first section, which is on the first page of the piece. They play freely—that means they don't coordinate their parts; they can even begin not at the beginning of the parts, but in the middle, and repeat from the beginning. It doesn't change at all my control of the pitch organization.

In what way is that possible? It's very simple. I established a sort of vertical aggregate of twelve different sounds in such a way that it made up a chord which has a certain quality, a certain character, a certain color. It's not just a collection of intervals. It's very carefully chosen in such a way that the twelve-note chord has its own very characteristic sound. This is the material for each melody played by one of the seven woodwinds. They play freely. They don't coordinate their parts. The melodies are very capricious, changing in tempo and in dynamics. And yet, what is the result? The result is nothing else but a rather sophisticated broken chord because all melodies are composed out of sounds that make up my precomposed aggregate. Of course, this is the simplest case. It's the simplest case because the final result is fairly static. To avoid this staticism, I had to develop some methods. But, nevertheless, it doesn't give a full result. That means if one wants to enrich the repertoire of means of expression by this kind of technique, what one gets is a great richness of rhythm, impossible to achieve in any other way, and also a sort of texture which is very flexible, and it can be paradoxically compared to sculpture in a liquid material.

But, for such richness and originality of sound, one must pay. What is to be paid is just this staticism of music because if I insist on controlling pitch organization, I can't go beyond some structures that last for a certain time, which makes music sometimes quite static. And that's why I can't just limit the repertoire of my means of expression to just this technique, because it would have been too static and to change the harmony faster in this technique is impossible. Then, of course, I write in a traditional way. That means with bar-lines and meters and so on and, in the orchestral pieces, with conducting, while the ad libitum sections in which there's no common pulsation—common division of time—are not conducted when played by an ensemble of an orchestra.

In the String Quartet, this technique predominates. I shouldn't say that there is a certain monotony or maybe staticism of harmony. It's because the music is organized in such a way that it's very continuous in spite of the very fact that it's composed of sections, each one being composed on one single aggregation. The passing on from one section to another is organized in such a way that the players mutually give some signs. For instance, at the end of a section it's written in the part, "Wait for a sign of the second violin," or "Give a sign to cello that you have finished," and so on and so forth. "Accompany the second violin," and the part of second violin is written and the part of the instrument—let's say of the viola or so—is written underneath. So, this system enabled me to compose a piece which is composed of several sections, but the continuity is assured, is kept.

A few words about the form of the piece. The ideal balance in large-scale closed forms, I think, is especially present in the Viennese classic music—the symphonies of Haydn for instance, where the right portion of music is presented in the right time and composed in such a way that you are never exhausted, never tired after a symphony of Haydn. So, I found it sort of ideal while, for instance, [although] being a great admirer of Brahms's music, I always feel tired after a symphony because there are too many movements. Yes? You know, I really love music of Brahms, but I can't listen to anything else after because it's too much. So, I wanted to find a solution for me which wouldn't be just imitation of classical form, but something which would correspond with the very nature of my music. I found the solution in the two-movement form; a very characteristic example is just my string quartet in which there is one movement which is introductory, it's called "Introductory Movement," and the other is "Main Movement."

What is the difference? The "Introductory Movement" serves here as a sort of preparation for the "Main Movement." That means it may engage, it may interest, it may involve the listener, but never satisfy. That means it's always something which doesn't develop enough to lead to something more important. So, after a certain number of such episodes, various episodes, there is a feeling of impatience, of low pressure, so to speak. Something important must finally happen! And this is the right moment to present the listener with the main movement, which requires more effort, more concentration, and possibly gives this expected satisfaction which the first movement doesn't give. That was my concept of the two movements, large scale, closed form. This is a characteristic example of it. It's being played *attacca*, without stop, but it's very clear, I think, for everybody when this continuity of music appears for the first time because the episodes are always interrupted by something, in this particular case by octaves played forte by all instruments, or two instruments, or the last time by one single and finally by all of them. So, that's about the form. I think it's enough. I hope the music will say better what it really is.

[Live performance of *String Quartet*]

Lutoslawski to the performers: Thank you for playing. Thank you so much.

So, now a few words about [*Partita for Violin and Orchestra*] which is composed much later, just a few years ago. Pinchas Zukerman and Marc Neikrug were people who wanted to have this piece and were the soloists of my concert in St. Paul with the St. Paul Chamber Orchestra.[15] I remember very well that the temperature in the wind chill was minus 45 Celsius! Nevertheless, the orchestra played beautifully and Pinchas Zukerman and Marc Neikrug made a wonderful first performance of

15 This premiere with Zukerman and Neikrug took place on January 18, 1985, in Saint Paul, Minnesota.

the piece. It's different from what you've just heard because it's a piece in which I wanted to make a sort of allusion to Baroque music. Of course, it's a rather distant allusion, but nevertheless it's recognizable.

The beginning especially is in the rhythm of a piece of that time and then the *Largo* may be sort of allusion to Handel's largos of his violin sonatas, and the last movement, the fifth, is in the triplet form, triplet rhythm. That makes it similar to a gigue. But, between the first and third movement there is a second and between the third and the fifth there is the fourth, and the second and the fourth are entirely different. They are written in the method that is similar to the quartet because it's written in the boxes. The boxes are independent for violin and piano and they are supposed not to coordinate their parts, but it's written in such a way that even when they don't coordinate their play, which is very capricious and without any definite meter and bar lines, nevertheless it fits to each other as in other pieces with the element of chance. So, that has nothing to do with any allusion to Baroque music and I wanted to just separate the first movement and the *Largo* and the *Largo* and the *Quasi-gigue*.

I don't think that there is much more to say about the piece, although in my work it played a sudden, rather peculiar role. During the 1960s (and earlier on) I was working with twelve-note chords and harmony (it has nothing to do with Schoenberg's doctrine—it's entirely independent). I thought that, always feeling that [Schoenberg's methods] were too one-sided a kind of harmony and it was good for big masses of sounds but not for thinner textures—for instance, pieces for an instrument with piano, a solo instrument and piano. So, I thought these thinner textures are to discover and to fit them to what I wanted to realize. I knew that there must be something of this kind around me and I didn't know where.

And one evening or afternoon, in a fraction of a second, I suddenly understood how to do it. I composed immediately a piece for oboe and piano. It was the first piece in this vein, a short piece called *Epitaph*. Then came other pieces where this technique was being used, like *Double Concerto for Oboe and Harp*, and many, many others. The elements of this technique are present in all my subsequent pieces, like the pieces that are in the program of next week's concert[16] (that means *Piano Concerto* and *Third Symphony*, and many others) and also they are present in the *Partita*. What it consists of I think it would be too long to explain and possibly I should systematize a little, but I don't need it for my purposes. Maybe it would be useful for my younger colleagues to possibly find some rules to begin their work.

16 The Los Angeles Philharmonic New Music Group performed a Lutoslawski program on January 7, 1991, with Lutoslawski conducting some of his pieces.

So, I just signal what happened to me. It completed, in a way, the collection of the procedures that I used in my music composed up to now.

But I must say that the work on the language I began in 1948, after a moment when I realized that what I was doing then wouldn't lead me to what I wanted to realize. That's why I began from scratch, from nothing. I knew only that two notes, one after another or one above another, can never be indifferent from the point of view of expression. That was the first premise, but only one. Then I began working on harmony especially, as I said, on the extreme cases (that means the harmony of twelve notes), but it was of course too one-sided and that's why I had to invent something which would fit to that, enabling me to compose thinner textures. So much so about the *Partita*.

[Performance of *Partita*]

Now Alan:

Did you see *The New York Times* this morning with the article that said, "farewell to atonality"?[17]

No, *Lutoslawski replies.* I haven't seen it.

Alan again:

Would you be ready to say farewell to atonality?

I don't know what "atonality" is, *Lutoslawski replies, which is met with applause from the crowd.*

This, *Alan starts*, is a very narrow minded, very bigoted critic who finds atonality under the bed before he goes to sleep every night. But today he has proclaimed the end of it.

Lutoslawski, chuckling:

Well, for me it hasn't existed at all. So, the end of nothing! I don't know what is "atonality." After all, "tonality" is not quite precise of a term. To me, tonality is major and minor and minor system and functional harmony. That's tonality. But, if there is a triad in music, it needn't be tonal.

Betty speaks out:

I have [a question]. What is your relation to John Cage?

My relation to John Cage, *he reacts*. Yes, of course, the question is very up to the point because if I use the element of chance always it's John Cage that comes to our mind. It was a very important moment in my life when I heard just incidentally a

17 Alan is referring to Donal Henahan, "And So We Bid Farewell to Atonality," *New York Times*, January 6, 1991, who writes, "While the abandonment of tonality may have been a perfectly logical step, what took its place was ridiculously constructed in expressive potential."

short section of John Cage's second piano concerto.[18] One must admit that a composer may listen to music in a different way than the listeners because we very often listen to music and what we actually hear is not what is being played, but what is in our imagination, but provoked by the sounds heard. And that was the case with Cage's second concerto because suddenly I realized that I could possibly use a lot of things that I couldn't realize in an entirely different way than it was before that. It doesn't mean John Cage's *music* influenced me, but it was a sort of stimulus. I wrote to him that he was a spark of a bottle of gunpowder in me.

I used this technique of chance operation, but not similar to those of John's because the goal was entirely different. His use of chance is the result of his philosophy, which is not the case with me. For me, the chance operations are only to enrich the repertoire of procedures, to enrich the technique of composing music and to free things that were, so to speak, accumulated in my imagination, but I couldn't realize them. But, with introducing the element of chance, finally I could compose entirely differently. That was very important for me, that moment. I wrote to him a letter. When he asked me to send something for his book, *Notations*, he asked me for one page or for a whole score or for a sketch or something.[19] So, I sent him the manuscript of *Venetian Games*, saying that without that moment I couldn't compose that piece. And I received a wonderful letter. Before that, I think that we met in Zagreb. We see each other from time to time. He used to come to Warsaw and to perform there.

18 Not to be confused with the 1953 *Concerto for Prepared Piano and Orchestra*, the title of Cage's piece Lutoslawski refers to here is *Concert for Piano and Orchestra*, which premiered in 1958.

19 John Cage, *Notations* (New York: Something Else Press, 1969).

Chapter 4

A Universe of Sounds

Pierre Boulez

"I WOULD SAY that the three B's who dominate the musical scene in the latter half of the twentieth century would be Babbitt, Boulez, and Betty."

Alan is setting up a salon, an unusual event in that it is dedicated to one figure—Pierre Boulez—flanked by a panel of fellow composers, critics, and friends. One of Douglas Wheeler's light constructions illuminates the Music Room's far corner. Stretches of tubes and colorful fluorescent light from Wheeler and Dan Flavin could be found in just about every room of Betty's home, and the Music Room was no exception. For this discussion about the spools of electronic music winding between Europe and America—mediated by no less than a *conductor*, all puns aside—these quietly humming art installations seem a fitting illumination.

Pierre Boulez served not only as a formidable composer but also as a conductor who was a fierce and loyal compatriot to new music both in America and in Europe. "It would be difficult to argue with the proposition that Pierre Boulez represents the predominant creative force of the previous half-century," Alan notes. "The sweep of his musical outlook spells out the flux of those five decades: his early experiments in musique concrète, the espousal (for a time) of total serialism, the activist years with the pamphleteering that called for, among other atrocities, the destruction of all opera houses or at least their repertories, the emergence of a symphonic conductor of peerless perception, the chilling splendor of his own compositions, the creation of the vast educational complex known as

The Music Room. Jake Johnson, Oxford University Press. © Oxford University Press 2025.
DOI: 10.1093/9780197775752.003.0005

IRCAM—perhaps it makes more sense to claim that Boulez actually created, rather than merely dominated, his epoch."[1]

Boulez appeared at the Music Room twice, preferring to talk rather than present any music. I chose to keep his manner of speech, including his irregular syntax and French expressions, mostly intact as a gesture toward the audience's experience navigating in real time this historic meeting of minds. The result is a voluptuous account of the formation of IRCAM and, in conversation with Stanford University composer and professor John Chowning and composer and cofounder of the San Francisco Tape Music Center Morton Subotnik, how Boulez found in Stanford's Center for Computer Research in Music and Acoustics (CCRMA) a model for further invigorating technology within European experimental music. It is through this conversation, in fact, that we learn the essential role Ligeti played in the development of IRCAM as a computer music center. John Chowning later highlighted the significance of this particular salon discussion:

> In the winter and spring quarters of 1972, Ligeti was invited to Stanford as a guest composer, knowing nothing of the computer music system we had developed at the Stanford Artificial Intelligence Lab over the previous eight years. He and I became very close as he visited the AI Lab and learned of the advanced state of our system based on Max Matthews's seminal article in the November 1963 issue of *Science*.[2] I had realized 4-channel surround with moving sound sources and discovered and developed FM Synthesis that Stanford patented and licensed to Yamaha.
>
> Ligeti knew very well the state of electronic music in Europe, having worked at Stockhausen's studio at the Westdeutscher Rundfunk (WDR). Except for a few research institutions, no one in Europe knew the digital domain. All of the electronic music studios—WDR (Cologne), EMS (Stockholm), RAI (Milano), etc.—were analog, and Boulez, in his initial plans for IRCAM, also planned for a large analog electronic music studio.[3]
>
> Soon after Ligeti returned to Germany in May 1972, he crossed paths with Boulez. Ligeti told him to pay attention to what I was doing at Stanford in our computer music studio. Ligeti told me of this encounter a month later when he asked me to give a lecture about the work at Stanford as part of his Darmstadt lectures. Without Ligeti's heads-up, IRCAM would have realized its plans and built the analog electronic studio, which would have been

1 Taken from *Il Salotto Musicale*, Los Angeles Philharmonic Archive.

2 M. V. Matthews, "The Digital Computer as a Musical Instrument," *Science* 142, no. 3592 (November 1, 1963): 553–557.

3 For a fuller account of these and other European electronic music studios, see Jennifer Iverson, *Electronic Inspirations: Technologies of the Cold War Musical Avant-Garde* (New York: Oxford University Press, 2018).

rendered obsolete by the time the center official opened in 1977. Boulez would have lost credibility and perhaps the Ministry of Culture's loss of confidence and IRCAM's funding source. It is difficult to imagine the state of new music in Europe had Boulez not succeeded.[4]

The Music Room gave space and audience for these kinds of revelations and conversations, documenting now for us all how, and when, and where, and why contemporary music took the paths that it did. Both the magnitude and intensity of the conversations here have no counterpart. For this reason, the Boulez musicales stand alone as a chapter unto themselves.

PIERRE BOULEZ

March 3, 1987

Alan:

What did [*Le Marteau sans maître*] mark for you as a composer?

The beginning of freedom, if I may say so, *Boulez responds*.

Alan again:

Freedom from what? Where were you before?

Well, I will tell you.

You know, I began with a great freedom in my writing. I mean, I was kind of wild at the beginning. I did not accept any discipline at the beginning. I accepted only my own discipline. The first works I wrote, especially the first two sonatas for piano and all the works which were written between '45 and 1950 approximately, were extremely expressionist, I would like to say. And possibly, under many influences, I noticed that I should go back to the sources of the musical vocabulary and try to analyze the components of the musical language. It came to a kind of very theoretical approach of language. Therefore, I was for a while in a kind of tunnel. Not that everything was dark. A tunnel is [for] bringing you from a point to another point. A tunnel is not a dead end. On the contrary. But it was very necessary to have theoretical inflections on the nature of the language, of how to renew the language, because I thought you could not go forever with classical forms and classical elements of the vocabulary. It seemed to me that was the kind of trap where all the preceding generations had fallen, that they wanted to renew the language, but to follow very classical patterns: for instance, the sonata form, the variations

4 Email to author, August 28, 2023.

form, and so on and so forth. I had for me the kind of thinking that on the contrary to go back to these forms, to these classical forms, would impair enormously the progress the language was supposed to make.

So, the kind of neoclassical tendency you find either in Stravinsky or in Schoenberg was not really very satisfying to me.[5] I asked myself why. I thought the answer was, "let's go down to the origins of the language and to the structure itself of the language." Then this theoretical approach materialized in exactly one work by myself. That was the *Structures, Book I*, for two pianos. I chose even neutral material for this purpose. I did not choose a theme or invention by myself to write this work, but I took a quote from Messiaen, the famous [*Quatre*] *Études de rhythme*, which was based on a series of twelve tones with timbre, attacks, and everything. I took that as a basis, which was kind of *Verfremdung*, as a German would say, I mean *disassociation* between me and the material. So, I had the kind of view on this material, which was not going with a personal involvement other than the beginning. Then I developed the ideas about language and it helped to find new forms, new ways of writing the music, not asking always for the same things, for the same categories as the ones I have learned. But it was very restrictive, very constraining.

Then I could not imagine that I would write like that for years and years and years to come. I mean, I could not be in a straitjacket like that. Therefore, when I began to develop the ideas, I wanted in the same time a certain discipline, but in the same time freedom, at each time. I think the composer has the right to be free at any moment when he composes. I think composing is not really filling a kind of categories which are already defined before he begins to compose because I think that's dead at the very beginning. But on the contrary, you have to discover yourself progressively what you want to do. You begin, maybe, with a definite path and you finish with quite another direction than the one you have chosen at the very beginning. So, this kind of freedom of past I wanted to recapture as much as the first years, [which] were very wild and undisciplined, but controlled anyway.

But controlled by things I have seen in other composers, by things I have inherited. I wanted to create my own vocabulary, my own image, but to be in the same time free at any moment of the composition. Therefore, *Marteau* was a very hard piece to write for me. It marks for me the beginning of a real personal language. That's funny, but it seems very pretentious to say that. But still now when

5 Boulez's disdain for Schoenberg was by then well known. In his scathing 1952 essay "Schoenberg Is Dead" (published only seven months after the composer's death), Boulez suggests the musical world move past Schoenberg—to "neutralize the setback"—and fears his outsized legacy will halt development in serial composition. See Boulez, "Schoenberg Is Dead," in *Stocktakings from an Apprenticeship* (New York: Clarendon Press, 1991), 209–214.

I am rehearsing, for instance, I think that no other composers were writing that before me. In the other pieces, on the contrary, I can trace many influences, obvious sometimes, taken from other composers, absorbed, but I can see them. But in this work, I think for the first time my language was really personal.

Alan:

Well, you bring up a kind of dichotomy here between freedom and awareness of the past. In other words, you say on the one hand that a composer must be free at every moment when he is creating a piece. And yet, in your own case you were conscious at this time—I imagine we're talking about early 1950s—you were conscious at this time of other composers in their tradition, music that you had listened to, so that you were not really starting from a zero point.

Boulez:

You cannot start from a zero point. I think that [André] Malraux said once, "You don't become a painter because you see nature or rivers or trees, but you become a painter because you have seen paintings."[6] You have seen van Gogh, you have seen Cézanne, you have seen Rembrandt, you have seen all these things. The nature through painters. That makes you a painter.

I think exactly the same way. In music, you don't become a musician because either you are just gifted or you have heard, I don't know, the noise of a river or the noise of the wind in the trees. You become a musician because you have heard a lot of things, even unconsciously. You are not aware, maybe, of your culture, but the culture where you are evolving has a great influence on you. For instance, a young Chinese does not, you know, have the same perception of sound as a young French or a young German or a young American because I think the whole environment brings a culture which is there already. You can fight against this culture, you can try to destroy it or to have this culture evolve at a more rapid pace than people expect, but you are anyway fighting against something. That's like a plane. Without resistance of the air the plane could not be airborne. I think the culture is exactly that for you when you are creating something. The culture is air. You are getting against it, but at the same time that is the culture which brings you up.

Morton Subotnick:

You know what we're seeing right now? We're seeing a prophecy come true, which looked to be nothing but the babblings of a strange, but excited man. That's [Marshall] McLuhan['s] media,[7] where he talked about everything being this

6 Malraux was France's minister of cultural affairs from 1959 to 1969. He and Boulez had a public falling out in 1969, which caused Boulez to exile himself from France for thirteen years only to be brought back to Paris at the request of French president Georges Pompidou to lead what would become IRCAM. See Donal Henahan, "Boulez Ending Exile with Post in Paris," *New York Times*, November 9, 1973.

7 Marshall McLuhan, *Understanding Media: The Extensions of Man* (Cambridge, MA: MIT Press, 1964).

FIGURE 4.1 Pierre Boulez, March 3, 1987. Photo by Betty Freeman, courtesy of the Los Angeles Philharmonic Archives.

bombardment of information where there would be no distinction between one thing and another, but rather the whole would become the object, the bombardment would be the object itself. That seems to be actually happening right now.

Alan:

Does this represent the philosophy at IRCAM, too?

Boulez:

Well, I am very careful about that myself, I would like to say, because we have seen—and one cannot avoid to tell this kind of truth—we have seen people who were fascinated by technology, but who had very little musical culture. It was a great handicap because you had in a way people who were brought up in a musical tradition, and who refused all evolution, who were saying, "Well, the instruments will remain the instruments and your technology will fade out," and so on. Well, that's not really a very clever attitude either because when you are confined in this closed tradition, you cannot go very much further.

But on the contrary, we had people who were excited especially by the new sounds, not very much by anything else, I find, or by a kind of poetic aspect. You know, they were attracted by the possibility of making *collage* in music. They took something and they edited that, they superimposed a thing with another thing. It gave across, of course, a kind of simplistic, naive, poetic atmosphere. But I mean, it was interesting, but interesting only from this point of view, either from the point of view of sound, they found some sounds, which were interesting.

It remains to be seen what is a sound in itself. I mean, is a sound really very important, or is a sound important because it is part of something else? Even if you touch a piano and you hear a "d"—what is a "d"? Well, a "d" is nothing unless there is a context. A bell has a marvelous sound—I mean, a very large bell, for instance—but what can you do with it? You cannot do very much because the sound is so rich. You can do only this kind of rhythmical regularity. The only thing you can do with bell is to superimpose a couple of bells with different phases, different regularity. Then it begins to be interesting, but it's a very reduced range of music because it is purely rhythm on sounds. You can tell me that's already the beginning of music, but that's not enough. I would like to say that if you are interested in sound you have to think about the relationship of sound and composition. I find that for me the beginning of working with sound—I mean, the sound in itself can be very beautiful, but absolutely useless, or it can be just for underlining some kind of very important point in the musical speech, in the musical work. For instance, we have examples of that in the instrumental literature. Look, if you use a tam-tam in the orchestra, you don't use a tam-tam every second. It would be terribly boring. The tam-tam has a very rich sound, but a sound which is so powerful and so unique that even you recognize the same tam-tam in the work of Mr. X or of Mr. Y. The tam-tam is really *the fact* and *not the music* at the same time.

Alan:

That's what's so thrilling about the Tchaikovsky *Pathétique*. We get the sound of the tam-tam at the end . . .

Boulez:

Only once.

Alan:

Only once, forty-five minutes into the piece.

Boulez:

Yes, because it articulates the structure, but you cannot use the percussion, generally, like you use a violin, for instance, because the percussion has a very strong center on the sound itself. It is very difficult. Mainly the percussion is, for me, to be mixed in a very difficult way with sounds which are more neutral. As long as you're not aware of this dialectic between sound and structure, composition generally, you are not really a composer. You are just adding. You add something, you add something, but that's not still composing. For me, composing is really trying to have the structure of sounds, even have an evolution, and meet other sounds and then combine, or on the contrary, fight, and so on and so forth. That's really complex.

I come back to what I was telling at the beginning, that some people who were coming because they were interested in technology have very little ideas about composition. What I do myself at IRCAM, I try to tell the people who are interested in this new technology, "Well, learn a language," and that's the main thing. Sound will come after. There are two things I try to avoid in IRCAM. People were only interested in technology because, you know, generally you find in this kind of conferences which take place once a year: last year we could do that in thirty seconds; now, we can do that in twenty-five seconds. That I find terrible because of course it's an improvement—I mean, that's better even if you can do it in two seconds, but that's not the core of the problem. The core of the problem is *how* to use it and what are the tools, which allow for instance a musical thought to be developed in a proper way. That interests me much more than "we do it in two seconds."

That's the first thing, and the second thing is if people are interested only in the sounds, I advise them, "Well, look at the relationship between sound and language." That, for me, is the main thing. That's a kind of philosophy I try to develop in IRCAM. That's not always easy, because it depends many times on the gifts of people. You have people who are very gifted for the ear, I mean for just creating sounds. We cannot do anything with them other than this kind of poetic collage, I would like to say. And there are people who are very brilliant intellectually, who can really explain and know very well what a language is, but they have no sense for sonority. But you find that also without technology, I suppose.

Subotnik:

Yeah. I think the biggest issue right now, which we're just beginning to face finally, and I'm really thankful for it, is exactly what are we going to do with the technology? The technology is clearly moving at such a rate right now that anything you could imagine you could almost do within some reason. The question really is now, what do you want to do?

But I'd like to just speak one moment to the idea of sound because I don't even see a sound as a sound, but rather as a gesture. The quality of sound, for instance, with an oboe, the quality of sound with a tam-tam, they're very particular because the nasal quality of the oboe already suggests a whole sense of possible expression, the very sound itself. If, for instance, one is drowning, and you say, "I'm drowning," it's not likely anyone will come to help you. But whether you understand the words or not, it's the way in which you cry for help that in fact communicates. So, one of the things that's attracted me to technology is the ability to not just make new sounds, but to make new articulations, new ways of communicating, which one does with orchestration, if you're working with orchestra. It's not just making a cloud of sound, but it's actually articulating the music or what it is that the music is trying to say. To create a sound which starts one way, opens up and changes, is interesting, but when it changes in such a way that it goes, "Uh–ooohhh," and turns into something that is very expressive is what [it's] all about for me. That I think is what I've been trying to teach, is what I've been trying to work with the students is not to think at all about creating a new *sound*, but to use the technology to create a *gesture*, to be able to articulate what it is they want to say. The issue is really there right now, what are [we] going to do with the technology and why are people using it? Most of the people who are using technology won't be using it in the future because they're just fascinated with new gadgets. And they will go on to other gadgets.

Boulez:

Well, you know the problem with technology is you have to work with quantities and quantities are not really very expressive for themselves. What is interesting in a performance, for instance, with a live performer, that's all the irregularities of a performing, the way the grid is distorted and it is personally distorted. When you make an accent, for instance, you have a regular rhythm, but also an accent or a crescendo, decrescendo. The performer does a rhythm quite irrational compared to what you have written very rationally, and also for the timbre. If you have a trumpet who makes an accent to the timbre on this particular tone, it changes completely.

But when you are faced with the technology, then you say, "Well, you have 1.5 and twenty thousand and so on," it doesn't mean very much in terms of expression. That's exactly the problem, to find the relationship between quantity and quality. The problem was not there when you wrote for the instruments because you have a lot of connotations which are in your mind when you write an accent with an oboe, to take the oboe again. You know very well that the instrumentalist will give this kind of gesture to make the accent on a certain note, especially for instance if it is a difficult register, if it is very high or very low. This kind of accent has an effort. If you make, for instance, very difficult articulation or jumps, irregular jumps, then you know that the jumps will be irregular because it is difficult to go from a tone to another one according to the distance. On a machine, you don't have any difficulties of this kind. You can make any jump you want. The machine will do it literally and as quick as you want. But it will mean nothing. So, you have to add something. That's this addition of epsilon you cannot really measure in a performance that you have to add. I have seen that sometimes for inventing new timbres, for instance. You have a timbre, but you add aleatoric elements to add this kind of irregularity that the performer brings into it. But I mean, aleatoric does not mean [anything] either because what the performers do is not really aleatoric. It is aleatoric within a certain field and for a certain purpose, but if you use aleatoric means like that it adds something, but it adds something without any direction. That's exactly the problem.

Alan:

Well, it seems to me as an observer that what seems to be happening among composers who are involved with the use of technology in one way or another is that within a very few years we've moved from the pure electronic piece, the *Silver Apples of the Moon* or *Wild Bull* kind of piece, to an exploration of how the live musician with the aleatoric quality of the fact that he plays differently every time can interact with technology.[8] A piece like *Répons*, for example, is a live piece in which technology becomes another instrumental resource along with the people playing in the corners of the hall and the people in the center.[9] Isn't that true?

Boulez:

Absolutely true. Therefore, I was aware of that. You know, I am performer myself, after all. I have done experiments myself with, for instance, in 1951, '52, '53 with pure tape music. Then I tried to mix in '58 tape music and instruments. But I played also music by other composers, especially when I was in London. With the BBC, we have done some experiments like that. As a conductor, I felt terribly under pressure because I had to follow a tape very precisely. It is not easy because you cannot really rely. You know that if you make, let's say, a performer's gesture, I would like to say, you are ahead of the tape or you are behind the tape. So, all your strategy is to go like that and as close as possible. Otherwise, your performance will be just purely mechanical. Therefore, when I saw this problem and I saw this problem a couple of times, I have lived through it, I thought I must go really to the core of the problem, which is to bring the gesture of the performer within the technology. The gesture of the performer is exactly the origin of the technology. Then I think we have solved part of the problem at least. I don't say all of the problem, but a part of the problem.

Or, you have to conceive another type of . . . that's not anymore a concert. If you have a tape music, which can be—not tape music, music stored, I would like to say, with a computer—that's very possible to do that, to store data and to have this

8 *Silver Apples of the Moon* was Morton Subotnick's debut album from 1967, and *Wild Bull* was his follow-up album from 1968.

9 *Répons* is a chamber piece by Boulez that premiered in 1981.

data modified as you want, which is possible now because you have, for instance, a trigger which will give the last data for all this data. This triggering system is also something very interesting because each time it will be modified and then you will never know exactly what will happen in a field that you have determined very precisely, but it will never happen exactly in the same way each time. But then for instance if you store some information like that then it is done like for an exhibition, a painting exhibition, an environment which will be live, very precise, but at the same time influenced by the way people are going in this space, and so on. That's again something which is completely different from a concert. But if you are in a concert situation with something which has to go from A to Z, then you are faced with this problem of interaction. I tried in *Répons* to do that, but I will do it more in the next works, to have a background which is completely amorphous, against something which has really a form.

My comparison is like with clouds. You know, suppose you are following a tennis match, and then you observe from time to time the clouds. These clouds have the same shape, but they constantly are changing. But you are not really observing the clouds unless you are a specialist in meteorology, you will not look at the clouds like that because it will be very boring, very rapidly. And you look at these clouds . . . .

Alan:

And you also will lose the tennis match.

Boulez:

Ha! But you look at the action. Then from time to time you look at the clouds again, and you say, "Oh, well, the clouds are not all the same shape formally, but they have the same general form." Then you go back to action. I think this contrast between music which is not made for being followed from the beginning to the end and the music which is on the contrary especially written for being followed from the beginning to the end is something which the machine, the technology, can produce very well. I suppose, for instance, I did that in *Répons*. That's just for a very short piece. But you know, I have music which is stored on tape in this case because we [were] not advanced enough when I did the work to store it on the computer itself. But we will be able to do it very soon. You have music which is stored on tape. Then the instrumentalist triggers the tape. When he plays loud enough, for instance. When he plays loud enough, the music just appears, this informal music, let's say. When the instrumentalist does not play loud enough or does not play at all anymore, then the informal music disappears altogether. This kind of game between informal and formal, which is for me very important, and the machine is unique to give that because an informal music cannot be created by human beings. It would be terrible to do some kind of class, for even half an hour, [where a] musician has to give a gesture. This music is the antithesis of gesture, in a way, but has to be in contrast with something which has a gesture.

Everyone wants to work in real time. Before, I remember, at the beginning of IRCAM in '72, '73, when we began to have some technology there in '73, '74, so if you wanted to make synthesized sounds really very complex—so you could work maybe five hours to have three seconds. And you were waiting these five hours for these three seconds. If they were not good, you have to wait again, something like maybe four hours to have the corrected three seconds. Can you imagine the frustration of the musician? It was really not only frustration, but it was discouraging completely. The musicians have the imagination, they want the response immediately. Even if you do synthetic sounds, purely synthetic sounds and purely synthetic scores, now you can have at least with a sketch a good approximation of something which can be a little more complex. On transformation of sounds, that now can be done, a very complex transformation, can be done in real time. That's very important for the musician, because if you have to wait or if you have no direct contact with the material of music, then you cannot go very far. And also, all the graphic developments [have] helped a lot. Before if you wanted simply a dynamic and you have to write 1.10, 1.08, 1.06, 1.04, and so on, it was terrible. You were like a cashier. Now, it's enough just to draw a line and the computer has immediately the figures which are corresponding to this line. It speaks much more to the imagination of the musician. When I am asked, and I am asked this question quite often, "Well, don't you think that the more you have technology, the more developed the technology is, the less human, the less inspiration you can have with this technology?" I say on the contrary. The more the technology is developing, the easier the contact will be with this technology. Before it was difficult to speak with these tools because you [had] to go through the process itself, but now when the language is at a higher level, then the communication is much more direct and the result is much more attractive, as a matter of fact.

Critic Paul Moor:

Developments in electronics with voice is still something I'm fascinated with. Any news on that? Reactions? What do you want to do? What do you hope to do?

Boulez:

The voice is the most difficult instrument, I would like to say, to deal with. I'm going very progressively. First, I have written *Répons* and I want to enlarge the work for its final end. I chose very carefully instruments in *Répons* which are rather easy to treat because the sound is a sound which is like that. With this profile, the sound is rather easy to manipulate. With wind instruments, the sound is already much more difficult, especially, for instance, when you have brass with mute because you have a lot of noise. To transform this sound, you have to get rid of this noise. That's not very easy. You have to put filters, and the filters transform already the quality of the original sound so much that the transformation will suffer from that. For the strings, exactly the same. Plucked strings, for example, pizzicato in a cello or pizzicato in a violin, easy to do because that's like plucked instruments, like the harp or even the piano. But with the voice, you cannot vocalize only—I mean, you can, of course, vocalize only, but if you are interested in transformation with the text and with the consonants, then it becomes extremely difficult. That will be the third step I will take. Now I am studying already, for the next work, wind instruments, the transformation of wind instruments. After [that] it will be strings, and the last step will be the voice. But I still have among my projects to do a real version of *Pli selon pli* with the voice.

Moor:

So that assumes the difficulty you're solving is total control of timbre, which is already something that's almost impossible with voice. One of the things that occurred to me was Mr. Subotnick's fabulous "Ghost Electronics" pieces I remember seeing Joan LaBarbara performing, her voice controlling what was happening with the electronics.[10] The complex envelopes that we do in speech, which we immediately react to, it's like everyone in the room would react to them without having to think about it, to be using that to control electronics and instruments, possibly is a simpler approach without having to develop total control of timbre?

Boulez:

Well, we have in IRCAM, a specialist of the voice. I am interested myself. He has done first the vocalizing that you have heard some sampling before by Morton, but he has also brought the consonant so you don't have only "ah," "o," or "a," but you have also consonants, words, the possibility of words. You can really take this artificial voice as an agent for transformation of instruments, for instance. You can really mix already the timbre of an instrument, synthetic or not, or imitation of an instrument, because it's easier for the [time] being, and the voice. You can cross them. That's possible to do it, but it doesn't go very far.

I think nobody in IRCAM has worked more than this very simple crossing. They have tried also crossing of instruments, the various instruments. For instance, you have the envelope of a tam-tam with the timbre of a trombone, things like that, which gives very interesting results, all this crossing. You know, that's like genetics of the sound practically. That gives sounds which are very interesting, but which are also difficult to manipulate because they are almost too complex already

10 Inspired by Marshall McLuhan's media theories, Subotnik's "ghost electronics" compositions such as *Parallel Lines* (1979) blend live and electronic elements in such a way that the performer's musical choices activate the electronic (or "ghost") sounds in response.

to compose with. They can be, for the time being, they can be only the exception, but they can't be really the rule, let's say. I am interested in the voice, but for me the voice is the most difficult thing to deal with.

Music critic Charles Shere:

I've always been curious to know your response to the invented instruments of [Mauricio] Kagel and his pieces. Do you consider him a real composer who's working with these things, in the sense that you were speaking of earlier, or collages? What is your response to those pieces?

Boulez:

You cannot speak about theatrical pieces as you would speak about just pure musical pieces. The music for the theater generally has other characteristics. Therefore, what Kagel's doing is very specific with the term. He had a great deal of evolution, also. The last pieces, for instance, in the last ten years, let's say, don't use very much this kind of rejected material. Before he was taking anything for the sake of it and the choice of the instrument was maybe for the sound. He took also the sound, but he took much more for the theatrical aspect of the instrument. For instance, the very example of that is the *Zwei Man Orchestrer*, when everything is distorted or when he takes real instruments he makes a caricature of them.[11] Like, you remember, we have seen that the harp which is played by two artificial hands which are slapping this harp, which is very funny to see. You cannot say that's a new use of an instrument. For him, that's like something from the tradition of surrealism, when you take something and you derive or you distort or you take it out of its function and you change the function and it acquires another meaning. This kind of poetic distortion, I would like to say, is the goal. Therefore, some music of Kagel is very difficult to hear on record, for instance, because as long as you don't have the visual meaning of things, the music itself—it's impact—is diminishing in proportion to the lack of the visual understanding.

Audience member:

[In thinking about] the ability nowadays of sonic technology to take the octave and divide it into any number of absolutely equal parts . . . When I say this, I'm reminded of an interesting lecture given by Leland Smith[12] at Cal Tech a few years ago—everyone in the audience except me, I think, were engineers, and Smith played a tape of a scale. He asked the members present to listen to that and see what they would notice about it, if they had any comments to make about it. What

11 *Zwei Man Orchestrer* was a sound sculpture Kagel created in 1973 that utilized a mixture of orchestral instruments, household items, and other found objects.

12 Stanford professor and cofounder of the Center for Computer Research in Music and Acoustics (CCRMA).

he did, he played a thirteen-step scale. It was very hard to hear something other than just half steps.

My question then, to any of the members of the panel, what is your feeling about the twelve discrete pitches upon which our music has been based for so long and the comparison of that treatment with our instruments and how they're built and how they relate to those twelve pitches, comparing that to what's happening in electronic music? Do you feel that when you write for instruments that the twelve-tone system of chromatic pitches has a continuing future? Are you writing in the twelve-pitch system? Does the music you write really relate to those twelve pitches as the fundamental points of references and all microtonal projects are just that?

Boulez:

Of course, twelve-tone is twelve-tone, but if you have played with an orchestra quite a long time you know that twelve-tone doesn't exist practically because all the intonation is just a matter of accommodating to each other. There is no real exactitude in the pitch, practically. The second thing I would like to say, that if you observe other cultures, you would see very easily that the intervals are not the same as ours, of course, but they respect approximately the same distance. I think it's been scientifically proved, as far as I remember, that the ear cannot really listen to an addition of intervals smaller than the half tone, approximately.

You can understand that very well if you take a comparison. I did that myself, for instance, with quarter tones, when I was younger. I was experimenting with scales, different scales. For instance, you can make the difference, of course, between one and two because you say one plus one is two. You make really the difference no problem. Four and five, still no problem. If, for instance, the difference between fifteen and sixteen, that's much more difficult. If you have a hundred pennies, for instance, and a hundred and one pennies, practically that's impossible to make any difference between the two. Therefore, the experiments of Leland Smith between the thirteen and the twelve where you cannot make the difference between a real seventh or a distorted seventh because the bigger the interval is, of course, the more the ear approximates, and they reduce. You have to have a perception of the interval according to what you estimate the distance. That's exactly, for instance, if you want to say, "How many meters?" You will say, "Well, maybe five, maybe six. I don't know. Between five and six." But you cannot really say it is exactly 532 centimeters. That you cannot really do. Exactly with music. The notion of grasping an interval in music is exactly like grasping space. You can measure it with rather big spaces. For instance, if you have absolute pitch, you say "Well, that's 'c.' That's 'f♯,'" no matter the interval. You don't calculate the interval then. You are really having the notion of the pitch.

The pitch is very funny material because that's the only material where you can have a very precise evaluation without comparing. For instance, rhythm, you cannot make any evaluation. You have to have a pulse for making an evaluation of a rhythm. But if you have absolute pitch, you don't need to have all the evaluation of the steps in between to know what distance is between a "c" and an "f♯" two octaves above. You know it immediately. Then the perception of the pitch is something very special. And I would like to add also that for the use of the intervals, young French composers who are now in their forties were very interested in having chords according to the natural intervals. They have made calculations of that and of course, rather precise calculations, and when they are writing for instruments they are writing "more or less a quarter tone down" or a "quarter tone above" and that's never precise because otherwise you have to have a notation which is impossible. Also, the speed has to do, or the density of the texture. If you see, for instance, instruments like in India which are making intervals much smaller than the half tone, but what are they playing? Homophony, a melody. They don't have any polyphony or they have just an interval of reference, the tambura, the bass. So, all the intervals can be judged, estimated, but there is no texture really. There is one line. The ear picks up the difference between the intervals much better.

Or you have to have a slow speed. When you have music which is written very slowly, then you can appreciate the intervals, very small intervals, even if you have a polyphony, if you have a polyphony not too complex, but two or three or four lines, a combination of three or four lines, and then you have very slow, then you can perceive maybe not always the detail of intervals, but you perceive the movement, the direction. But if you go, and I made some experiments with myself, if you go to very small intervals then you lose the direction and you don't know between two notes if that's going up or down, if you have very, very small intervals, let's say a thirtieth of a tone, for instance. That's really impossible to appreciate. You don't know where you are, practically.

I would like just to add to that, with our instruments the material conditions are not made to have intervals smaller or more precise. There's a very famous saying that the harpist spends half of their time tuning their instruments and spends the other half of their time playing out of tune. You know, a piano, for instance, is stronger. It's built differently. The piano tuning is different, but the instrument is built in such a way that you cannot change the tension along the table without distorting completely the instrument and it will not sustain the chord because the distance is made for this tension. If you change very much the tension, the string will either break or just not sustain the tuning for very long. So therefore, if you want to go this way, that's better to find something which is adequate. Our instruments are not adequate for that. So you have two ways: either you transform the sound of instruments, with a computer, with ring modulation, with all kinds of devices you have to your disposal, and you give half tones, chords based on half tones, but the results will be completely nontempered because if you add 200 Hertz to any pitch, then the scale you will have will be completely different [from] a tempered scale, or you have to go in purely synthetic sounds where, for instance, you can define the scale and you change the scale at your wish. You have, for instance, a program which does this type of scale. Next five seconds you can change the scale completely. That's adequate and that's reliable, because if you do that with our instruments you just change the tuning and you have to change it for the complete piece. That's not reliable. But you want to bring some kind of relativity in the world of pitches, then the synthetic sound is much more adequate for that.

Therefore, you know, I think that our instruments can be improved. For instance, for flutes we are having somebody develop at IRCAM a flute with special keys for quarter tones. But you cannot destroy completely the fingering of a flute because the fingering is not really the fancy of somebody. The fingering on a flute or on a wind instrument is the result of many centuries of evolution and that's the optimum realization for such an instrument. If you introduce something new you have to be very careful that this new thing does not interfere with the past of the instrument, but adds something without destroying something else. Therefore, you can improve some aspects of the instrument, but not change completely their nature, for the time being, unless we invent something new. But I think if you go into a new field then that's better to find the field where you find an adequate response and a reliable response.

Rand Steiger, composer and faculty member at CalArts and UCSD:

There's been a proliferation of articles written the last couple of years about the idea that the concept of modernism no longer really pertains to music and that embracing the past is much more important than progressing into the future. I would like to ask the panel not only their personal attitudes about my question but also why is this in the air and why is it being written about these days?

Subotnik:

What he means is, "What is postmodernism?" Have you come across this term? What does it mean?

Yes, *Alan snorts*. It's the watchword of the critical studies department at Cal Arts.

Subotnik:

I think there's some seriousness to it, but I'm afraid that some of it comes because in the visual arts it was a way to create a new market at a certain point.

Boulez:

I prefer this word: *transavantguardia*, the Italian use, much more colorful than "postmodernism."

Subotnik:

Well, there's no question that something's happening that's different, but I think the fact that putting labels on it and creating a kind of philosophic closed door, which says, now we're going to go to the past, or now we're going to the future, now we're going to the left, or now we're going to the right and anything else is wrong is, I think the word's *hogwash*. It's very useful if you're trying to sell something, or to say this is the car of the future and so you sell the car because it's the car of the future. "We're no longer selling cars of the future. Only Model T Fords." So now, you know, the thing to do is now to buy a Model T Ford. It's very easy when you classify things, but when you really get right down to it people are still doing pretty much what they've always been doing: struggling to find new ways of being themselves. It's different than it was. I find it difficult. The labels are difficult for me. I don't understand them completely.

Alan:

Well, as the working journalist of the group, I have to apologize. I am thoroughly and sincerely embarrassed by all this because, of course, we are the people who force it upon you, that you have to give us names for what it is you're doing because we cannot just sing a piece of Boulez or Subotnick onto the pages of our magazines. We must give them names. The quick, easy handle, whether it's "postmodern" or "premodern," or "post or neo something else" is really the invention of the editorial office. I regret having to be a part of this, but one must eat.

Music critic Charles Shere:

I'm curious about your relationship to Los Angeles and southern California. You've been here now a long time. I'm wondering, what has it meant to you? Has it been in any way inform[ing] your work?

Boulez:

You go to cities not just for their own value, but for the people you meet in this city, which is the value of the city, as a matter of fact. If I would not have known, these three persons [*gestures to Ernest Fleischmann, Lawrence Morton, and Leonard Stein*] then I certainly would not have been as early as '57 in this city, first, and I would not have come regularly back, because I find an environment which is friendly, which gives good conditions for working, which is for me necessary.[13] Friendliness is not

13 All three men Boulez points to were regular attendees of Betty's salons and dynamic figures in the West Coast new music scene. Ernest Fleischmann, whom music critic Mark Swed credited with having "transformed a provincial second-rank orchestra into one of the world's best," was executive director of

enough. Good, professional conditions are the things I appreciate the most. When these professional conditions are there, I have a tendency myself to be friendlier.

WITH JOHN CHOWNING

May 17, 1992

John Chowning:

Just to form a point of departure, when Alan mentioned my studies with [Nadia] Boulanger I must say that being in Paris in 1959, '60, '61, studying with Boulanger was only a small part of my education, because those were also the years that Pierre had placed the Domaine musical series at the Théâtre de Lyon.[14] I guess that in some sense was a major step because of the nature of the Théâtre, etc. A few of us who were studying with Boulanger, in fact, went to these concerts regularly at which I heard some of the most wonderful pieces of the post–World War II era. I heard performances of [Berio's] *Circles*, I heard *Kontakte* by Stockhausen—*Le Marteau*, of course, I heard. The interest in the loudspeaker as a new and important sound source and representation of a medium of electronic music was well represented and, I found, very compelling.

When I came to Stanford as a graduate student in 1962, I then became involved with computers as a poor alternative to that which the big studios had in Europe in those days. As it turns out, that was a critical and fortuitous circumstance. So, I thank Pierre for the larger cultural context in which much of my education took place. Though we are in years not so distant perhaps, I think we really are [of] two different generations in terms of our musical evolution. After all, I was thirty years old before I saw my first computer. That's a rather late age to make a contact that seemed to be forbidding, but finally workable somehow.

the Los Angeles Philharmonic from 1969 to 1998. See Claudia Luther, "Ernest Fleischmann Dies at 85," *Los Angeles Times*, June 15, 2010. For seventeen years, Lawrence Morton directed the Monday Evening Concerts (formally known as Evenings on the Roof) and later directed the Ojai Festival. And, perhaps most pertinent to Boulez, Morton introduced Boulez's music to the United States in 1957 with the American premiere of *Le Marteau sans maître*. Lawrence Stein was a music scholar, composer, and composition teacher, and a tremendously well connected and respected figure among many composers of the time, including Arnold Schoenberg, Robert Craft, and Igor Stravinsky. He also ran the Encounters concert series, which took place at the Pasadena Art Museum and was where Betty first met Harry Partch.

14 Boulez established this concert society, active between 1954 and 1973. Composers as varied as Stockhausen, Messiaen, Berio, Bussotti, and Pousseur were represented at these concerts.

Boulez:

Well, I would like to speak specifically if we can because we cannot speak about everything tonight. I would like to speak about what an institution, like your institution at Stanford or like my institution in Paris, can do for music now. I mean, I think that's a very important problem. These institutions at least are recognized as important. Well, there were some fights, of course, but I mean, one has to ask oneself what is the necessity of an institution right now—an institution like IRCAM in Paris or your institute at Stanford.

I would like to go back to when we met about building an institution. My idea of building IRCAM goes back quite a lot of time. I think the first idea of an institution for that did not come from me, as a matter of fact, but came in Germany from some scientists of the Max Planck Institute. Some of the scientists of the Max Planck Institute wanted to create in 1966 a big music institute to have different sorts of things. First, certainly teaching, or I mean reflection on pedagogy. That was very important to them. Also, the performance: How can you perform the relationship between performance and theory? And then the third department for contemporary music and new technology. That was really the basic plans of these scientific people.

They asked me, because I was living in Germany at this time, "Why don't you make a plan for the part of the institute which will be devoted to contemporary music?" I had, of course, connections with German studios before, with the French studio, with German studios and the latest one which was the most important; therefore, this name came to me first, the Siemens studio, which had a very short life in Munich. Siemens, the big manufacturer, was ready to spend money for creating a very important studio there in Munich. Then unfortunately it was in weak hands so after a while they say, "Well, why do we spend all this money when it [is] used the way it is?"

So finally, the Siemens studio had a very short life, but it impressed very much when I saw the technicians, especially, and the engineers there, to see the direction in which somebody could work. It remains on my mind because I was visiting Munich regularly between '60 and '65, especially conducting some concerts of a series which was called Musica Viva, [and] did contemporary music.[15] So it remained in the corner of my mind, but no more than that. So, you know, I say, it would be marvelous if that developed. When the question came from these people of the Max Planck Gesellschaft, "Are you ready to work with us?" I say, yes certainly. We had a couple of meetings. I wrote, I don't remember how many pages, but quite a number of pages of how to organize an institute for contemporary music in Germany at this time.

15 Munich's Music Viva concert series was founded by Karl Amadeus Hartmann in 1945 to program contemporary music that had been banned under Nazi rule.

Chowning:

Contemporary research.

Boulez:

Contemporary research, and contemporary music generally. I mean, with the research, of course, but contemporary music generally, to bring forward contemporary music, which has always its difficulties. Everybody knows, and I'm really well situated to know that. So certainly, I said, I'm for that. It was in a bad time. You know also this word, *recession*, and it was a time of recession in Germany, '66, '67, '68. So finally, the board of the Max Planck Institute decided, well, it can wait. Finally, it came to nothing. I had still a copy of things I had written with me. I said, well maybe, you never know, in life it can be useful another time.

Chowning:

Was it not the case that it was a well-known German physicist who led the defeat?

Boulez:

It is. It is. He's a very great scientist, one of the best scientists of our time. It was [Werner] Heisenberg, who was at the time president of the board. That was Heisenberg who was really very instrumental to kill[ing] the plan because for him that was like [it was] for Albert Einstein. You know, music was go home and play Mozart sonatas with his daughter, which was nice. But he could not conceive—and he told that—he could not conceive music as an object of research. Music is spontaneous and only spontaneous and nothing else. So that was it.

Chowning:

It's an important point because I think this arrogance that exists in the scientific community in regard to the arts—where the arrogance is based in a kind of superior knowledge of the physical world—is untenable today. I think it's in part because of the consequences of these institutes that have made such great contributions not only to music, but to the very sciences themselves and the engineering sciences. Anyway, an aside, but I think an important one.

Boulez:

Oh, yes, certainly, but you have to confront the fact that for some people music is just a kind of, well, high-level entertainment—no more than that, no less, but no more than that. Of course, the kind of plans we had were not really in phase with this kind of view. So, the plan remained with me.

In '69, just a couple of years later, the president [Georges] Pompidou in France decided to have a center for contemporary art. They decided to have a department for music. The first plan was just to have a department for having tapes, scores—a kind of documentation center on contemporary music. I say, no, no, no, it's not enough, certainly not. I will not come back to France to just run a kind of shop, you know, with tapes and with scores. Certainly, for me it was much more important to have something that I would do for the first time in my life, also. Therefore, I said, well I have worked in Germany on a plan which was not realized. So, if you agree with that, assuming I will just think about it again to put it in a new environment with new circumstances, then assuming I will think of it and I will bring something, I think, in a few days, maybe one month.

Then I really wrote quite a long paper on how I conceived the center of research for music to bring together technicians, scientists, and musicians, because at this time I had the experience in the music life that the music life is very good, but does not allow composers to be in peace and to think and to really have time, not only for success, but have time also for failures. I think that's the main thing because in the music life you are always pushed forward and you have to bring something, so there is absolutely no time and especially the conditions of the music life are very demanding and you don't have this kind of time to conceive and to think. I think always of a comparison because I have good friends in Basel. I taught in Basel for a while. The people were the head of the chemical concerns there. They told me for one invention which is successful, we have to have a hundred failures. Like that the success compensates really the time we spent also on these failures. I think in music it is exactly the same. You must have time to have maybe a hundred failures, but you have one success and a real one. So therefore, the institute was planned in a way that composers could stay there, work, have commissions, or work only on some technical problems or some relationship of the technical problems, and musical problems, of course. The institute was built around this idea and was given, you know, subsidies for that.

Never enough. But certainly substantial, I would like to say. We could build our building according to what we thought. You know, we did not quickly project a kind of building just like that. We built this building according to our needs and also to the future because I did not want the building to be so rigid that it could never change. On the contrary, the building has accepted many changes already since it exists. It's now fifteen years. I think it's very lively because we can change the destination of this studio, or this studio, or this studio. The size has changed. When you think at the beginning the computers were in all this room. Now, they are on this table only. Simply the dimensions have changed enormously, the speed has changed. Before you had to have time sharing, so you were waiting for a quarter of an hour before one result was there. It was terrible. It was very discouraging. The progress of IRCAM came a lot through the help of Stanford. I remember the idea was there and we wanted to have a model. Through Ligeti, as a matter of fact, I began to know about John Chowning and we invited him to come to a symposium in the south of France, which was pleasant as far as I remember.

We decided then to go the other way, to go to Stanford to learn about what was going on. It was quite hard, I remember, not only because you had to learn things. Especially, I was already fifty at this time, so that's beyond your thirty, long beyond even. You had to get up at five or four o'clock in the morning.

Chowning:

We had to begin at five, so we had to leave the university and drive up in the hills, about four miles to the artificial intelligence quarters.

Boulez:

Yes, because you were squatters then.

Chowning:

That's right. Again, this arrogance of the scientist that is not ubiquitous, but from the point of view of an artist it can be overwhelmingly discomforting. In any case, we succeeded, however early the hour.

Boulez:

We were beginning at five, and at nine we are finished because at nine the real scientists came! So, it was hard because you had to be awake, very much awake about the thing you did not know very well. And you did learn, you did begin to learn at five o'clock in the morning. It was quite hard. But it was very pleasant. Therefore, we kept really a very good relationship with Stanford and people of

FIGURE 4.2 Audience at Betty Freeman's home, 1987. Photo by Betty Freeman, courtesy of the Los Angeles Philharmonic Archives.

Stanford, John Chowning especially; we got on well with the scientific committee, we meet each year practically. Therefore, I think we had a good start because we had this push at the beginning. Otherwise we would have had a much more difficult start.

I had heard, of course, through Jean-Claude Risset especially and Max Matthews (we met when I was in New York), I heard about the importance of the computer.[16] I was not aware of that before. Therefore, I thought at the beginning of IRCAM I had a couple of departments. I had the department for instrumental research, I had the department on electronic research, what I call electronic research because it was still the time of the old studios. I had foreseen, anyway, a department of computer. Consequently the computer ate everything else because after maybe two or three years nobody could work without computer.

So, we went on. I think the good thing there that we had in the same time, I created with the help of the Ministry of Culture of this time, Michel Guy—I created a group, Ensemble InterContemporain, of thirty-one musicians exactly for performing contemporary music. I am always, my practical side, I am always very careful about being only in the laboratory. Performance is extremely important, not only because you must have the approval or disapproval of an audience, of the contact with an audience, but because it forces you out of yourself and it brings you to confront the practical problems of having this technology with the world of instruments which we know. To have a kind of communication was to me excessively important. I compare it to you know a kind of convent where people were working in peace and they could do whatever they wanted, but from time to time they are to go out and be missionaries, let's say—I don't say martyrs! They had to go out and be present in the musical world. That was my preoccupation.

Therefore, I brought together these two groups. I think we had in the beginning two streams of thinking which were looking at each other with not great respect or great friendship. They were the people [for whom] everything had to be electronic: "We don't need anything beyond the computer, we don't want to hear anything about instruments, we can do everything with the machines, and why do you bother with the instruments?" Other people say: "Well, the instruments are there and the moment of the performance must be there and the sound world is richer in one case, so why do you put yourself in just a small cell like that?" Really,

16 Composer Jean-Claude Risset helped pioneer the use of computers in music composition. Max Matthews was an electrical engineer responsible for developing sound programming software like MUSIC and GROOVE. It was Matthews who in 1961 arranged the song "Daisy Bell" to teach a computer how to develop a computer-synthesized human voice, which was the inspiration behind HAL-9000's death song in Stanley Kubrick's *2001: A Space Odyssey*.

there were some very lively discussions, I remember. It came especially between some Americans and some Italians. It was, you know, the south, against the big industrial countries. But it was interesting because this confrontation progressively disappeared. Everybody knew that one cannot do everything only with the technology, and the instruments are good for something still. Progressively there was an interest to mix both worlds. I was pushing very much into this direction because I thought it was maybe the way of getting people together and to have a project, a common project, which would put IRCAM really on the map. That's how it happened.

Of course, there are people still working more on synthesis, on purely artificial sound, and people who are more interested in a kind of spontaneous gesture of the instrument type to the technology. I think there is no hostility anymore. I think one of the difficulties, speaking of scientists especially, is to have dialogue between people of science and people of music, because their education is not the same. They have a completely different education. They have completely different backgrounds. They have a different type of imagination.

Sometimes, you know, a kind of technician or scientist is just going, imagining in one direction and the musician stays in front of it and says, well, I don't use it, I will not use it. Because suddenly, you know, he's inventing in his direction which is not directly interesting for a musician. Sometimes a musician thinks he has found something absolutely exceptional, and the scientist says, but that's very trivial, I can do it in two seconds. You have this kind of differences in the language, in the imagination, and in the culture. Therefore, one of my big preoccupations—and it remains still a preoccupation—is to have a kind of language which is possible for the musicians and for the scientists to speak together.

I think the evolution of the technology has allowed that much easier than before. I remember in the beginning when I saw all this spitting of figures, of numbers, and you have to imagine a sound with these numbers. You don't imagine anything. Or you had to wait quarter of an hour before the sound was there. Then you say, oh, only that. So, I begin again. Then you have to wait again a quarter of an hour to be more satisfied than before. So, for a musician that's not very exciting, especially if you can hit a piano and you have the sound immediately. So, I think the methods have changed in two ways. Certainly, the technology is much more sophisticated, but the language is much more accessible than before. So, musicians can communicate now without going through this nightmare of accumulating numbers, numbers, numbers, and figures. The second thing that you can use also: graphics. Graphics speak also to the imagination of the musician in a very different way, in a more intuitive way. I think the more sophisticated the technology is the more intuitive[ly] you can work. That's exactly the point where we are now. We are trying to mix the sophisticated language with a very intuitive manipulation of this language.

I'll just continue to tell, for instance, how the music has benefited from it. I see by the works which were done by myself or by other composers at IRCAM, especially the conjunction of instruments and technology, I think you can give quite another perspective to the instruments because what you can do, you can take an instrument and you can expand its range, expand its range of dynamics (that's very simple, of course), but expand its range of space (you can put the sound in the kind of perspectives of space), and then you can change the sound itself, the spectrum itself of the sound so you change really the nature of the sound. But not only you can change instantly what happens with the instrument, but you can change also what follows the instrument because the instrument can dictate a score, the score which has been prepared.

For instance, you have the material on paper and you have that in your computer and you can really, for instance, decide on precise notes that the score can be triggered. So, for instance, you have first a kind of passive triggering. You say, for instance, that a note, an "e♭" at this point in the score performed will trigger a score which has been prepared completely already. So, you know, that's a passive thing. When you play the note, then it happens without really any kind of quality, a special quality. You know, the quality is independent of the quality of the performer. The performer plays an "e♭," the "e♭" will trigger this score. But that depends. You can already make quite a lot of things with a kind of passive interaction because if the interaction is, you know, on very small notes, then if you play a lot of notes for instance, each transformation would apply to each unit you are playing. Then you can have interferences between the time of the performer and the time of the transformation. Then you can really have this kind of dialectic between something which is flexible and something which is inflexible.

For instance, you have the tempo of the performer, which can be flexible with an accelerando, ritardando, something, you know, a curve. But the transformation would remain exactly the same according to the same duration or the same division of the duration, division of time. So, you have the kind of fight between something which doesn't move and something which moves constantly. Therefore, it can give really very interesting results and sometimes results you cannot really analyze so quick they are, especially if you have a succession of really quick notes. Then the transformations are there, but it makes a kind of block of sound which is perceived as a complete thing and you cannot analyze each component. That's one thing. But you can also modify your tempo and have things triggered differently. We have a score-follower. The performer is not obliged to comply to a rigid tempo or to follow some conditions. On the contrary, he is the one who says to the machine what to do and the machine reacts sometimes according to what you have said, of course, reacts according to how you are playing. For instance, if you are playing very loud, the score will be triggered. If you don't play loud, the score will not be triggered. For instance, that's one of the parameters. Or another parameter is, you say, you have a long trill for a flute. I say that because that's my case. You have a long trill on the flute and then you say if the trill is longer than three seconds, or is longer than two seconds, *then* the score will be triggered. But if you have a trill under this duration the score will not be triggered, the artificial score will not be triggered. Therefore, you can play with the technology. You are not really waiting for things to happen. No, on the contrary, you are yourself the one who says, I want that, I don't want that.

We are working also now on what I call virtual scores because that is real score. You have a real score, you have the data, you have everything. But virtual scores are for instance a score which has data, but not completely fixed. So, for instance, if you have a very slow tempo, events are happening in a very slow tempo. So, you say then the intervals will be very small, let's say quarter tone or eighth of tone, anything, because the duration of signals which are sent by the machine are very slow, so the intervals on the virtual score will be reduced. If you take a quicker tempo, then the intervals of the artificial score will be bigger because you don't hear. To hear really small intervals, you have to have a slow tempo. Therefore, the tempo of the performer can influence completely what you hear in the virtual score and also the complexity of a score. You have a virtual score which is done with four layers. If it is very slow you have the four layers because you can hear the four layers. If you are playing quicker, then you are reducing the virtual score to one layer, two layers, according to the speed you are playing. That's a kind of interactive process between the performer and what you have written before. Then it becomes very interesting, because then the performance itself—the way the intuitive sense of performance is of course very active in the transformation of a score, but also the determination of the player to play this way or this way—will also induce some consequences which are really very important.

Chowning:

In the past, one would have had to have several scores when you think of all these conditions, so it's impossible. In the middle of a performance, one can't.

Boulez:

Which for me was very important because I am also a performer. I suffered also quite a lot, I must say. When I was performing scores where you had to follow a tape, to follow strictly a tape, because your gesture is completely nil then. Oh, I am ahead. No, I am behind. Oh, I am ahead again.

Chowning:

You have to have a click track in your ear, which is impossible.

Boulez:

I will tell you the worst of my experiences. I had not a click track, but a flashlight, a small flashlight and I have numbers, but the numbers went to twelve thousand. Can you imagine if you are beginning to beat 4/4, where I am? Twelve thousand? 11,999? That was a really dreadful type of experience to be tied with a music which was already established and you could not do any gesture about that. You think you are strict, and many people think I am [a] very strict conductor. When I was confronted with these tapes I knew really very well how nonstrict I was because you had always a small difference between the tape.

Also, I remember this same experience in London, that was a piece I had to conduct in London. The flashlight was not in phase with what I had to conduct. For instance, you had the second and for instance, I had to conduct for four seconds I had to conduct six or I had to conduct five. I don't remember. So, I was looking at that. I am there, yes, I am there. I did not pay attention at all to what was performed. Only if there was a very big goof I could listen to it. Since this experience, I wanted therefore my contact with Max Matthews. I say, could you make these things possible, even some score which has been recorded, which is completely already in storage? Can it be really made flexible? That was my dilemma. When you are performing, you want some intuition to be there. You want to modify the tempo. You want not to be very strict. You want to accentuate, for instance, more, you want to go further.

It depends also upon the acoustics of the room, the acoustics of the hall. Sometimes when you have a very dry acoustic, well, you go quicker because you have nothing to fill the hall. When you have on the contrary a hall very reverberant you want to have the relationships more distant from each other. Then you could notice. Whatever you played, you were just obliged to get there. I find that a kind of straitjacket which was absolutely impossible. Therefore, my obsession when I came to IRCAM was to have the instruments related to a virtual score, or an artificial score, but related in a way that the instrumentalist has his say, his possibility of expressing himself.

Also, I found before in some experience I have done with myself with *Poésie pour pouvoir*. It goes back in '58. The sound I could get before when you projected them with a loudspeaker and you had the orchestra it did not fit at all. It was two worlds completely apart. You could try, but you had this world of the loudspeaker and the world of instruments. I don't say that's still solved because if you have loudspeakers you know, you will accept a type of sound which does not match the instruments exactly. I think the loudspeaker is a kind of machine which is very anonymous, which makes everything anonymous particularly because the radiation of an instrument goes many directions, the radiation of a loudspeaker is very much directional. So, if you have a loudspeaker which is there and which sends you music from here and you hear an instrument, then it's not the same type of perception you have. Also, when you are conducting concerts you are more and more aware of this type of fact. It's very disturbing. Sometimes you say, oh well, there is a source and another source. You want to relate them as closely as possible.

Therefore, for instance, in my work *Répons* that some of you have maybe heard in 1986 when I performed it here, you have transformation of keyboard instrument (piano, harp, vibraphone, and so on).[17] When we began to rehearse this piece, first there were places in the score when you don't have any transformation. So, I say, well, no loudspeaker at all. Then with the transformation, yes, of course, with loudspeakers. When we began to rehearse, the difference between no loudspeaker and loudspeaker was so enormous and so difficult for the perception to accept as such, then even when there were no transformations at all, all the keyboard instruments were amplified because then you have a kind of unity of the sound. That's very important. There are some problems which have still to be solved, I suppose, but we come closer now to a very interesting and lively relationship between instruments and synthesis or sampling. I remember at the beginning of sampling, oh horror! You never use samplings, you know. Now, we use samplings, also.

Chowning:

I don't use sampling.

Boulez:

But we use. No, no, I mean before, between the different schools there was this kind of contempt for each other. The ones who were using samplings were impure and the other one was pure and the other one were in-between, so we have neither pure nor impure.[18] Now, I think if you need a sampling you can

17 This performance took place February 11, 1986, on, surprisingly, a basketball court at UCLA's Wooden Center. See Martin Bernheimer, "Boulez in a Basketball Stadium: Electronic Avant-Garde at UCLA," *Los Angeles Times*, February 13, 1986.

18 In this discussion of sampling, Boulez is referring to a fierce debate about the use of musique concrète, or pre-existing recorded material, in electronic compositions. Pierre Schaeffer, who is not mentioned here at all, is considered the founder of musique concrète, which he and fellow composers, including Boulez, explored under the auspices of the Groupe de Recherche de Musique Concrete (GRMC). By 1953, Boulez and Schaeffer had parted ways. According to composer and fellow member of the GRMC François Bayle, Boulez "had an idealistic and abstract vision of composition" and that technology should "be neutral and transparent in order to realize abstract ideas." Schaeffer, on the other hand, was willing to pursue the new medium to its limitations. Bayle also admits that Boulez and Schaeffer were similar personalities, "aggressive fighters who could not tolerate the existence of strong-willed people in their immediate circle." See Sandra Desantos, "Acousmatic Morphology: An Interview with François Bayle," *Computer Music Journal* 21, no. 3 (Autumn 1997): 11–12.

use a sampling. You don't need to be ashamed of yourself. That's what I meant. Therefore, the possibilities are very big now, I think, of getting purely synthetic sounds to purely instrumental sounds and you have all the possibilities of using all the possibilities in between. I think that's very important. I find much more relaxation in our people, especially the youngest ones, than they were twenty years ago, fifty years ago. I don't know if that's the case with your people, but in IRCAM it's like that.

Chowning:

It's common. Every composer I know except for myself uses sampling. Some of us are pure, Pierre, and some of us aren't, *he laughs*. No, I quite agree that that's a false issue. That is, musical material is musical material and it's used well or not depending on not its source, but it's how it's used, I believe. That's no different than it always was.

I guess I'd be interested to ask Pierre about his feelings in regard to the evolution of the Western instruments. I had the feeling that probably with the nineteenth-century orchestra, the late Romantic orchestra, and the advent of electronics of such flexibility, even with the limiting factor of loudspeakers ultimately being the transducer, I've had this feeling that probably there will not be further evolution of acoustic instruments. That is, that's it, and all new instruments will be of an electronic nature, but closely coupled to traditional performance, which involves technique, technique driven by repertoire. But we won't see new kinds of string instruments that are of the family of the violin or the viola, but we may see violinists using their technique playing—their vibrato may mean not just pitch shift, but also could have other effects on the timbre, or the spatialization of sound, or many other things. But I guess I would like to know what your thoughts there are, in regard to the ultimate evolution of the media.

Boulez:

Well, I think the instruments are what they are because they are the product of an evolution. You don't have a violin because it's born like that out of nothing. You know, the violin is a result of thinking and in the same time using it. I think our fingers, for instance, are just limitations. If you want to have an interval smaller than a half tone, let's say, well, if you are in the high register of the violin then you have to cut your fingers in two or in three to have the intervals you want because your finger is too thick for that. Also, if you want to tune a harp in quarter tones, which I did so I know the trouble, you are sure that after a quarter of an hour or half an hour the instrument is completely out of tune, which justifies the usual joke on the harps. When you perform harp, we used half the time to tune the instrument so as not to play out of tune the other half of the time. That's more true than ever when you have small intervals because these instruments—given their reaction, given their construction—are not really done for that. You can say, well, but if the instrument cannot do that, why do you write something like that because you are unable to produce it? Therefore, I think your conception is right because your ear can listen to it. You are really very much aware of the small intervals. If you produce them through actual technology, then you hear these small intervals. You need time. I mean, the speed is not the same, as I [said]. The time of perception is longer and to hear really you have to pay more attention. So, there is more attention. You can do a lot of polyphony. Therefore, in cultures where you have use of intervals which are more sensitive, then there is no polyphony because this instrument would disappear. It's a result of perception studies that the half tone is the minimum you can perceive when you have polyphony. If you go under that then you have to simplify the polyphony and to go back even to a melodic line.

Chowning:

It sounds out of tune.

Boulez:

Yes, because it sounds out of tune and you could not perceive anything. You perceive just wrong intervals. That's all. Under some conditions, you can use the instruments, but use them with the expansion of the technology. For instance, in *Répons*, I used two pianos finally among the keyboards. I thought at the beginning to use a piano normally tuned in half tones, normal tuning, and the second piano would have been tuned in a special way. But when I used the piano through the technology, then I can have much more interesting intervals and I can change. Suppose that I would have tuned the piano a certain way, then it's done for the whole work and I cannot change anymore, even if I prepared it and it stays as it is, not like the harp. You know, if you prepare a piano long enough ahead of time, it can sustain the tuning if you control the tuning with a kind of electronic device. But I mean, this you cannot change. With a transformation, you have a certain set of intervals, depending from the piano, of course, the notes you pick. Then you push another program and you have another set of intervals. Not only is it much more precise and accurate but also you can change, which is in phase with what we think of music now.

You cannot depend on one system, a kind of rigid system. You can develop a system, or another system, another system. The technology is able to do that. Therefore, I think for me that certainly the instruments as we know them will survive because they are the result of generations of people who found the best way of using these instruments, with lips, with fingers, or with any kind of production of sound. You have a kind of development of the instrument you can see in the orchestra. You can see that the importance of these instruments has grown and grown and grown. First you have the string instruments mainly with some wind instruments. The winds have augmented quite a lot. Finally, the last development is in the percussion, either keyboard percussion, pitch percussion, or nonpitch percussion. You see, for instance, that the development of the percussion brings you in the direction of the thinking of the technology because with pitched instruments you have a kind of standardization, a very highly organized code.

For instance, if you say "d," the note "d," well, "d" is a "d" on a violin, is a "d" on the oboe, is a "d" on the bassoon, any kind of thing. That's a code, is "d." But the more you go into the use of the timbre itself, then—for instance—if you hit very hard a "d" in the low register of a marimba, that's not a "d" like a "d" of a violin. You hear quite a lot of harmonics and sometimes you hear an "a," you hear a "c." If you take bells, for instance, or chimes or big bells, then the harmony components are so complex that you hear maybe a main note, but you hear quite a lot of them in the same time and there is an evolution of the spectrum. I think the more we go, the more we have a tendency to go into specific sounds which are created for a specific purpose for such a composition.

There is a danger, of course. You know, the "d" is very convenient because it is a "d" and it is nothing at the same time. You can recognize it on each instrument, but its originality comes from what comes before and what comes later. If you have a "c♯," "d," and "a♭," you say, oh well, that's atonal. The intervals are very dense and you cannot attach to anything. But if you have "a" and "d," well you'll think of the tonality of D major. The "d" can take many personalities. It has no personality in itself. It has the personality which is given by the context. With the importance of percussion, you have much richer sounds, much more interesting for themselves. But the danger is you recognize them because they are what they are and no context can absorb them. For instance, I take the example of a tam-tam. You have a big tam-tam. Wonderful sound. It's much richer than the "d" of a violin in itself. Much richer.

Chowning:

It's a universe.

Boulez:

That's a kind of universe for itself. But once you have heard it once, it returns, oh that's a tam-tam again. You recognize it. It is so individual, so personal, that you cannot really make it part of a context. Therefore, you use it with parsimony because you use it for articulating, for having a climax, for telling, "yes this introduces a new type of sonority, maybe a sonority more metallic," and so on. So, you use it as a kind of way of articulating, but not as a kind of sound just like the other one.

I think with artificial sound that's exactly the point where we have difficulties, or higher difficulties, because I want to have sounds which are rich, but I want them neutral enough to be part of a context. I think that's this difficulty, to have the richness of the sound and in the same time the interest of the context. If you have a sound too rich, it will not mix. If you have a sound much less rich, you can act with it, you can manipulate it because it will be part of a context more easy. In the instrumental world, you have also this possibility from the completely codified (what I called in French *déréalisé*—out of reality), this "d" is a pure abstract. This is very funny because what we think is the most familiar music is in reality based on the most abstract concepts. The music of today is based on a much more realistic concept of the sound. That's exactly the turning point when we were more interested in having interesting sounds, but we did not know how to manipulate them as easily as we did before with the sounds, which were much more codified.

Chowning:

I think that one of the important attributes of these machines today in music-making relates directly to this question of percussive instruments and their kind of overwhelming idiosyncratic nature. They have a personality which is so well-defined that it's hard to break in a sense. Now, the percussion instruments are very special because unlike the pitched instruments, they're composed of what are called enharmonic partials. That is, they are not orderly as violin strings and piano strings and you know, tubes of air, etc. All the pitched instruments have one thing in common and that is they are made out of partials that are harmonically related, what's called the harmonic series. Now, percussion instruments, bells, drums, and marimbas are tuned, but only to a certain extent. That is, the low "d" on a marimba is tuned by size, by shaving little bits of wood out of its lower surface, but the tuner can only manage about, I don't know, I would say about four or five of the significant partials in a complex that may include twenty, thirty, or more. It's these other twenty or thirty that are disorderly, in some sense, that give this overwhelming personality to these instruments, whether it's a big church bell, a tubular chime, or a marimba.

What we can do with machines, however, is for the first time we can make orderly sounds that are enharmonic. I think that was seen early. I did some experiments—in *Stria*, in fact, was an attempt to do that.[19] Others have pursued that as well. It's a region of exploration, I believe, that is yet unfulfilled, and one that I think uniquely identifies the computer in this kind of control over the fine structure of the sound in a way that no other musical source does. So, I agree that there's something very special about the abstraction of pitch, but I think we don't yet know enough about the whole domain of enharmonicity to be able to make very general characterizations in regard to potential. I think there's a lot for us to learn.

19 *Stria* is Chowning's landmark composition, from 1977, that is generated by the computer.

Boulez:

I see just from the practical point of view because you know very well when the sounds don't match. You have a kind of intuition of that. Later, you can find a kind of rational explanation for that, but immediately when you are a musician you say, you know, something does not work. Or, what's very disturbing to me, for instance, I had the so-called Darmstadt courses of the '60s. Then people had really an organization with the pitched instruments, extraordinarily complicated, and then you had three percussion instruments which were so primitive on the contrary that it contradicted completely the pitch organization. Therefore, I think that's the difficulty. You want to mix these sounds. They are not easy to bring together. In one case, you have, as I said, a strong personality which you cannot manipulate very easily and in the other case the personality comes because you can manipulate them. Therefore, we're always between these two extremes.

Chowning:

One of your early interests, as I remember, had to do with breaking this deadlock over the tempered system and having the availability of arbitrary microtonal tunings. Now, in this evolving technology at some point we had a contact with the music industry that allowed us to impose a tiny bit of influence over what might be considered largely a vulgarization of the research that was done. But one of the successes was having Yamaha allow the user to retune its electronic keyboards, that is to open up the keyboard such that any key stroke that, while related physically to the traditional pitch associations, in fact, could be assigned to any frequency within one—just a little bit more than a cent of difference, which is more than the ear can detect. Left-handed pianists could play backward or the keyboard could turn such that the eighty-eight keys would encompass the span of a minor third, or successive keys could produce a melody, in fact. Did this, finally, you find useful and if not, why not?

Boulez:

Well, I find [it] useful, but I mean you have only one kind of instrument which can do that. It cannot be very useful because generally you cannot use [it] just for a melodic instrument. I remember the experience I did at this time goes very far back, I mean, in '45, '46, that was with the ondes martenot.[20] That was long before the days of Yamaha. You could have instruments which had five octaves. You could tune it, of course, maybe a minor third also for five octaves. It has to be, of course, given the principle of the instrument, you had only register because, you know, that was an exponential. So, you had to be in the high register to have this

20 An instrument played with a keyboard or by moving a ring along a wire that produced a theremin-like sound.

kind of difference, which was an experience I did with some friends. I was in the Conservatoire still at this time, '45, '46.

For instance, when the intervals are very small, you lose the perception of direction. You don't know if you are going up or down, when it is very small. You can make a test. Somebody, students like me, was playing and I say, what I play? Say, well, I think up. No, that's down, and so on. You were completely out of touch with the relationship. That's like a very, very small distance. You don't appreciate them anymore. We made tests: to what extent can we make sense of an interval, going up or going down. But after when we tuned the instrument again in half tones, then it's absolutely gigantic. We were making experiments for one hour like that, you know, then you say, Oh, my God! I never thought a half tone would be that big. Very funny. You can go into this direction, but I think also you have to know really more precisely what the perception can take. I made quite a lot of experiments on scales, doing on the computer, which was very interesting. At one point, especially if you make chords with these scales, you cannot make any distinction at all because everything is so tight that it does not work as a kind of perceived object.

Chowning:

Well, you know, I have always felt that [Edgard] Varèse was one of the real visionaries in regard to music, not just music and technology. His thoughts about this were much deeper, I understand, but the idea really of connecting the musical evolution to the insights that could be gleaned from scientific thought. The problem always was getting the sciences to take this issue seriously. Varèse found a couple, one was John Pierce and one was Max Matthews at Bell Labs, both very amateur musicians I might add, but incredibly insightful.

Jean-Claude Risset did a recent article, I don't know if it's been published yet, about his experience and his acquaintance with Varèse in the few years before he died.[21] Jean-Claude's article speaks of quotes from Varèse and his thoughts about the kind of rigor that would be required for music to engage and evolve in the way that he hoped it would. He was extraordinarily sensitive to these issues of timbral richness and kind of breaking the classical notions of timbre. But he was pushed away by very well-known people like [acoustician Harvey] Fletcher, I guess, and others. Finally, Max and John Pierce engaged him, but it was already so late in his life that he was really unable to make a substantive impact. But I think he represents a kind of vision and view and his works are almost iconoclastic, one might say, in regard to traditional underpinnings of compositional practice. So, I think with many others we revere him and his music. Pierre, on his death, wrote

21 Jean-Claude Risset, "Some Comments about Future Music Machines," *Computer Music Journal* 15, no. 4 (Winter 1991): 32–36.

something like, "Adieu, Varèse. Goodbye. Your time is at an end, but then too it's at its beginning," which was poignant.[22]

Boulez:

I must say for tomorrow evening when we perform [Varèse's] *Deserts*, you know, I've performed sometimes this piece with the interpolations of tape, but the tape is so miserable now, that [it's] impossible to perform particularly, first because that's also the type of thing he had no time really to realize. He was very unhappy about his working in Paris in the studio, *musique concrète* there. He recorded some sounds from the exterior world, let's say, and he recorded that with a very small tape machine, amateur tape machine. So, the quality already was not good.

So, after that the transformations were not better. Now, after thirty years, forty years almost, the quality of the tape is really dreadful. The last time I performed it, because it was an old festival, around ten years ago, we say, you know, we'll do the original version. You know that he put a note in his score, which is quite telling about what he thought himself, that you can perform the piece without the tape interpolations. I do that without the interpolations because I think now to hear the tape in the middle of this work, first: does not match the level of the instrumental writing, and second: the technical quality of this tape is really almost not to be heard.

Chowning:

Is the tape available through the publisher? Is that it?

Boulez:

Yes, the tape is available through the publisher. When I was in Paris I asked the radio studio to give me a tape and they provided me the best tape possible apparently, but the best was not really very high [quality]. All the tape pieces of the '50s, '60s have suffered quite a lot. If you hear, for instance, *Gesang der Jünglinge* by Stockhausen, especially if it's projected in a hall with a kind of level, you hear the hiss constantly. If you have the space projection, then you hear already the hissing before the sound comes.

Chowning:

There's hope, however. There's a project that Max Matthews began with support from the Mellon Foundation. It's a joint project now with a new center to record in digital media all of these tapes that are rapidly deteriorating and especially to engage the composers because there are things that one can do, to clean them up and sharpen the attacks, for example, of some of the early Stockhausen works, at least to guarantee that they will not get any worse because the medium

22 Boulez's comment reads, "Farewell, Varèse. Your time is finished and now it begins." Quoted in Andrew Ford, *Illegal Harmonies: Music in the Modern Age* (Collingwood, Victoria: Black, 2011), 132.

is sufficiently reliable that we believe that that's possible. So that is a project that's being done just now in these years and I think within a year or two, beginning with the oldest of course because they're the ones that are most in danger, but Berio's pieces that were done in multichannel, which have only been recorded in vinyl on two channels, like *Visage* and *Hommage à Joyce*, to get these in the original four channel form and in digital media. So that's a project.[23]

William Kraft, composer and percussionist on faculty at UCSB:

I don't know if you were aware that there were two tapes that Varèse had made for *Deserts*.

Boulez:

Yes. We had in Strasbourg when I performed it in this festival, we had the latest, you know, revised one, the best one.

Music critic Jim Farber:

My question has to do with the computer as what I might call an impersonal Pandora's Box. The computer doesn't care what you set it at. Every setting creates a new variation. Therefore, is the role of the composer a channel switcher or an active creator?

Chowning:

I will give you a short answer and then Pierre can give an answer. Well, I'm sure there are many views on this because it has to do with an essential question which I was asked very early on, which is why are you using computers? It's dehumanizing music. My feeling is that it's rather the contrary. Computers used in music result in the humanization of them. Remember, the very best violin placed in the hands of a person who doesn't play the violin has absolutely zero meaning. I think exactly the same thing applies to the computer. It takes a great deal of time to build the details of control, let's say the fine structure of sound manipulation, whether it's manipulating sampled sounds or synthesis. That, in the early years, was our primary activity, in fact. But now, after nearly thirty years, we're building up bodies of knowledge which are a part of the whole package, which comes to a composer who is new in the use of these machines just as the tradition of violin performance comes for free. That is, we don't expect composers writing for fiddles to explicitly state every detail of the actions which are to be used in the performance. There's a great deal that's understood and we take for granted as a result of the tradition that's passed on through the master–student relationship. And so, with computers. One does not begin at the level of detail necessarily any longer. There are circumstances where one must if one wants to engage the medium at a

23 This project would eventually become the International Digital Electroacoustic Music Archive (IDEAMA), which is now housed within the Center for Art and Media (ZKM) in Karlsruhe, Germany.

very low level, but as we begin teaching students today, they have a very rich palette from which they can begin.

Boulez:

I think exactly the same. I think simply the computer is a tool among other tools. What is important to understand is the mechanism, how it can work because if you're writing a work like that, of course you don't write anything and then you say to an assistant, well do that for me. No, you are asking about how the programs are working, for instance, how you want that, you prepare something. Then when you are writing, you are writing in this direction, of course, but you are not obliged to be a programmer by yourself and to be a kind of wizard of computers. You know, that's like exactly when you are having to orchestrate something. Well, I've never performed the oboe, but I know very well the articulation of oboe, the range of the oboe. I've never made an oboe in my life, certainly not. So, you know what the instrument is able to produce and then your imagination works into this direction. You know very well that you will not write for an oboe like you write for a trombone, for instance. For the computer, it depends on the program you use. You don't write this way or this way, according to what you want to do. I say that's a tool. That's a very sophisticated tool, but that's a tool.

Chapter 5

In Memoriam

John Cage
Anthony Braxton
Libby Larsen

PLAYING GRACIOUS HOST alongside his wife Betty, Franco Assetto was a largely unseen force of cheer and good at Betty's salons. By all accounts, he rarely stepped out of the kitchen during the salons, happily content to be out of earshot of music he never cared for himself—cooking "saves him from listening to the music," according to Betty.[1] Instead, the Italian sculptor used the salons as opportunities to experiment with his pasta creations. Melinda Wortz, in her poem tacked to the front of this book, memorialized Franco's contribution as one of humor, of love, and, fittingly, as adding a dash of colorful harmony to the gatherings:

> From the kitchen—the Cageian sounds
> of Franco's deep toned swearings
> and finely tuned seasonings
> bring anticipations of oral delectations
> to enrich the already sensuous fare
> a synaesthetic mix that knows no simile.

John Adams agreed. "Franco's participation in the Freeman Sunday Music Rooms was a key element to their success," he wrote to Betty.[2] From the looks of those

1 Letter from Betty to Gavin Bryars, August 3, 1990.
2 Letter from John Adams to Freeman, February 19, 1992.

The Music Room. Jake Johnson, Oxford University Press. © Oxford University Press 2025.
DOI: 10.1093/9780197775752.003.0006

guests milling about with bowls and plates of his pasta experiments in hand after each salon, I'd wager most were happy with the arrangement.

So when Franco died in 1991, things were never quite the same. Betty found it difficult to continue hosting the salons. She began them shortly after she and Franco had married in 1981 and it seems that his spirit and their marriage fueled and were fueled by the kind of gatherings their home boasted. Without Franco, Betty wasn't sure how to continue things as they were. Judith Rosen offered her home in Van Nuys to keep the series going for what ended up being only a few more years. The setting changed, but Betty continued organizing the salons and photo-documenting them up until the end.

One year after Franco died, so did John Cage. Betty and Cage shared an uncommon bond. She supported his work, of course, and in several ways. From 1965 until his death she gave him an annual grant to cover living expenses—a rare type of gift for Betty, who later in her career supported composers in less conspicuous ways ("the necessity in those days was just to keep them alive," she once explained)—and gave a number of grants to cover the costs of recording Cage's compositions.[3] Cage, in turn, dedicated to Betty his set of thirty-two etudes for solo violin (known as *The Freeman Etudes*) and, as included in this chapter, was a featured guest in one of her earliest salons. But Betty and Cage were also close friends. In a letter to Cage's long-time partner Merce Cunningham, Betty placed Cage among the most important people in her life. "When you love someone you love them living or dead," she wrote. "So it is with John and others close to me such as Franco and my father. They are never gone, only on a little trip."[4]

Two months after his death, John Cage was memorialized at the Music Room. Following the memorial, Anthony Braxton and Libby Larsen presented their respective work. It is a testament to Cage's wide influence that these two composers, whose music represents drastically divergent or, at times, incongruent styles, would both use the memorial to trace their influence back to Cage.

Alan begins introductions.

Alan:

"As varied as these afternoons have been in the twelve years since Betty Freeman first began them at her house, the one common denominator that they have all shared is the spirit of John Cage, who was the great pioneer of our time, most of all because he constantly asked the question, 'Why not?' Since there was no logical answer to that question, he was the great enabling force behind anything that has happened in music in the last fifty years."

3 Interview on WNYC, October 28, 1988.

4 Letter from Betty Freeman to Merce Cunningham, October 30, 1992.

Alan steps aside as he gives the floor to Betty, "John's great friend and patron and supporter and sponsor and everything else that a composer requires in order to subsist in these troubled times."[5]

I first met John Cage in 1965, *Betty begins*, when he made a concert at the Pasadena Art Museum. I think I must have been ready for him then because everything he did made absolute sense to me; I didn't understand why it didn't make [sense] to everybody. What he did was very similar to what Harry Partch did—with whom I was involved at the same time—which was to question why music had to be played on a string with a bow, why couldn't it be played on anything. The first concert I heard of his was sort of a mind opener. It didn't have to have black and white keys. It could be played on anything. I heard a concert of his played on a cactus one day with a pick up mic. I heard other concerts played on mixing bowls, blowing bubbles, seashells—he did a beautiful ballet score for Merce [Cunningham] just pouring water from one seashell of a size to another. It was so refreshing to me. There was just no problem with responding to what Cage was doing.

I'm going to just tell you two or three incidents because they're very revealing. About 1967, which would be a couple of years after I met him, I went down to his apartment in Greenwich Village. [He was] very poor. You had to go downstairs six stairs and the apartment was half underground, half above. I was with my daughter who was at that time fifteen. There was no furniture. There were plants: that's all he had in the living room. No furniture at all except a studio couch which was also his bed. So, my daughter, coming from Beverly Hills, said to him "Mr. Cage, how come you live so poor if you're so famous?" because in '65 he already was who he is today. People don't realize that. He was already world famous; he just had been written up by *Time* magazine.[6] He answered wonderfully. He said, "I have everything I need. I don't have to teach for a living. I have enough money to cover copying my scores. That's all I need." That was kind of a revelation.

Another story about the *Freeman Etudes*. It was 1977 and John called me up and said that he was going to dedicate a piece he just finished—of violin solos. He was going to dedicate it and call it the *Freeman Etudes*. At that point I was very modest, and I said, "No, I don't think so. In the dedication, why don't you just say, 'To B.F.' or 'To Betty.' But don't call it the *Freeman Etudes*." "Well," he said, "if you really don't want your name attached, I'll just dedicate it to Thoreau. I'll take away the name entirely, the whole thing will be for Thoreau because he's also a Free-man." At which point he called my bluff and I said, "No, no, no, keep it!"[7]

5 Taken from *Il Salotto Musicale*, Los Angeles Philharmonic Archive.

6 "Anarchy with a Beat," *Time*, March 21, 1960.

7 *Il Salotto Musicale*, Los Angeles Philharmonic Archive.

FIGURE 5.1 John Cage, March 8, 1982. Photo by Betty Freeman, courtesy of the Los Angeles Philharmonic Archives.

JOHN CAGE

March 8, 1982

Cage:

I'm going to read a text which I wrote last August when Merce Cunningham and I were invited to the University of Surrey in Guilford.[8] There were professional choreographers and composers brought from different countries—Greece, Germany, Holland, France, Ireland, and so forth. We were to conduct a two-week intensive course. My feeling was that those people all knew what they were doing since they were professional in this society and that it wasn't a proper thing to do to teach them. So, what I did each morning was improvise a review of my work. I divided the history of my composing into twelve talks. I talked for an hour and a

8 The work Cage presents here is titled *Composition in Retrospect*, first published in *John Cage: Etchings 1978–1982* (San Francisco: Crown Point Press, 1982). Brent Reidy calls this text Cage's "autobiographic mesostic." See Reidy, "Our Memory of What Happened Is Not What Happened: Cage, Metaphor, and Myth," *American Music* 28, no. 2 (Summer 2010): 211–227.

half to the students. Then I gave them an assignment. The first assignment on the first day was to make a four-minute piece which would be performed that evening. Through chance operations I assigned the musicians that they would use. There were a number of musicians available and the composers themselves played instruments. All of that was subjected to chance operations. Each one knew at 10:30 what he was to do for that evening. The second day of the assignment was a five-minute piece. The third day a six-minute piece, and so forth. On Saturday, there was a kind of revolution. Some people maintained the idea of writing a piece a minute longer each time, but the others were free then to go to any time length they chose.

After giving them the assignment, I then sat down and wrote this text that I'm going to read to you [and read it] in front of whichever of the students wanted to be there. Most of them didn't want to be there at all because they immediately went to work on their projects for that evening. But there were three or four who were generally there. I then tried to put in poetry what I had said in the improvised talk. It was rather difficult. I didn't know whether I could do it, but [I decided] to follow this discipline of a mesostic and to write the mesostic on the subject that seemed to me to be the subject of the talk that I had just given.

The first day determined the shape of the whole lecture that I'm going to read. The first subject seemed to me to be on method. So, I wrote a mesostic on the word *method*.[9] I'll show you what one is. The first one here is, "My memory of what happened is not what happened." The "m" of method is the "m" of "my." The "e" is on the next line and there's no "e" between the "m" and "e" so it's "my memory." "Of what" is the first "t" after the "e." "Happened" is the "h." "Is not" is the "o." The "d" of "happened" finishes the word.

I was able to write six such mesostics and more or less cover what I had said in an improvised fashion in the previous hour and a half. Then I used a principle which fascinates me, which I call *Renga*, which is derived from Japanese poetry that's written not by one poet, but by several—it's somewhat like those drawings that we make when someone draws a head and then you fold the paper, and someone draws the neck and then you fold the paper and someone makes the torso. I then subjected the six mesostics which I had written to chance operations and was able that way to get as a bonus a seventh mesostic. The first line of which came from a chance determined one from the previous six, the second line from another, so that the seventh mesostic doesn't make ordinary sense. So that as I read it to you now, when things go nonsyntactical, you know that we're coming to the end of the chapter, so to speak.

---

9 A type of poem arranged so that text running vertically intersects with lines running horizontally.

The first one is on the subject of method. The second is on the subject of structure. The third is on the subject of intention. The fourth is on discipline. And so is the fifth. And so is the sixth. The seventh is on the subject of notation. The eighth on indeterminacy. The ninth on interpenetration. The tenth on imitation. The eleventh on devotion. And the last on circumstances.

My
mEmory
of whaT
Happened
is nOt
what happeneD

i aM struck
by thE
facT
tHat what happened
is mOre conventional
than what I rememberеD

iMitations
invErsions
reTrograde forms
motives tHat are varied
Or
not varieD

once Music
bEgins
iT remains
He said the same
even variatiOn is repetition
some things changeD others not (schoenberg)[10]

what I aM
rEmembering
incorrecTly to be sure

10 Cage is referring to Schoenberg's concept of "developing variations," which Schoenberg explores most deliberately in relation to Brahms in his 1947 article "Brahms the Progressive." See Walter Frisch, *Brahms and the Principle of Developing Variation* (Berkeley: University of California Press, 1990).

is wHatever
deviated frOm
orDinary practice

not a scale or a row but a gaMut
to Each
elemenT
of wHich
equal hOnor
coulD be given

iMitations
invErsions
iT remains
motives tHat are varied
deviated frOm
than what I remembereD

the diviSion of a whole
inTo
paRts
dUration
not frequenCy
Taken
as the aspect of soUnd
bRinging about
a distinction bEtween

both phraSes
and large secTions
many diffeRent distinctions
coUld be thought of
some for instanCe
concerning symmeTry horizontal or vertical
bUt what I thought of
was a Rhythmic
structurE

in which the Small
parTs
had the same pRoportion to each other

that the groUps of units the large parts had to the whole
for instanCe
64 since iT
eqUals eight eighths
peRmits
division of both sixty-four and Each eight into three two and three

in *Songe d'une*
nuiT d'été
satie divided fouR
foUrs into one two and one (four eight and four)
and in other pieCes
he worked symmeTrically
coUnting
the numbeR
bEtween

Succeeding numbers
following addiTion six plus two
with subtRaction
six minUs two
and/or reaChing
a cenTer of a series of phrases
continUing
by going backwaRds
six Eight

four Seven five
seven four eighT six six being
the centeR horizontally five vertically
thUs
a Canvas
of Time is provided hospitable to both noise
and mUsical tones upon which
music may be dRawn
spacE

in which the Small
inTo
the centeR horizontally five vertically

foUrs into one two and one (four eight and four)
and/or reaChing
of Time is provided hospitable to both noise
as the aspect of soUnd
peRmits
a distinction bEtween

musIc
for the daNce
To go with it
to Express
the daNce in sound
noT
beIng able
tO do
the same thiNg

gIves the possibility
of doiNg
someThing
that diffErs
liviNg
in The same town
fInding life
by nOt
liviNg the same way

the dancers from malaysIa
a theatrical crossiNg
from lefT to right
so slowly as to sEem to be
moviNg
noT at all
the musIc meanwhile
as fast as pOssible
togetherNess

of opposItes
purposeful purposelessNess
noT
to accEpt it

uNless i could remain
aT
the same tIme
a member Of society
able to fulfill a commissioN

to satIsfy
a particular Need
Though having no control
ovEr
what happeNs
accepTance
sometImes
written Out
determiNate

sometImes
just a suggestioN
i found iT
workEd
therefore i Nap
pounding The
rIce
withOut
liftiNg my hand

gIves the possibility
a theatrical crossiNg
Though having no control
that diffErs
uNless i could remain
in The same town
the same tIme
as fast as pOssible
togetherNess

to sober and quiet the minD
so that It
iS
in aCcord
wIth

what haPpens
the worLd
around It
opeN
rathEr than

closeD
goIng in
by Sitting
Crosslegged
returnIng
to daily exPerience
with a smiLe
gIft
giviNg no why
aftEr emptiness

he saiD
It
iS
Complete
goes full cIrcle the structure of the mind
Passes
from the absoLute
to the world of relatIvity
perceptioNs
during thE

Day and dreams
at nIght
Suzuki
the magiC square
and then chance operatIons
going out through sense Perceptions
to foLlow a metal ball
away from lIkes
aNd
dislikEs

throw it on the roaD
fInd it in my ear

the Shaggy nag
now after suCcess
take your sword and slIt my throat
the Prince hesitates
but not for Long
lo and behold the nag Immediately
becomes agaiN
the princE

he haD
orIginally been and would never have again
become
had the other refuSed to kill him
silenCe
sweepIng fallen leaves
sweePing up
Leaves three years later
suddenly understood saId
thaNk you
again no rEply

to sober and quiet the minD
goIng in
iS
in aCcord
returnIng
going out through sense Perceptions
with a smiLe
lo and behold the nag Immediately
becomes agaiN
aftEr emptiness

He sent us to the blackboarD
and asked us to solve a problem In counterpoint
even though it waS
a Class
In harmony
to make as many counterPoints
as we couLd
after each to let hIm see it

that's correct Now
anothEr

after eight or nine solutions i saiD
not quIte
Sure of myself there aren't anymore
that's Correct
now I want you
to Put in words
the principLe
that underlIes
all of the solutioNs
hE

haD
always seemed to me superIor
to other human beingS
but then my worship of him inCreased
even more I
couldnt do what he asked Perhaps
now thirty years Later
I
caN
I think hE

woulD agree
the prIncipIe
underlying all of the Solutions
aCts
In the question that is asked
as a comPoser
i shouLd
gIve up
makiNg
choicEs

Devote myself
to askIng
queStions
Chance
determIned

answers'll oPen
my mind to the worLd around
at the same tIme
chaNging my music
sElf-alteration not self-expression.

thoreau saiD the same
thIng
over a hundred yearS ago
i want my writing to be as Clear
as water I can see through
so that what i exPerienced
is toLd
wIthout
my beiNg in any way
in thE way

Devote myself
(superIor)
to other human beingS
a Class
now I want you
so that what i exPerienced
is toLd
I
my beiNg in anyway
choicEs

he maDe
an arrangement of objects In front of them
and aSked the students
to Concentrate
attentIon on it
until it was Part
and parceL
of hIs or her thoughts
theN
to go to thE wall

which he haD covered
wIth paper

to place both noSe and toes
in Contact
wIth it
keePing that contact
and using charcoaL
to draw the Image
which each had iN mind
all thE

stuDents
were In
poSitions
that disConnected
mInd and hand
the drawings were suddenly contemPorary
no Longer
fIxed
iN
tastE

anD
preconceptIon
the collaboration with oneSelf
that eaCh person
conventIonally
Permits
had been made impossibLe
by a physIcal
positioN
anothEr

crossleggeDness
the result of whIch
iS rapid transportation.
eaCh student
had wanted to become a modern artIst
Put out of touch
with himseLf
dIscovery

suddeN
opEning

of Doors
It
waS
a Class
gIven by mark tobey[11]
in the same Part
of the worLd
I walked with him from school
to chiNatown
hE was always stopping pointing out
things to see

which he haD covered
was In
and place both noSe and toes
to Concentrate
mInd and hand
in the same Part
with himseLf
I walked with him from school
suddeN
anothEr

turNing the paper
intO
a space of Time
imperfections in the pAper upon which
The
musIc is written
the music is there befOre
it is writteN

11 Cage crossed paths with American painter Mark Tobey when both men worked at the Cornish School (now Cornish College of the Arts) in Seattle in 1938. Cage continually cited Tobey as a lasting influence on his work. Along with painter Morris Graves, Cage and Tobey, sharing intersecting interests in Eastern philosophies, became known as the Northwest Mystics. See Wulf Herzogenrath and Andreas Kreul, eds., *Sounds of the Inner Eye: John Cage, Mark Tobey, Morris Graves* (Seattle: University of Washington Press, 2002).

compositioN
is Only making
iT
cleAr
That that
Is the case
finding Out
a simple relatioN

betweeN paper and music
hOw
To
reAd
iT
Independently
Of
oNe's thoughts

what iNstrument
Or
insTruments
stAff
or sTaves
the possIbility
Of
a microtoNal music

more space betweeN staff lines representing
majOr
Thirds
thAn minor
so That
If
a nOte
has No

accideNtal
it is between well-knOwn
poinTs in the field of frequency
or just A drawing in space

piTch
vertIcally
time reading frOm left to right
absеNce of theory

accideNtal
majOr
To
stAff
The
vertIcally
finding Out
oNe's thoughts

you can't be serIous she said
we were driNking
a recorD
was bEing played
noT
in thE place
wheRe we were
but in another rooM
I had
fouNd it interesting
And had asked
what musiC it was
not to supplY

a partIcular photograph
but to thiNk
of materials that woulD
makE
iT
possiblE
foR
soMeone else
to make hIs
owN
A
Camera
it was necessarY

for davId tudor
somethiNg
a puzzle that he woulD
solvE
Taking
as a bEginning
what was impossible to measuRe
and then returning what he could to Mystery
It was
while teachiNg
A
Class
at wesleYan

that I thought
of Number II
i haD
bEen explaining
variaTions
onE
suddenly Realized
that two notations on the saMe
pIece of paper
automatically briNg
About relationship
my Composing
is actuallY unnecessary

musIc
Never stops it is we who turn away
again the worlD around
silEnce
sounds are only bubbles on iTs
surfacE
they buRst to disappear (thoreau)[12]

12 Thoreau's writings on sound and silence, in Cage's words, "possessed" him. Here Cage refers to a passage in Thoreau's journal: "All sound is nearly akin to Silence; it is a bubble on her surface which straightway bursts, an emblem of the strength and prolificness [*sic*] of the undercurrent." See Bradford Torrey, ed., *The Writings of Henry David Thoreau* (New York: Houghton Mifflin, 1906).

when we Make
musIc
we merely make somethiNg
thAt
Can
more naturallY be heard than seen or touched

that makes It possible
to pay atteNtion
to Daily work or play
as bEing
noT
what wE think it is
but ouR goal
all that's needed is a fraMe
a change of mental attItude
amplificatioN
wAiting for a bus
we're present at a Concert
suddenlY we stand on a work of art the pavement

musIc
Never stops it is we who turn away
i haD
as bEing
noT
surfacE
foR
all that's needed is a fraMe
It was
amplificatioN
wAiting for a bus
my Composing
not to supplY

musIcircus
maNy
Things going on
at thE same time
a theatRe of differences together

not a single Plan
just a spacE of time
aNd
as many pEople as are willing
performing in The same place
a laRge
plAce a gymnasium
an archiTecture
that Isn't
invOlved
with the makiNg the stage

dIrectly opposite
the audieNce and higher
Thus
morE
impoRtant than where they're sitting
the resPonsibility
of Each
persoN is
marcEl duchamp said[13]
To complete
the woRk himself
to heAr
To see
orIginally
we need tO
chaNge

not only archItecture
but the relatioN
of arT
to monEy
theRe will be too many musicians
to Pay

13 "All in all, the creative act is not performed by the artist alone; the spectator brings the work in contact with the external world by deciphering and interpreting its inner qualifications and thus adds his contribution to the creative act." See "The Creative Act," in *Salt Seller: The Writings of Marcel Duchamp*, ed, Michel Sanouillet and Elmer Peterson (New York: Oxford University Press, 1973), 140.

thE
eveNt
must bE free
To the public
heRe
As elsewhere
we find That
socIety needs
tO be
chaNged

I
thiNk
That
many of our problEms will be solved
if we take advantage of buckminsteR fuller's[14]
Plans
for thE
improvemeNt
of the circumstancEs of our lives
an equaTion
between woRld resources
And human needs
so That
It
wOrks
for everyoNe

not just the rIch
No
naTions
to bEgin with
and no goveRnments at all (thoreau also said this)[15]

14 Cage met American architect Buckminster Fuller at Black Mountain College in the late 1940s. Later in life, Fuller became an outspoken advocate of renewable energy sources as a means of accomplishing greater and more sustainable relationships with the planet and universe more broadly.

15 See Thoreau's writings on government, including his famous essay "Civil Disobedience," in *The Higher Law: Thoreau on Civil Disobedience and Reform*, ed. Wendell Glick (Princeton, NJ: Princeton University Press, 2004).

an intelligent Plan
that will hEal
the preseNt
schizophrEnia
The use
of eneRgy sources
Above
earTh
not fossIl fuels
quickly air will imprOve
aNd water too

not the promIse
of giviNg us
arTificial
Employment
but to use ouR technology
Producing
a sociEty
based on unemploymeNt
thE purpose
of invenTion
has always been to diminish woRk
we now hAve
The
possIbility
tO become a society
at oNe with itself

not just the rIch
of giviNg us
That
at thE same time
theRe will be too many musicians
to Plan
a sociEty
the eveNt
thE purpose
To the public
has always been to diminish woRk

Above
The
not fossIl fuels
we need tO
chaNge

the past must be Invented
the future Must be
revIsed
doing boTh
mAkes
whaT
the present Is
discOvery
Never stops

what questIons
will Make the past
alIve
in anoTher
wAy
in The case
of satIe's
sOcrate
seeiNg

It
as polyModal
(modal chromatIcally)
allowed me To
Ask
of all The modes
whIch?
Of
the twelve toNes

whIch?
renovation of Melody
In
The

cAse
of eighTeenth-century hymns
knowIng the number
Of
toNes

In each voice
to ask which of the nuMbers
are passIve
which acTive
these Are
firsT tone
then sIlence
this brings abOut
a harmoNy

a tonalIty
freed froM theory
In *chorals*
of saTie
to chAnge
The staff so there's equal space for each
half tone
then rubbIng the twelve
intO
the microtoNal (japan calcutta etcetera)
whIch?
as polyModal
revIsed
allowed me To
these Are
firsT tone
of satIe's
Of
the microtoNal (japan calcutta etcetera)

a month spent failing to finD
a nEw music for piano
haVing characteristics

that wOuld
inTerest grete sultan[16]
fInally left my desk
went tO visit her
she is Not as i am

just concerneD
with nEw music
she loVes the past
the rOom she lives works and
Teaches
In
has twO
piaNos

she surrounDs
hErself
with mozart beethoVen bach
all Of
The best of the past
but lIke buhlig[17]
whO first played
schoeNberg's opus eleven

and also arrangeD
thE art of the fugue for two pianos
she loVes new music
seeing nO real difference
beTween
some of It
and the classics she's sO devoted to
theN

i noticeD
hEr hands
conceiVed a duet
fOr

16 Grete Sultan was an influential pianist within Cage's circle. She introduced him to Christian Wolff, igniting a significant friendship and exchange of musical ideas, and Cage dedicated some of his piano works to her.

17 Pianist Richard Buhlig, Cage's teacher in the 1930s.

Two hands each alone
then catalogued all of the Intervals triads and aggregates
a single hand can play unassisted by the Other
sooN

finisheD
thE first of thirty-two etudes
each haVing
twO pages
showed iT to grete
she was delIghted
that was eight years agO
the first performaNce of all thirty-two will be given next year

she surrounDs
thE art of the fugue for two pianos
each haVing
that wOuld
showed iT to grete
she was delIghted
whO first played
sooN

aCt
In
accoRd
with obstaCles
Using
theM
to find or define the proceSs
you're abouT to be involved in
the questions you'll Ask
if you doN't have enough time
to aCcomplish
what you havE in mind
conSider the work finished

onCe
It is begun
it then Resembles the venus de milo
whiCh manages so well

withoUt
an arM
divide the work to be done into partS
and the Time
Available
iNto an equal number
then you Can
procEed giving equal attention
to each of the partS

or you Could say
study beIng
inteRrupted
take telephone Calls
as Unexpected pleasures
free the Mind
from itS desire
To
concentrAte
remaiNing open
to what you Can't
prEdict
“i welcome whatever happenS next”

if you’re writing a pieCe for orchestra
and you know that the copyIng costs
aRe
suCh
and sUch
take the aMount of money
you’ve been promiSed
and divide iT to determine
the number of pAges
of your Next
Composition
this will givE you
the canvaS

upon whiCh
you're about to wrIte
howeveR

aCceptance of whatever
mUst
be coMplimented
by the refuSal
of everyThing
thAt's
iNtolerable
revolution Can
nEver
Stop

even though eaCh
mornIng
we awake with eneRgy
(niChi nichi kore ko nichi)[18]
and as individUals
can solve any probleM
that confrontS us
we musT do the impossible
rid the world of nAtions
briNging
the play of intelligent anarChy
into a world Environment
that workS so well everyone lives as he needs

upon whiCh
It is begun
howeveR
aCceptance of whatever
mUst
can solve any probleM
to find or define the proceSs
of everyThing
Available
iNtolerable
Composition
procEed giving equal attention
"i welcome whatever happenS next"

18 One of Cage's favorite Japanese Zen Buddhist proverbs, it translates to "Every day is a good day."

The crowd applauds.

I have a tape recording of a piece that I wrote that was first played last November. It's called *Thirty Pieces for Five Orchestras*. I divided the full orchestra into five groups of between fifteen and twenty instruments so that the paper could become a canvas such as I mentioned here. Any mark on the paper became a sound. I then used a means similar to the means I've been using recently to make etchings. I found that a great difference between graphic work and music is that the vertical dimension in graphic work is useful for producing changes. For instance, if a template that you're using goes off the top, that can indicate the need to cut the template and produce two images rather than one whereas the same thing done in music would be senseless because it would only affect the piccolo. The important dimension in music is not the vertical dimension, but the horizontal one, of moving through time. And so, a template going off the side, either to the left or to the right, suggested to me the possibility of a different kind of rhythm than the template would have if it was not going off the side, that is to say existing in the space.

Existing in the space, it could be signaled by a conductor, whereas going off the sides, it could become metrical music, the joys of which Nicolas Slonimsky has already demonstrated for us. So, the *Thirty Pieces for Five Orchestras* combine the pleasures of metrical rhythm and what is now called proportional rhythm.

[Tape performance of *Thirty Pieces for Five Orchestras*]

ANTHONY BRAXTON

October 4, 1992

Thank you very much. I am very grateful to have an opportunity to come to the West Coast again and to have this possibility to talk to you about my work. I would, as far as historical background, go back to the '60s. My work is directly linked to restructural musics that opened up in the 1960s, especially the work of the great Sun Ra, who, in this time period, is very sick and many of us are wondering if Mr. Ra is moving toward transformation. He's given us so much. My work is linked to his work as well as the work of American master Ornette Coleman, John Coltrane, and Cecil Taylor. I also see my work as connected to the thrusts of trans-European progressivism, especially the work of the master Arnold Schoenberg, Karlheinz Stockhausen, and the American master John Cage, who has recently left us. I will never stop thanking the great masters who have worked to bring us to this point in time. Because of their efforts, I was fortunate enough to find something in my life that would become more than what I could possibly say. What I've received from the restructural musics of the '60s would set the tone and direction of my life and clarify my own balances.

Before talking to you about my work, I would first seek to describe it to you in terms of the definitions I have come up with in the past ten years. At this point in time, I have come to refer to my work as a tri-partial sonic entity that seeks to establish a context of architectonic reality, a context of philosophical reality, and a context of ritual and ceremonial activities. I've taken this route because, like the early masters—the early African and European masters from the mystic tradition—I would, after experiencing the work of John Coltrane, come to understand the early definitions: the concept of music as not separate from composite evolution, the concept of music as not separate from spiritual evolution. I would in the '60s make my decision to practice music as a life's work based on the dynamics of the '60s and what opened up.

What opened up? Well because of the work of John Coltrane and Cecil Taylor, we would find ourselves in the '60s with the possibilities to research and better understand new definitions. Here we are now eight years away from the next thousand years. I believe that the work in the '60s and the response to it in the '70s would give us some indications of the new balances of the next thousand years, a chance again to better understand the thrusts of the trans-African musics and what was opened by Charlie Parker.

As such, in the middle '60s I would, in the same way as Johann Sebastian Bach or Duke Ellington would, move to create music that would demonstrate a relationship between body and mind, spontaneity in the sense of improvisation and moment improvisation, and from that point like Bach and like Ellington, I would, from improvisation, seek to better understand recognition and the role recognition would play for better understanding the challenge of form in the next time cycle. This in my opinion was necessary because the dynamics of music and music science in the middle '60s would transport us to a very fresh place in time, one the emergence of computer technology and the new information would give us the possibility to think in terms of dynamic extended music logics. The question then would become for musicians like myself: what would constitute fundamentals of the next time cycle as it related to architecture? What would the new breakthroughs mean in terms of language vocabulary? What are the challenges of the next thousand years and how can we as musicians and composers move to solidify a base and an aesthetic context that can help us on the third plane (that being the plane of the individual), on the second plane (that being the community), and how we can seek to bridge the complexities of this time period and have our children understand the evolutionary implications of creativity and the role of creativity in the next time cycle, and finally on the first plane that being with respect to purpose and the ritual dynamics that underlie sonic fundamentals?

As such, in the middle '60s, after making the decision to deal with music seriously, I would find myself attracted to what had opened up in the middle '60s, that being the dynamics of collective improvisation. Not freedom. I was never interested in freedom or not freedom, but the challenges of the open space because of the possibilities of redefinition and reconstruction. As such, the genesis progression of my music would involve the work in the early period, in the solo musics, and in that context I would seek to, through improvisation, better understand what constitutes structural identity. I would look for better understanding of language and vocabulary. And by 1970, through improvisation and from that point translating that information into the stable logic context—stable logic being my term for notated music—I would begin to categorize the components of my system. I would take that approach because I felt that the next cycle would not be separate from the early cycle in terms of the challenges it would open up for the creative person, that is personal involvement on the third plane. I was only interested in self-realization as I sought through my work to better understand myself.

On the second plane I would try to, with my information, erect a context that would give me possibilities for understanding interaction dynamics as it related to the possibilities and the beautiful dynamics of communication between individuals. Finally, I would, in my system, seek to establish a context to better understand polarities—micro-macro polarities—in the sense that in my system I would define or come to recognize twelve states of identity that would not later be separate from the twelve basic paths in my music. I seek in my structure to establish a prototype that in terms of architectonic particulars would give a better understanding of interaction dynamics and structural dynamics in an extended sense as it could relate to the next thousand years. Also, I would seek to build a context that would give me the possibility to—like modern-day physicists—combine structures, combine logics so that I might have a chance to better understand the implications of structure and what structure could mean in the next time cycle.

Finally, in terms of the ritual and ceremonial implications of the system I've been working on, I seek in my system to develop a model that can give hint at the similarities which unite us as a species, that give hint at the oppositions so that a given individual in my system can find his or her own way. I bow to the polarities but in fact the system I seek to erect does not attempt to tell anyone anything about what they should think or what they should do but rather because I've only defined two-thirds of the components of my system—and this is consistent with a trans-African aesthetic position—I have with my system left room so that the individual can find something of his or her own in the system and as a result give me the possibility to better understand what I'm learning from the work that I've been doing myself.

So, this would be the background to my decision to become involved in the exploratory musics and more important, my decision to become involved in categories—looking for categories to better understand the context of structural architecture and decision-making on the third plane. I wanted to stay interested in my own music and as such I would in my system seek to build a model that would help me stay interested in my own work and help me find my way toward a spiritual position that could make sense for me.

Okay, today I would like to talk with you then about this tri-partial model and I would like today to talk to you about this model through the plane of repetitive logics—repetitive logics as a point of definition to understand form-building as it relates to this particular system. [Saxophonist] Steve Lacy says, "Well, you practice and practice over and over again and this is why repetition is so important." Of course, while Mr. Lacy will always tell us the truth, my decision to look at repetitive logics this afternoon would be so that I could give you some sense of how my system connects.

I should also say that, at this point in time, my system is comprised of 380 compositions which are cataloged into 169 structures. The uniqueness of the system, this being a tri-metric system, is that in my system the bass part in *Composition 63* can be separated from *Composition 63* and can itself become an orchestra piece. By the same token, a completed structure in my system is only complete in the traditional sense of I approach a composition as a composition but after the composition is finished then I use it for solo material. I believe that the challenge of the next time cycle will involve a more flexible approach to composition organization as well as interaction dynamics. And so, using *Composition 63* as a point of definition, *Composition 63* is a tri-metric structure that can be a solo piece—the flute part can be taken out and played by a sousaphone.

I have come to talk of this as a context of models like building blocks, where a given interpretation can be approached in any way depending on the needs of the instrumentalists, depending on the needs of the improvisers, and depending on the needs of the moment. As such, a composition that was composed that takes four hours to be performed can be taken and three minutes of it can be used. It doesn't matter. It can be looked at as genetic material based on the twelve components of my system that can be reordered to fulfill the needs of the moment. This is consistent with the breakthroughs of Duke Ellington, and this is also consistent with the breakthroughs of Ornette Coleman, Cecil Taylor, and the great Sun Ra.

The first example I would like to play you would be an example of repetitive logics on a solo plane. This example, in fact, is consistent with what took place in the '60s—that is by 1967, after experiencing the solo musics of Fats Waller, solo musics of Arnold Schoenberg—in particular Opus 11—and the work of Karlheinz Stockhausen—especially *Klavierstuck* 6 and *Klavierstuck 4*—I would make the decision to begin to investigate and look for the components of my music in the solo space, in the solo context. And *Composition 26F* would come about in that time period. I will play only a part of the composition and from there seek to demonstrate repetitive logics and the relationships between how I have come to utilize material in my system. This is in the language music group of structures, and it's performed on the alto saxophone.

[tape performance of *Composition 26F*]

The composition itself is made up of additive repetitive fragments as a point of definition to establish a sound space. *26F* would be an example then of one form of repetition. There are no notes composed, only a set of terms. As such, a given performance of *Composition 26F* can go for as long as necessary. I have tried with the solo context especially, with the language music context especially, to give myself those kinds of components that can challenge me as an improviser. I would later develop another context of solo musics that would involve notated postulations, and this would give me the possibility to establish a tri-metric relationship to that information. Later [in] the twelve language components of my system I would find the twelve related attitudes and states of character in the ritual and ceremonial musics. *26F* then would be one of the early examples of the language music studies, the language music exploratory possibilities, and from that point I would as an improviser see what I could find.

I should also say, before *26F*, before the language musics, I would try to give concerts of solo music—just improvisation—and I found that for the first five minutes it was very interesting but after the first five minutes I found myself repeating given ideas. It was at this point when I discovered that the concept of existential freedom might not be the most advanced state for what I was looking for. But rather than existential freedom I tried to look for those areas of unity that could help me understand what an identity state could mean. *26F* then would be the repetitive logic example of the language musics in that time period.

The next example I would like to play would be an example of a repetitive logic music in the second plane, that being on the plane of the more than the individual, of the group. *Composition 40O* is performed by four musicians. I didn't realize when I was coming that [musicologist and trombonist] George Lewis would be here, but the example I brought of *40O* would be the example that we did in 1976.[19] *Composition 40O* is a phrase-grouping structure, written in a time space of 10 1/2 beats. *40O* was conceived as a point of definition for an ecstatic repetitive state that would give interaction possibilities for the quartet based on the identity state of one phrase-grouping rhythmic component. And so, I would like to play part of *Composition 40O* as an example of the musics which, after coming through the solo improvisational dynamic, I would begin to forward that information. *40O* is notated, but in fact once the piece is played, we can take any part of it and a given performance of *40O* involves using the shape, working against the shape, taking out aspects of the rhythm, going against the rhythm, focusing in a particular register or with a particular timbre or even with one pitch. *40O* would open up for me many possibilities and, for the next fifteen years, I would become involved with repetition on three different levels: *Kelvin*, that being phrase-grouping repetitive logics; *Cobalt*, that being static sound block logics; and *Kauffman*, that being multiple repetitive logics. The example I've chosen to play for you today would be *40O*, phrase-grouping logics.

[tape performance of *Composition 40O*]

Okay the next example that I would like to play that continues the repetitive logic musics would be an example of the tri-metric musics from the late '70s. Tri-metric in this context would involve multiple logic situations put together. Multiple logics in this context would be the traditional terrain of *Composition 134*, which is a repetitive structure based on five pitches. In that context, I would bring to that *Composition 96*, which is a line forming structure composed for orchestra and four slide projectors. Parts of that composition would go into this structure, and also a tri-metric in *134* would involve the use of open solo, extended solo dialogue. *Composition 134* involves vamping material and, added to that, *Composition 96*.

I would find myself more and more fascinated by multiple logic situations—multiple logic situations having to do with different components happening at the same time. I remember John Coltrane before he died talking of his need for more and more rhythm. Even in that period I found myself trying to understand what Mr. Coltrane had opened up in compositions like *Ascensions* [Editions 1 and 2] and compositions like *Meditations*. Later, the work of Sun Ra—especially the concerts

---

19 Braxton is referring to the live album he and Lewis recorded in 1976 called *Donaueschingen*. Lewis wrote a brilliant accounting of Braxton and other experimental composers and performers in the Association for the Advancement of Creative Musicians (AACM) during the period Braxton is recounting. See George E. Lewis, *A Power Stronger than Itself: The AACM and American Experimental Music* (Chicago: University of Chicago Press, 2008).

in Central Park dealing with multiorchestral dynamics—would greatly affect me. At that point, I would begin to move in the early '70s to multiple logic situations as a way to understand what Mr. Coltrane talked about when he talked of playing in a "sea of rhythm." I found for myself, too, a multiple logic situation would give the kind of definition that I found that I sought in my music and yet at the same time the summation music would transcend any of the components in terms of the various possibilities for mixtures.

I would like now to play you *Composition 134* as an example of a tri-metric repetitive model and as an example of combination music. I will play maybe five minutes of this so that you can get some sense of the material and how that material is treated and also the open space implications of this particular composition.

[tape performance of *Composition 134*]

In the future, my hope is to create a music that will establish twelve tracks in great environments with musicians who are moving. Imagine a giant choo-choo train system with switch tracks where trains of musicians can come in, switching into smaller groups, larger groups. Imagine a music stage, like our country where there are large structures like Chicago or Los Angeles, in which its internal geometry is defined in terms of what that means for interaction dynamics and experiencing, as well as corridors of trajectories where musicians can come together and hook up. This is ultimately the kind of state that I dream about, that being a music that contains menu logics, where a given individual connects with the orchestra for maybe part of the time and the other part of the time that individual is fulfilling his or her own particulars in terms of menu directions that would involve connecting in to *134* in time spaces twelve and three. But in time spaces 5 and 8 you're on your own, and good luck.

The next example I would like to play for you would be *Composition 151*, as a stable logic model that demonstrates multiple repetitive possibilities. *Composition 151*, unlike *134*, seeks to establish extended time space parameters, that being in the same way that Saturn takes more time to circle the sun than Mercury, in *Composition 151* there's a dynamic of repetitive logic devices which are coming back quicker, repeating quicker, as opposed to longer time spaces. And *151* is constructed as a tri-metric model that demonstrates the twelve vocabulary components in a fixed time space scheme that is conducted. I have in the past ten years found extended structural time space musics to be very effective for the kind of musics I'm interested in. Extended time space models in this context would involve the use of extended notated music materials—given in this context to the three clarinetists—and they are able to use that material in any way, playing it forward or backward. There are repetitive signatures inside that material, and it is placed in the city of *Composition 151*; a given correct performance of *151* would see three clarinetists in costume with 27 positions of choreography. This will seek to fulfill the imagery of the Ashmenton musics.[20] The example I would like to play today would be *Composition 151* of the extended repetitive multiple musics.

[tape performance of *Composition 151*]

At this point in time in my system, I feel somewhat like a highway city construction person in that for the past five years I approach composing based on what is needed in the system, in the same way that city planners talk in terms of, "oh, we need a highway going from Sacramento to Los Angeles." At this point in my system, I approach a given composition based on what components I need to bridge given identity spaces in my work. As such, five years ago I began to work on what I would come to call the "C-class prototype" structures. C-class prototype structures are multiple cyclic structures, and I have found that this particular group of compositions can be very important for connecting given spaces. I would like to hope in the next ten years to concentrate on connector logic structures. I would like to focus more on song musics, especially musics from the image and ritual spaces as I seek to clarify and fulfill the mythology of my system.

The last example I would like to play—and then after that if there are any questions, we will deal with that—would be *Composition 158* as an example of the C-class prototype structures, the connector structures. I have chosen *158* because it's a multiple repetitive structure—multiple in the sense that *158* is scored for four musicians and the repetitive cycles for each instrumentalist is of a different time length. As such, a given performance of the work will see different cycles repeating, only this is in the mutable logic space as opposed to *151*. This is material that I use in the quartet as we seek to kick it about and also to always have a context that we can use for identity's sake.

[tape performance of *Composition 158*]

I was not able to remember to bring *Composition 95* (for two pianos). Had I brought that composition I could have played an example of the signature logic

20 Ashmenton is one of the twelve character archetypes of the Trillium Opera Complex.

musics—that is, *Composition* 95 (for two pianos) is part of the ritual and ceremonial musics. It serves as a password logic that would enter into one of the territories in the same way that we talk of, "you get on this road, and you go to Los Angeles, but you have to go through a toll booth," or something like that. For the kind of structure and structural materials that I've been trying to develop I'm looking for those materials which can synchronize events, those materials which can give polarities, those materials which can help me better understand the twelve tendencies of my system, and also what that information could mean in its most optimum sense to world unification and dynamic evolution.

I believe that the next thousand years will see many new projections open up. I feel grateful that I was able to discover a discipline that's never-ending where I can be a student for the rest of my life. I believe that if we are able to have some good luck that our country in the next eight years will seek to rebalance itself and reenergize itself as we seek to move out and fulfill the challenge of our species consistent with our ancestors and with the hope that we have for tomorrow for ourselves and for our children. My work is merely an attempt by a guy to stay in tune with music. The more I discover about the discipline of music the more I find I'm not interested in music. I'm interested in what's *behind* the music. I feel very grateful to have discovered something so wonderful and evolutionary.

There are other musicians, many other musicians, who are working on some of the challenges I've tried to define today. George Lewis, his work on electronics. David Rosenboom, his work on electronics. All these people are helping to change the next time cycle. Miss [Libby] Larsen—I feel very grateful to be able to see her again. This is a very exciting time in music, and there are many people who are working to fulfill the challenges opened up in the '60s even though it is clear at this point that no one is going to make any money at it. In a way, that's kind of nice because it clarifies intentions. You are doing this because you must be serious; there's no money in it.

Audience member:

You talked about learning from masters, teachers, other people. Where else do you look as you try to change and move forward?

Braxton:

I have been trying to better understand, for instance, the Ankh Valley African mystery system and the relationship of that information to Pythagoras and what the Europeans really got out of Africa. I've also found myself very attracted to better understanding Plato and the *Republic* and the foundation of what in this time period is referred to as Greek philosophy, although among those of us who care very much about this subject, we tend to emphasize the fact that the Greeks did not simply solidify our context of information separate from the world group. Their information has its genesis in world information. I have in the past and now sought to study that information because I'm very concerned about the challenge of dynamic spiritualism. Also, the work of Hildegard von Bingen is very important to me. And the work of [American–Puerto Rican doo wop group] Frankie Lymon and the Teenagers. I feel that that music is all part of our great heritage and I as a professional student of music try to study and learn as much as possible about my discipline.

Audience member:

I don't think it needs that much explanation. Music should talk for itself. I think there should be less explanation and it should be left to each individual to try to figure out what the music says.

Braxton:

I can relate to your viewpoint. If we were in a culture where it was possible, for instance, for most people to have exposure to the nonmarketplace musics, I feel that the music would carry its own weight. Yet because of the complexities in this time period, there is a need to talk about some of these things. I think there's a need to educate the public and there's also a need to talk about these things as we seek as artists to better understand what we're trying to do and also there's always a need for dialogue because as the students of the discipline, we have much to learn from each other.

LIBBY LARSEN

October 4, 1992

Anthony Braxton and John Cage are both heroes of mine, and yet when you hear my music, you'll hear a very different manifestation of why they are my heroes.

When I began composing in earnest, really studying composition, it was in 1973. I was invited back to the University of Minnesota by the physics department to teach, as a lab technician, "The Acoustics of Music," which I had taken as an undergrad just for fun while I was getting my degree in music. I love physics and especially acoustics, and so I was invited back, and I decided, well, I think I will study composition.

Why I am bringing this up is because—I think what will be important while listening to these two works that I want to present to you today is—for me, my work is as a bridge builder. It's a place that I have thought very carefully about and

FIGURE 5.2 Libby Larsen at the home of Judith and Ron Rosen, October 4, 1992. Musicologist and musician George Lewis (wearing a tie) sits before her. Photo by Betty Freeman, courtesy of the Los Angeles Philharmonic Archives.

decided to plant my feet there and build bridges not to the next thousand years, but from the last thousand years to the present day. Those bridges have to do with the fact that I believe that since 1970 there has been a revolution in sound and that revolution is over, and yet the instruments that I deal with, which are acoustic orchestral instruments, have not really taken part in that sound revolution except for in the recording industry. And yet it is the fact of this revolution in sound that is really influencing, I believe, a great disparity between the possibilities and potential of composition to communicate something about the world in which we live and the audiences who value listening to music in acoustic concert spaces and who choose to invest themselves and gain meaning through it. It's this disparity that I want to address with my music. And so, I thought that would be an interesting point of view to talk about today.

Let me talk a bit about the revolution in sound the way I see it and the effect that I think it is having on music. When I was in graduate school, one of the challenges that was given to me by my professors was this: if I was to receive my doctorate, I was required to study the history of tuning from Carthage to present day and write a paper on that. None of my other colleagues had to do that, and all my other colleagues were male. But I completed the assignment, and one of the things that I discovered was a curious sociological tendency—at least in the writings and the tuning systems that I could study—to want to evolve tuning systems which help [a] society explain its own sociological functions to itself. I discovered that it appears that the society evolves the tuning system, and it's the composers who define the possibilities of that tuning system ultimately adding, through their compositions, some kind of sense of order and meaning to the world of sound in which we live.

Case in point: In 1923, which is an interesting year for me because there were some landmark pieces produced that year, among them the Schoenberg Opus 23. Also, Stravinsky was, correct me if I'm wrong, but I think that was the year the *Pulcinella Suite* came out.[21] One of the great scandals in music history was that, present in that suite, Stravinsky used a nonfunctional, added sixth chord. [What] was accepted and credible in the classical music world of 1923 is this chord [*plays major triad*]. The added sixth chord is this chord [*plays major triad with added sixth*]. Now, just think societally of the difference when we hear this chord [*plays major triad*] and when we hear this chord [*plays triad with added sixth*]. This chord [*still playing sixth chord*] in 1923 smacked of what? Dissonance. Smacked of also what else? Where do you hear this? Jazz. And that's a sociological differentiation based on a simple arrangement of notes.

So, what occurred to me as I studied the history of tuning from Carthage to the present day, which at that time was 1978, was that societies need and evolve orders of sound, perhaps unconsciously, as one means of defining themselves. At the same time I was thinking this way, I was also studying Schoenberg and Varèse, an interesting pairing. Schoenberg of course was extending the possibilities of the twelve-tone system, the equal twelve-tone system, and was talking about whole universes of sound. Varèse was talking about the theoretical existence of an infinity of sound within the trajectory of sound—positing the fact that you can literally slide from one pitch to another for as long as you want and define the center of a pitch at will. Out of Varèse's work came many possibilities concerning microtonal tunings and all kinds of systems. We can think of Varèse as a person who is forecasting what finally happened by 1980—the evolution of electronic instruments which realize what Varèse was talking about at the beginning of this century. It was then that a society which was beginning to mechanize itself and was developing myriad motorized machines and vehicles, such as airplanes to fly around, a society that was really basing itself around the motor—and consequently around the sound that motor produces—*needed* its own, fresh musical vehicles to study and reflect upon what that means.

---

21 *Pulcinella* premiered at Paris Opera on May 15, 1920, and the suite was first performed in Boston on December 22, 1922.

As I was listening to the Cage [*Freeman Etudes*] and I was thinking of how marvelous it is in these etudes—and in all of John Cage's music but particularly in these etudes today—that the simple discrete detail of a quadruple pianissimo pizzicato was so meaningful because he was saying we can discretely listen to *this* sound as evolved on *this* vehicle, the violin. And I think at the same time an airplane was flying by, and it was a perfect counterpoint to that simple tiny pianissimo pluck. Of course, therein is Cage's genius, in being able to articulate to us the importance of our world of sound and to allow a person like me who was beginning to really study composition in the 1970s to feel absolutely free to incorporate all that thinking into my thinking.

At the same time, I also made a choice to create my own music as this bridge builder. I grew up in the Midwest and as such, much of my listening experience was not live, it was by recorded music. When I did attend live concerts with the Minnesota Orchestra and the St. Paul Chamber Orchestra, which was just beginning to evolve into what it is today, I really wasn't hearing the broad spectrum of music being performed live that I was hearing in other venues: the record player and the radio. And I realized that the sonic parameters of the music I was hearing outside of the classical concert hall were reflecting more of what was happening with sound in the world at large than what was happening inside the concert hall. And I thought about and realized that this could be a life's work for me as a composer, to try to build some bridges between 100 years of acoustic sound and the next thousand years of technologically mediated sound—because if we are going to get to the thousand years from now that Anthony Braxton is talking about, we have to have a way to get there. It's genius what he describes, and yet I feel feet in cement as to how to get there from here, you know? I listen to the music, and I think, How can we listen to this music next to Mozart? How can we build this context which is so important? And that's where I come in.

We're going to play two pieces today. The first one is a piece called *Up Where the Air Gets Thin*. It's for cello and bass. The piece explores the concept of what happens to sound when you're in an atmosphere in which sound waves can't be successfully transmitted. When you're above about 35,000 feet, if you're a mountain climber and you happen to climb that high, there are many reports of a person speaking a sentence: I speak to George [Lewis, seated in front of her] and he only gets a few phonemes of what I actually said because that's all the air can support. That's really interesting to me: the atmosphere and the way it affects how we receive sound. At the same time, when these instruments were developed—these vehicles of the bass and the cello—the rooms in which the instruments evolved were much more this size than they are the size of [the] Hollywood Bowl. I believe that societies evolve instruments along with the chambers in which to perform.

This piece is a study of the phenomena of sound in a large space and a high space, placed in the context of sound as it was when these instruments evolved.

[performance of *Up Where the Air Gets Thin*]

Just to relate back to this whole question of bridge-building and sound: I brought up the airplane drone for a reason, and my hope was that when you heard that opening note from the cello that somehow you also remembered the airplane drone and that you made a connection between this instrument and the sound of the instrument and the world in which we are living right now this very second—in a way that you might not have made if you were thinking about the cello in the context of the repertoire which is standardized for it at this point in time. It is the instruments themselves that a culture evolves to study the sound world in which we live.[22]

Another case in point. As a chamber piece, there's a great deal of almost improvisatory interaction—a great deal—which is written into the score. Since you don't really feel a 4/4 meter or a 3/4 meter, there's a great deal of give and take and breathing which comes much more out of a jazz and improvisation creative music tradition than out of the tradition in which these instruments evolved. At the same time, I had begun to study samplers which were just beginning to be standardized. What I was about to say too is that, to take this sound and translate into the larger vehicle of the orchestra is very difficult because of the improvisatory nature of these little tiny *sul ponticello* tremolos: to get a whole cello section to do that is hardly the purview of the larger vehicle of the orchestra and the way we evolved it so that it's meaningful. But now we can do that because now we can sample the sound (and pay all the royalties, and the copyrighting, give all the credit to the sound maker) but put it on a sampler and amplify that very soft detail.

And there's the possibility (I don't know if this will work or not, this is the risk) there's the possibility that those audience auditors—"artful auditors" is the way I like to speak of when I listen because I also am an audience member, an "artful auditor"—that those auditors who have been listening to sampled sound, to film scores, to music outside of the traditional concert hall, then come to the concert hall and can experience some kind of bridge to these instruments that they couldn't experience before we had samplers and the possibility of amplifying these

22 For more on the relationship between instrument development and cultural change, see Emily Dolan, *The Orchestral Revolution: Haydn and the Technologies of Timbre* (Cambridge: Cambridge University Press, 2013) and Thomas Patteson, *Instruments for New Music: Sound, Technology, and Modernism* (Berkeley: University of California Press, 2015).

tiny little details of sound. Then they come for Mozart through the sound, not through the music. It's through the sound of the instruments.

The other piece that I wanted to play today is my piano concerto which was premiered in both October and May with the Minnesota Orchestra last year. That was because we premiered it on the same night we got, I think, 39 inches of snow in October.[23] We were absolutely snowed out—it was the most amazing thing—we couldn't even get home from the hall. The whole series of concerts [was] canceled. But it actually turned out to be wonderful because then we had all that time for the piece to really sink in to the performers, which makes a difference and because of the way this piece is. This piece also talks about the development of instruments as vehicles for a culture to study itself. I think of the orchestra as an instrument. It's an instrument with an amazing sound potential.

Another thing my professors asked me to do was to also present a paper on the history of the development of the orchestra, which, again, proved to be instructive. It also proved to be wonderful in parallel with my history of tuning investigation especially in relation to the overtone series of an instrument—when an instrument plays a low note, it generates its own series of overtones. What's really fascinating is that throughout the history of Western music and tuning, societies have defined as dissonant the next available overtone, and then after about fifty years considered it to be consonant and then moved on to the next overtone as dissonant. So right now, in orchestral music we are up to—let me just play an overtone series: [*plays series of pitches on piano*] You would hear this, right? And from there on we get smaller and smaller, and we can't produce them on the piano. The history of tuning tells us that at first we accepted this [*plays fundamental pitch*], and then we accepted this with this [*plays first two overtones*], and then we accepted this, this, and this, and then this, this, this, and this [*plays successive overtones*] and then lo and behold, there it is the major chord. Then a reinforcement of the major chord, but then, and this is where our century starts to come into play.

At the beginning of the century, unless you approach this kind of a chord in a certain way, it was considered dissonant, but of course by now, it's considered pretty consonant. And what's considered dissonant [*continues to play highest overtones in the series*] is way up here. Now we have Jimi Hendrix and the electric guitar and samplers and the trombone; we can have glisses that go [*demonstrates gliss sound*]: which doesn't work at all on the piano, does it? And all of the nuances of tones within there. Now, why? Because a culture evolves the instruments it needs to study its own system of sound. With the sampler, the whole question of

23 *Piano Concerto: Since Armstrong* premiered October 30, 1991, with Janina Fialkowska as the soloist.

twelve-tone systems is a moot point because you can digitally divide the distance from this note to this note into an infinite number of fractions, so it's a moot point. It now becomes a study of social systems, a study of interactive systems, the kind of systems that Anthony Braxton was talking about. But how do we get there from here?

In my residency with the Minnesota Orchestra, the piece that I wanted to write was a piano concerto and the reason that I wanted to write a piano concerto was because, of all the instruments in this century that I can think of, that cross all the various stylistic boundaries and all the various cultural boundaries and all of the many boundaries we have cut out for ourselves in which to study ourselves, the piano seems to be it. I wanted to ask the question: Then, what is a piano concerto? This wonderful vehicle that evolved to study the piano studying itself. So, I thought what I would do is read you program notes and first I'll just read you the titles of the movements, because it's important.

This is a concerto, it's in three movements and about twenty-five minutes long. *Piano Concerto* has a subtitle: the subtitle is *Since Armstrong*, meaning since Louis Armstrong. The first movement is titled "Freely-Allegro-Deep Purple-Allegro-Funk." The second movement is entitled "Rock Dance." The third movement is entitled "Allegro-Chamming-Dialogues-Honky Tonk/Rag-Allegro-Raucous." I'll just read the notes quickly:

> Over the past few years, I have become increasingly preoccupied with the questions of evolved vehicles and the contemporary artist. What vehicles do we choose to transport the content of our vision? Which ones? Why? I have come to view the symphony orchestra as a paradigm for the twenty-first century. In this paradigm, we (audience and performers) witness again and again a large group of disciplined, talented, intelligent people coming together with the faith that through their combined efforts, led by a singular vision, they will produce and experience something of value. Value is a question of social validity. And it occurs to me that in the wake of post-1970s changes in sound production, the value of the orchestra concert as it was before the 1970s has changed dramatically. And while the vehicle of the orchestra concert and all its attendant forms, including the symphony, the concerto, the overture, the tone poem and the suite, remains of great value to us, the contents of the vehicle are in serious question. Should the musical language be tonal, or atonal? Does the question of tonality matter at all in the light of the synthesizer? Should the rhythm be Western or Eastern? And to whom is this question significant? Should the sound of an orchestra be purely acoustic? Or should we begin the task of incorporating an electronically treated instrumental choir into its body?

In my study of the history of orchestration, the percussion choir has evolved in the orchestra over this century. That whole battery of percussion that we all use—"we" being composers that work with orchestra—use either by not using it or by *really* using it, we use it. I think that by the end of the next century if we kind of evolve in the slow way we seem to evolve, we will have an electronic choir as part of the orchestra. That's the next step. Of course, that frees up all kinds of parameters for the composer.

> Do we compose the music of our time for minds and ears only? Or may we reunite the five senses in the listening experience? In fact, if we do not reunite the five senses in the listening experience, will we lose the vehicle of the symphonic concert altogether?

Case in point: If you go to a rock concert, one thing you'll find are subwoofers, which means the enhancement of the bass, a part of the sound. With subwoofers, you find a floor that is vibrating, and you find your feet vibrating. And it feels wonderful. You're getting a foot massage and of course the foot is where all the nerve endings of the body are come and are significant and you listen—we think that we listen with our ears and our brain, we also listen with our hair follicles and salivary glands and our muscles.[24] And because of the sound revolution this is more and more and more important, I think.

> I see the piano as the quintessential musical vehicle of our culture. It alone regularly transcends all the barriers of class, economy and religious belief in our country. Composers across genres have amplified their voices through this instrument in halls of all kinds to all kinds of audiences. It has been used as the purely essential contrapuntal-tonal machine in the music of the second Viennese School and its descendants. It has been used as an alternative guitar in the early rock and roll music of Chuck Berry, James Brown, Jerry Lee Lewis, et al. It has literally telegraphed cultural messages in the music of ragtime. It is comfortably as monophonic as polyphonic, monometric as polymetric, tonal or polytonal as atonal. It is a one-design vehicle with cross-cultural potential. It is so potent that many people own the most

24 Music scholars have recently taken an interest in the materiality of listening. See, for example, Nina Sun Eidsheim, *Sensing Sound: Singing and Listening as Vibrational Practice* (Durham, NC: Duke University Press, 2015); J. Martin Daughtry, *Listening to War: Sound, Music, Trauma, and Survival in Wartime Iraq* (New York: Oxford University Press, 2015); Martha Feldman, ed., *The Voice as Something More: Essays toward Materiality* (Chicago: University of Chicago Press, 2019); and Bettina Varwig, *Music in the Flesh: An Early Modern Musical Physiology* (Chicago: University of Chicago Press, 2023).

expensive concert grand pianos for the sole purpose of reminding them of the meaning of discipline. On the other hand, you find pianos in shambles in places where they are played constantly and jubilantly by people with no formal training.

My piano concerto is a bit like a dinner party. The guests at the table include the contemporaries Louis Armstrong, Igor Stravinsky, Maurice Ravel, Arnold Schoenberg, Jelly Roll Morton, and Robert Johnson. There are no singers, which accounts for the lack of women dinner guests. You are there too. After dinner, we pose this question to our guests: Look ahead to the last decade of the 1900s. Who is the soloist and what is the piano concerto at the end of the twentieth century? My piece, *Piano Concerto: Since Armstrong*, is the conversation which results from our question.

Now we can listen to the piece.

[tape performance of *Piano Concerto: Since Armstrong*]

Chapter 6

West Coast Undertow

Lou Harrison
Pauline Oliveros
Morton Feldman
Esa-Pekka Salonen

LIKE THE SOUNDS of the salons themselves, Betty's artwork spilled everywhere, including into the backyard. Just off the back patio and within eyesight of guests in The Music Room perched one of Claes Oldenburg's enormous sculptures of everyday objects. This one, *Typewriter Eraser* from 1976, sits on the corner of the patio and leans toward the yard, too tall to fit under the awning. The larger circular rubber portion, what would be used most familiarly like a pencil eraser to scrub out typed mistakes, is as big and round as a table. The feathery brush portion attached to the eraser leans and spills and arches over itself, like it was either caught in a current or caught in a moment of repose. Maybe both.

The eraser feels at home but also out of place here. By enlarging everyday objects into life-sized wonders, Oldenburg in part magnifies those object's eventual obsolescence (who uses a typewriter anymore, let alone makes a mistake using one?). In this imaginative display, Oldenburg's sculpture rhymes in a way with Betty's salons: they, too, feel bygone and of another age. Perched on the edge of erasure. At the same time, the very conversations churning under *Typewriter Eraser*'s unsteady watch were, it was hoped, changing the narrative, scrubbing and brushing away the encrusted aesthetic boundaries of another time and making room for their own story. An eraser, like a salon, can be both a thief and a builder of worlds.

The Music Room. Jake Johnson, Oxford University Press.
DOI: 10.1093/9780197775752.003.0007

Which brings us to the final chapter. This grouping of composers is pulled together as misfits, truly Californian in their adventurousness if not through birthright. These composers stand here as a testament that what Betty and Alan and others on the West Coast built pulled like an undertow—an artistic force working under the surface, largely unobserved, and yet powerfully in opposition to what seems matter of fact.

Morton Feldman felt the pull. And, perhaps more than most composers featured in these pages, he understood how much Betty's gatherings charged his batteries and echoed, as musicologist Ryan Dohoney has beautifully explored, elements of friendship key to his early career in 1960s New York. Feldman needed people. "For all its austerity, fragility, and abstraction," Dohoney reminds us, "Feldman's music is bound up with human relationships."[1] In 1986, Feldman was composer-in-residence at the California Institute of the Arts, known also as CalArts, which was founded by the Walt Disney family in 1970 as a space where "different creative disciplines come together under one roof, inspiring and elevating each other."[2] The same year Feldman was on faculty, CalArts awarded John Cage an honorary doctorate. Faculty and student composers from CalArts were frequently in attendance at Betty's salons, and Feldman's consequent proximity to Betty fostered a deep kinship between the two—he even appeared, as he does in this salon, on his sixtieth birthday, ushered into the room by the crowd singing "Happy Birthday" in his honor. The appreciation was mutual. As Feldman wrote once to Betty, "your letters are like a shot of vitamin D without the smog."[3]

Morton Feldman and Lou Harrison are the kind of personalities Betty most easily gravitated toward. They were not the wounded pups of the Harry Partch and Conlon Nancarrow type, but rather held a boisterous and commanding gratitude for the chance Betty gave them to do the work they loved. Harrison tried to return the favor. In 1979, Harrison built a large gamelan that he later named Gamelan Si Betty and the year before composed the beautiful *Serenade for Betty Freeman and Franco Assetto* as a wedding present for the couple. Betty adored him, and his appearance in her home spilled all over the house, with instruments and musicians lining the foyer and magnificently extending up the front stairs.

Pauline Oliveros, on the other hand, led the audience through a more intimate experience. Oliveros engaged the crowd in a tuning meditation before listening to some newer works on tape. For whatever reason, Betty did not often invite women

1 Ryan Dohoney, *Morton Feldman: Friendship and Mourning in the New York Avant-Garde* (London: Bloomsbury, 2022), 3.

2 "History," CalArts.edu/about/history.

3 Letter from Feldman to Betty Freeman, March 29, 1966.

composers to be featured in her salons. But those women she did support—most significantly Libby Larsen, Pauline Oliveros, and Kaija Saariaho, whose opera *L'Amour De Loin* was commissioned by Betty for the Salzburg Festival—remain among the more compelling and distinctive musical voices Betty ever surrounded herself with, which is, we might all agree, saying something.

While united by this proximity to cultural institutions in California, none of these composers could claim the state as the place of their birth. Rather, these composers represent, in a span of several decades and generations, the thrust of creative minds upon the West Coast. Lou Harrison was composer-in-residence at San Jose State University during the 1960s, and Pauline Oliveros—after leaving her position at the University of California, San Diego, in 1981—returned later to the West Coast as part of the San Francisco Tape Music Center and then as composer-in-residence at Mills College in Oakland, California. Esa-Pekka Salonen's position as composer, but also conductor of the Los Angeles Philharmonic from 1989 to 2009, similarly places him, like the others featured in this final chapter, in connection with larger California institutions. Salonen helped champion the new music scene in Los Angeles under the auspices of the city's most prominent and powerful musical organization. His dual role as composer and conductor also placed him and his interconnected networks of young and established composers on a higher platform than ever before. Salonen and the orchestra's development between his first appearance at Betty's salon in 1989—only months after being named the orchestra's tenth music director—and his last appearance in 1994 shows in this chapter the gains Los Angeles made in becoming a respected haven for new music during the period of Betty's salons.

His salon at Judith Rosen's home in 1994 was the final one. It is fitting that this book ends there, too. As Judith so poetically puts it in the final moments of the salon, *I think that's a wonderful place to stop.*

LOU HARRISON

March 6, 1983

I suppose there's nobody in this room, this is such a brilliant gallery, that doesn't know what a gamelan is, *Harrison announces*. So, I needn't demean you. Even though you may know what a gamelan is, you may not know the incidental fact that the instruments themselves are the gamelan. Gamelan really means "orchestra ensemble," so it's almost useable as "orchestra" or "ensemble." But the

FIGURE 6.1 Audience gathers on the front foyer steps to see and hear Lou Harrison's gamelan performance, March 6, 1983. Photo by Betty Freeman, courtesy of the Los Angeles Philharmonic Archives.

instruments themselves are the gamelan, not the players. The players come and go, but the gamelan remains, which is a new concept to the West, one that apparently fascinated Debussy. Debussy who said, "This music" (he meant Javanese music which he studied at the fair in Paris), "makes European music sound like a barbarous noise, suitable for accompanying a traveling circus."[4] That's rough, but that's what Debussy said. That's rough on some of us, huh?

Apparently, this is an English-speaking thing because France doesn't have gamelan, Germany has one and it's in Munich, a Balinese one. But the English-speaking peoples are acculturating to the gamelan at a bewildering rate of speed as a matter of fact. There are nearly a hundred gamelan in this country now. To indicate the concentration of them, Santa Cruz County (which is where I live) is the smallest county in California and has a dozen gamelan. So, you can get some idea for it. Young people are writing for it. I'm happy to report that older generations have, too.

4 Debussy's full statement reads, "Thus Javanese music obeys laws of counterpoint which make Palestrina seem like child's play. And if one listens to it without being prejudiced by one's European ears, one will find a percussive charm that forces one to admit that our own music is not music more than a barbarous kind of noise more fit for a traveling circus." See *Debussy on Music: The Critical Writings of the Great French Composer Claude Debussy*, trans. Richard Langham Smith (New York: Alfred A. Knopf, 1977), 278. Annegret Fauser writes more about this and other musical exchanges at the fair in *Musical Encounters at the 1889 Paris World's Fair* (Rochester, NY: University of Rochester Press, 2005).

FIGURE 6.2 Lou Harrison, March 6, 1983. Photo by Betty Freeman, courtesy of the Los Angeles Philharmonic Archives.

There was a feeling about the gamelan in the first generation that it was not to be touched. It was part of anthropological observation, but you couldn't touch the cultures or the music or anything like that. But some of us got bumptious and decided we would do it. I as a matter of fact got into writing for gamelan at the invitation of [Pak Cokro, one of] the greatest composers and musicians in Java who simply said at a cocktail party down here, "I would like you to write for gamelan."[5] And I have scarcely looked back since.

So, we're going to play for you first an opening piece which is *Jagung Jagung*, and I don't know what that means.[6] Nobody seems to know.

A woman standing near Harrison speaks up:

Cornfield. It's a pun on cornfield.

Harrison:

Okay, we're going to have some corny music this weekend. This is my assistant, Jody Diamond. Then we're going to go on to a piece written by Jody. This is an example of the spreading of writing for gamelan. This is a younger generation which

5 Pat Cokro is the familiar name for K. R. T. Wasitodipuro, who was Harrison and Diamond's teacher.
6 *Jagung Jagung* is a traditional piece from Central Java.

you can see. Of the older generation, we now have pieces by Alan Hovhaness for gamelan, two of them, by Virgil Thomson, one cocomposed by Jody Diamond, and I just received a manuscript from Mantle Hood, who founded the society, the Institute for Ethnomusicology here in Los Angeles, who imported the first Javanese gamelan into this country, and who held off composing for, lo, these many years.[7] Colin McPhee of course was interested, but he was one of the scholars; he never wrote for gamelan. But now there's a sense that we can do it.

And what's more, we can build them. So, [Harrison's partner] Bill Colvig can build everything in this gamelan that you're going to hear, with one exception: that's the gong which we borrowed from the *Gamelan Si Betty*, which is named after Betty Freeman. The gamelans bear names. This particular one you'll be hearing is the *Gamelan Si Darius*. With permission of Madeleine Milhaud [widow of Darius Milhaud], it is named *Si Darius*. The pelog section (this is half of the gamelan), the pelog section of it is named *Si Madeleine*. So, we've married them off. She's fascinated by this and enjoys what we do.

So I suggest that while we play *Jagung Jagung* you could perhaps circulate around the stairs and around in other rooms.

[Performance of *Jagung Jagung*]

Harrison:

Now, a piece by Jody Diamond. It is after the American folk song ["Wayfaring Stranger"] and called *In That Bright World*. She wrote it in '81. And now we also get a demonstration of singing in the gamelan. While we are rearranging ourselves, I would like to talk to those of you who are interested in intonation. This gamelan is generally a form of just intonation, based on 8-7-7-8. At any rate, it is a classic formation from the Mediterranean.

[Performance of *In That Bright World* by Jody Diamond]

Harrison:

And now something else of mine. This is part of a longer piece, a concerto for two solo Western instruments, which happen to go very beautifully into the world

7 The two gamelan pieces by Alan Hovhaness are *Stars Sing Bell Song* and *Pleiades*, both from 1981, while Virgil Thomson's piece featuring the gamelan, also from 1981, is titled *Gending Chelsea*. The piece by Mantle Hood was likely *Marta Budaja* (a work that Harrison had commissioned) which would be premiered May 8, 1984. Hood founded the Institute for Ethnomusicology at UCLA in 1960 and would go on to write several more works for both Javanese and Balinese gamelan.

of the Javanese gamelan. I don't pretend that this is any kind of native Eastern or Western music. Instead, it's a hybrid, which is the very best thing it can be.

[Performance of Movements II and III from Harrison's *Concerto for Violin, Cello, and Javanese Gamelan*]

PAULINE OLIVEROS

November 9, 1986

Oliveros:

Since Lucky [nickname of composer Stephen Mosko] talked about his name, I want to talk about mine. It's the only name I have—two names, "Pauline" and "Oliveros." The "Pauline" comes from my grandmother. It's a family name and was spread around a number of my female relatives and is also carried by my niece, so there's another Pauline Oliveros. The "Oliveros"—the ancestor Bartholomew Oliveros landed in St. Augustine [Florida] with Ponce de Leon and de Avilés, and so Oliveros is about the third-oldest name from Europe in the United States. I didn't find that out until recently, until I sat with a relative of mine in St. Augustine who was 101, Miss Nina Oliveros. She had a citation from Pope John because she had lived so long.

Anyway, Oliveros means "one who grows and gathers olives." The coat of arms is an olive tree with its roots in the air and there [are] olives all over the tree, but it's upside down. That, I guess, is my relationship to the field. Anyway, one more note on names. Something you might find interesting to do, I've done it on many an airplane, is a mediation on the sounds in my name and the meanings—all of the sound meanings and all of the letter meanings and all the ways the letter meanings change into more sounds. And so, I find that the name—be it Lucky Mosko or Pauline Oliveros—will have a rich variety of sounds and meanings and words, which resonate very deeply in one's being. I spend a lot of time thinking about that. Maybe you could take it home with you or play with it as I did.

I want to do three or four different things today. The first thing is going to be a piece which I hope you will do, and I'm going to play a little tape piece for you also after that. Then I want to tell you about a few projects that I have, and then I want to play my accordion for you. So those are the things that I'll do.

In California, beginning around the '70s, I began a series of work which I call sonic meditations. These meditations have sort of grown to number about sixty-four. They've been very important to me because it was a way of relating to people who were not trained musicians as well as musicians who had a great deal of training. The challenge was to find ways of making music with people without the training and also to make it interesting for musicians.

I'm going to ask Arthur Stidfole and Lauren Pratt, who are here with me, to pass out the score for *The Tuning Mediation* and I'll talk to you about it a little bit before we do it. Tuning, of course, is of major importance to musicians and it has many, many aspects. Tuning is not only just playing in tune, or tuning up an instrument so that it meets the certain expectation of a musical community, but it's also tuning to one another in an ensemble, tuning to the space you are in, tuning to life, tuning to the world, tuning to the universe. The metaphor of tuning, for me, has a great deal of meaning and, again, deserves a lot of contemplation and consideration.

In this little piece that you have in your hand now are some basics for me and for many. The piece has a history of about sixteen years—I think that I first thought of it in about 1970; I've done it with people all over the world in many different forms, many different occasions. I guess the most modest occasion was with about six people working together in a small room and the most magnificent occasion was doing it at the Cathedral of Saint John the Divine in New York during a festival called One World Music, and there were a thousand voices taking part. I realized when I decided to do *The Tuning Meditation* on that program that people were going to love to do it because everybody wants to hear their voice in a cathedral, especially [one] like Saint John the Divine because the reverberation time is so long, so you just want to go in and shout, but you're not supposed to, I guess.

A couple of things I'll say about it: the meditation begins with just listening and then it's a good idea to be very comfortable, to pay attention to your breath for a little while to see what it's doing. There's no specified time but maybe we should go for about ten minutes or so, and you'll feel the time when to stop. I'm going to ask for the lights to be turned off while you're doing this piece so that you'll feel less self-conscious. My role in *The Tuning Mediation* is—as I said, the olive tree is upside down—I'm going to listen, to demonstrate listening.

[the audience performs *Tuning Meditation*]

So, you may have noticed a few things in performing that piece. I, through all of these meditation pieces, have learned a lot about the structure and form of human attention. One of the things that you experience at the end of the piece was that everyone stopped at, it seemed, the same moment. That's the phenomena of group consensus. Some people think it is time to stop and others wish it had stopped long ago and there are some who wonder why it had to stop. That's group consensus. And it works like that all the time. It always works that way. I have come lately to think that one should overcome that, one should think about group consensus and try to be sure to question it.

Alan:

The interesting thing is how it all ended. I'm sure all of us were ready to start again but we hesitated because everyone else had stopped.

Oliveros:

Yes, and that's the question part, which is: could you go ahead even though everybody else has stopped? The essence of music, as far as I'm concerned, is leading and following. And doing one or the other but knowing when to lead and knowing when to follow. That happens in a little instance, and it happens in the big time as well.

I want to move on from these meditations now—I want to play a little piece for you that is on tape; first I have to refer a little bit to the San Francisco Tape Music Center. I'm currently in residence at Mills College at the Center for Contemporary Music, which, twenty years ago, I was the first director of—and it was [during] the transformation of the San Francisco Tape Music Center to Mills—and now I have the great pleasure of being there without any obligations. I don't have to worry about whether it works or not. I just have been able to be there and to make some music in a place which I had a hand in starting and I'm really happy that it's still going. A lot of people have benefited from being able to be there and being able to work there.[8]

I had a commission from the German radio in Cologne, the WDR,[9] to do a little piece for John Cage's 75th birthday, along with a number of other composers. I took the opportunity to make this piece, which is called *Dear.John: A Canon on the Name of Cage*. The reason for the title—it's kind of a play on computer terminology. This piece is generated from a program which I designed, a computer program. The computer program, each time it's activated, makes a new version of the piece. The piece is five minutes long. It will be set up in Cologne—hopefully we'll try to do it this way—so that a person could go into a room, there will be a computer there which they can type *Dear.John:* and get their version of the piece which is all theirs for that particular five minutes. The program that I designed uses the notes which are in Cage's name and chooses a variety of ways of playing it.[10] Without further talk about it I think I'd like to just play it for you.

---

8 For more on the San Francisco Tape Music Center and interviews with the composers who intersected with it, see David W. Bernstein, ed., *The San Francisco Tape Music Center: 1960s Counterculture and the Avant-Garde* (Berkeley: University of California Press, 2008). See pages 95–111 for an interview with Oliveros.

9 Westdeutscher Rundfunk Köln (WDR).

10 As in C-A-G-E, the pitches that correspond to the letters in Cage's name.

[tape performance of *Dear.John: A Canon on the Name of Cage*]

Before I play for you, I would just like to tell you a little bit about a lot of the projects that I am doing, coming up. I left the University of California [San Diego] in 1981 and I left with the purpose in mind of establishing a foundation of my own, a not-for-profit so that I could work out some of the ideas that I had. The foundation has come into existence, called the Pauline Oliveros Foundation (POF) and we hope it will be a magic dragon especially for some of the people that I'd like to involve in it. Over the years I have collaborated with a large number of artists and I have asked all of them to be artistic advisors to the foundation (that includes people like Merce Cunningham, Deborah Hay, Allan Kaprow, and so on—Jerome Rothenberg), because my collaborations have been with a variety of kinds of artists so I wanted my foundation to be an umbrella for interdisciplinary activity and also for a way for me to help some of the younger, more innovative artists, to work, and to establish a place for myself to do my work as I really like to do it. So, the foundation is established and among the projects that are happening, the charter of the foundation says the artists should be innovative in making original efforts and that they should receive state of the art support in technology and in administration. That's the ideal that we have, and we are working toward it.

One project is a film which is going to be a film about my work because I'm using my career as a model, not so much as what one should do but what one needs in a way of being supported. Because I was—going back to my roots in the air—doing things that are dangerous artistically and, on the edge, it's hard to find a place and to be supported for that kind of work. As you well know you have to have risk takers. If you don't have it there's a chance things calcify and don't grow and change and expand. That's what [the foundation] is for. So, one of the projects is the film which will, I believe, show a lot of the history of the connections and networks and things that happened in California, since thirty years of my career have been here. As Alan says, we go back to 1952–53, when the radio KPFA started in Berkeley and was a major force in contemporary music, and still is today. All across the country and the world, I found that there are people who are really very interested in what new things are happening and have very little way of finding out about that. Betty Freeman's work is certainly instrumental here in LA, and there are others everywhere I go, which is a lot of places, so I hope the film will show some of these connections and the way it works and then be a model for the way the foundation can work.

There's the project, which is the Artists Support Network, which will help distribute materials because one of the worst problems we have is we have products of our work over many, many years and they don't get distributed, so it's very hard and we're going to try to do something about that. Betty has her own distribution system here, which is very, very helpful, and there are many around the world that do that, but they need to be networked together. Then it's a very powerful distribution center. This can happen now because we have that possibility with computer communication.

For my own work, I have a project called *Echoes from the Moon*, which will happen in Boston in June.[11] This is supported through the foundation and is in collaboration with an artist named Morgan O'Hara. It's an installation, where people can walk into the installation, and if everything is working well, we'll have a homemade network of antenna which transmit the voice of the person in the installation to the moon. The voice will bounce around a particular crater in the moon, will pick up that pattern of reverberation, and then come back to the earth and be recorded. And then the person can take it home, having been to the moon.

The audience laughs.

At least their voice went to the moon, right? You can see an artistic realization of this. There will be a model of the moon so you can look at the crater and imagine where your voice is going. So that's one project.

And then I have a number of projects with a writer named Carole ["Ione"] Bovoso, who happens to be here. Carole is a wonderful writer, and we have a piece which is going to be called *Nzinga*, which is about a seventeenth-century African queen who became a king.[12] It is a play with music and with pageantry. Then there's a mythic opera concerning Io and Hera, which we'll be working on. Io and Hera do sing to each other, and they sing in such an extraordinary way that flowers just pop up in front of them, so those are a couple of the projects—the mythic opera and the play with music.

I now want to move on to playing for you. My instrument, the accordion—which when it's mentioned everyone's eyeballs roll around in their head. I want to tell you something about the accordion. I have a friend in the audience who will, I'm sure, verify this. One of the emperors of China was very enamored of the cry of the phoenix and he sent his instrument maker out to listen and he wanted the instrument maker to bring back an instrument which would emulate this cry. So, the instrument maker dully arrived, and he had a gourd instrument which had bamboo pipes. The pipes represented the wings of the phoenix. The player would play this instrument, the *sheng*, with breath. Inside of the pipes was a metal reed which vibrated. That principle of the vibrating reed in a pipe is the predecessor of

11 *Echoes from the Moon* opened at Mobius Gallery in Boston in 1987.

12 *Nzinga, the Queen King* was completed in 1993.

the accordion. It has a very ancient and illustrious ancestor, so I consider my instrument to be the Western phoenix.

The piece that I want to play for you is called *The Roots of the Moment*. I was in Israel in June for a festival, and I had the opportunity to walk in the old city for part of an afternoon, in Jerusalem, and I was to play that night at the American Cultural Center. And when I went back to where I was staying, I was just resting and meditating and I heard a scale, it was an eight-note scale, not a seven-note scale. This scale was very interesting to me and so I decided that I would play it that night. The title, *The Roots of the Moment*, came to me and I felt that there was something very, very special in the air there. Of course, the roots are there and the Mount of Olives, which I feel very close to. The moment is—when I perform, sometimes I make a piece at that moment, although the roots of the moment are very deep.

And so, I'm going to ask you to participate in the making of this piece in your listening and in your imagination. I've played *The Roots of the Moment* before, I've used this scale before, but the piece will manifest itself as it will here. I want to dedicate this piece to my former teacher and colleague who I appreciate a great deal because he taught me to be courageous and pay attention to my ear and rely on it. His name is Robert Erickson.[13] I want to play this piece with the feeling that anything of benefit in this piece, any vibration that is good, will go to him in support of his health and his well-being. That will be my purpose as I play today. One other thing that I'll say is that I like to listen with my eyes closed and I like to play with my shoes off and so they're coming off so I can hear better.

[performance of *The Roots of the Moment*]

MORTON FELDMAN

January 12, 1986

Feldman:

This reference to my New Yorkese and the New York raconteur psychologically is going to leave me speechless by my next birthday. I had a morning to reflect on *Piano*. Notice that the title is kind of Beckett-ese. It's part of a trilogy—I didn't realize it until this morning—of three pieces which capture the [Samuel] Beckett

13 Erickson, a frequent guest at Betty's salons, helped Oliveros found the San Francisco Tape Music Center.

mood, if only because he wrote the text for one of them. I was very fortunate that Beckett wrote something called *Neither* (like German "ie") or *Neither* (like German "ei"), depending where you come from. Then, there was a flute and orchestra piece, and then there was this piece. They're very involved, not only with the same atmosphere, but with the same compositional strategies, if I may use that term.

This piece, metaphorically, is a fugue. I'd rather think of it that way rather than just saying that I'm layering in some kind of a collage effect, superimpositions on top of each other as the piece goes along. I actually thought of it as a fugue. I was interested, being as I'm so nuts about the Stravinsky fugue in the *Symphony of Psalms*, which I think was the last great fugue written in the century. And I always wondered: is it possible still to write a fugue in some way or another? Not formally, but maybe just expressively in some way. All three pieces, including this, are involved with that particular idea. I think it was the only idea in the piece. [*Long silence*] That's not a silence, that's a cadence! [*laughs*] Thank you very much.

[Performance of *Piano*, circa 30 minutes]

Alan:

You talked about this as a fugue.

Feldman:

Metaphorically.

Alan again:

Metaphorically, okay. So much of the actual sonority is chordal. Is this a fugue that one follows the lines of in listening or is it a fugue for the eye?

Feldman:

You mean as opposed to say Beethoven's [Opus] 101?

Alan:

Or Stravinsky.

Feldman:

Well, that's another story.

Alan:

Yeah, you hear lines moving in that.

Feldman:

Actually, I don't want to appear to be pretentious, but I thought of the fugue in this metaphorically, as having expressive elements like you would find in a late Beethoven fugue—in that sense, that it was done for expressive elements. Not for architecture, or something like that. I mean, it's not really a fugue. You have to stretch it. It's metaphorically a fugue, obviously, but the layering of it, you see, is what interests me, in the bringing back of different kinds of materials. Very difficult to hear it. You have to hear it a few times, then you would hear these things.

Alan:

In other words, these aren't chords like a Chopin Polonaise.

Feldman:

No, but they're chords like a Chopin Ballade. [*laughs*] I think one can be both chordal and linear at the same time.

Betty:

How come it's never been recorded?

Feldman:

Oh, there are thousands of my pieces that have never been recorded.

Betty:

Why?

Feldman:

The record industry couldn't afford it! [*laughs*] Oh, I don't know. I got a million of 'em. I wrote three pieces very much of the same character. Then, it was really Beckett [who] took over. I was in another body in this piece. To me, there's that kind of didactic poetry that Beckett has. I kind of had to shake it off, and I immediately went into something completely different and something that I never did before just to get out of it. It was as if it took over.

Ernest Fleischmann, executive director of the Los Angeles Philharmonic:

What was the year of *Neither*?

Feldman:

The same year.

Fleischmann:

The same year? I thought it was later.

Feldman:

They're all the same year. The flute and orchestra—they were all done in '77.

Betty:

I was at the performance in 1977 at Columbia University. I was there.

Feldman:

That's right. That was right after I wrote it. Where was it?

Betty:

Manhattan. What's the connection between *Piano* and *Neither*?

Feldman:

They're constructed very much the same. And so is the flute and orchestra piece, very much the same.

Betty:

In what way?

Feldman:
Well, just in terms of superimposing things. I just brought more furniture into my work than I usually ever had before. I was just very interested in seeing if an extensive copying job will pay off to some degree. The piece was more a copying job than a composition really, especially in *Neither*. It just took me, say, four days to copy a page. I was just very interested in doing it. And also, there was another element that I never did before: I never wrote a piece with beginning, middle, and end. And I thought, being that I didn't do it when I was sixteen, or twenty-six, or thirty-six, or forty-six, I should do it late in life. That was exciting, just to approach beginning, middle, and end for the first time. That's why the ending is so long on this. I had a feeling that endings were always too brief in most music and that it takes a long time to get off the mountain, so to speak.
Fleischmann:
You set us up for the ending with this one.
Feldman:
But that's because of all the years I didn't work with beginning, middle, and end. I could work a little bit.

Well, *answering Fleischmann*, but I do that, I do that in all my music. Maybe it's to aggravate composers, I don't know. But I'm always interested to what degree a cul-de-sac, so to speak, might help the piece rather than destroy it, and I look for it in my music. It's one of the reasons my pieces are becoming so long is that I find another place and I go that way. But this piece is a very favorite piece of mine because it was very new for me to write, where a lot of my music in a sense, even when I write not something like it, but in the same world, perhaps five or six or seven years later, it's reminiscent. This piece, when I hear it, is not reminiscent. I think it's the one piece of mine that I actually refer to more as an object than the kind of music I usually write or that I'm interested in writing, only because of the beginning, middle, and end aspect of it.

I was also interested—and the reason I say a fugue—I was interested in writing a middle. After all, what is a middle in music? It's usually some aspect, you know, development, or this or that. And I was very interested in: how do you write a middle that doesn't sound like a middle? I mean, the problem with beginnings is that usually beginnings sound like beginnings and endings sound like endings. Some composers are great with beginnings and some composers are great with endings and some composers are great with middles. It's marvelous to hear these pieces—like Fred Astaire's "I won't dance, don't make me." Like, I won't begin. I heard a percussion piece by [Hans Werner] Henze start off and it's not like a beginning, you know. He's not going to be conventional and write a beginning. And the whole piece was like that.

It's very interesting that when I work, I memorize more or less the piece because my eyes are so bad. When I was a kid, the only way I could learn the piece was by memorizing it. I brought that into composition, too. I find, I always try to tell my students how they have to become familiar with the notes, that they should try and memorize. In other words, if you write a row, memorize it. So, in a kind of cabalistic way you could move it around like this and that, you see. I feel that part of the aspect of the piece is the kind of concentration that goes into the performance as well as in the composing of it because of that memory. It's hard to play unless you really learn those. You know, you just can't play it. You just can't fit it in.

But what happened was that—I was wondering when I was going to insult Boulez, but Boulez's copyist copied this and, in a way, she helped me out with this piece—what happened was that when she copied it, she put it on one line and it looked like a demented [Charles] Ives.[14] And I didn't write it as a visual aid, of course, but I wrote it in a sense so you could see the architecture and the terracing, so to speak. When she put it all on one line it looked awful. It not only looked awful, but it was not the right idea of the piece.

Okay, any other questions?

Betty:

Has *Neither* had many performances?

Feldman:

Neither dropped dead in Berlin some years ago. Very nice. The problem with *Neither* is that it's expensive to put on and when they put it on, they're sorry that they did it. It seems simple because it's only a one-person thing, but [it requires] a lot of rehearsals and things like that.

Musicologist Wiley Hitchcock:

Morty, is this piece published in the copyist's copy?

Feldman:

No, no! They had to throw it out. You know, they put a lot of money in it. No, it's in my copy, except it's printed.

Pianist Robert Krupnick:

The printed version is not as easy to play from as his hand, either. Much more difficult because they tried to line it up. The editor tried to count it, if I'm not mistaken, and actually tried to fix some things that Feldman had done.

14 Feldman's joke about insulting Boulez points to a sore spot when Boulez insulted Feldman because he worked at his family's coat factory until the age of forty. When asked by Earle Brown why he didn't program music by Feldman or Christian Wolff, Boulez responded "without any hesitation at all, 'Well, they're not composers! Feldman works for his family, and Christian Wolff is studying the Classics. They're dilettantes.'" See Amy Beal, "An Interview with Earle Brown," *Contemporary Music Review* 26, nos. 3/4 (June/August 2007): 350.

FIGURE 6.3 Morton Feldman speaking with Loren Rush over a bowl of Franco's pasta, November 3, 1985. Photo by Betty Freeman, courtesy of the Los Angeles Philharmonic Archives.

Feldman:

Well, they're going in different meters, Robert. It's very interesting. If it's going in different meters, it's polyrhythmic, obviously. Though it's not that obvious. But, when you line it up, it's polyrhythmic. Actually, Harrison Birtwistle learned from this kind of copying when he had [pianist] Roger Woodward do this piece originally. He decided that he wasn't going to line his up in a polyrhythmic way. That was for a clarinet quintet he wrote.[15] When the Arditti Quartet did it, he told them to *shmear* it up a little bit—that they should be exact, but not exact as they progress, you see. He learned that actually from watching the score of this piece. So, it's very difficult because, well, it's very difficult. If you want to really be precise you get into trouble, too. That's one of the problems in the sense that I learned from Schoenberg about the whole generality and precision going on at the same time in notation. It's very hard to know when to generalize and it's very hard to know when to be precise. You have to develop an instinct about it.

15 Harrison Birtwistle, *Clarinet Quintet* (1980).

ESA-PEKKA SALONEN

December 3, 1989

Good evening. This program starts with a series of solo works called *Yta*. It's a Swedish word; it means "surface." I'll come back to that point later. Anyway, I started to compose this series in the early '80s after I had been studying in Milano for about a year or so. After having returned to Finland I felt that in order to test, to try out new musical ideas I had in mind, I would like to write a series of solo works, partly because I wanted to write solo works, partly because of economies, because if you try out something and in the end it turns out to be a failure, the loss is small if you want to write a solo piece. If you write an opera, that takes five years to write and then you realize that it didn't work in the end. So, you know, it's a major problem. As a matter of fact, I was quite satisfied myself, at least at the time, when I completed these works. My idea from the beginning was to write a long series of solo works for basically every instrument. But, so far, I've only written three. The first one is for alto flute, the second one is for piano, and the third one is for cello. I have no idea of the fourth one. This might be the end of the series!

Yta means "surface." I chose that title partly because I felt that most of the solo pieces in the European avant-garde I had heard were too complicated structurally. Most of the composers I knew tried to create a multilayer musical texture and expression in their solo works. I feel that if you have one flute, it should sound like one flute. If you want to create something which is more complex, you take two flutes or twenty-four flutes. I mean, that's my basic idea about instrumentation. Also, it was a comment in a discussion that was going on in Scandinavia in the beginning of the '80s, when people spoke a lot about hidden structures, superstructures, and all sorts of microthings that one actually couldn't hear. I wanted to create a structure where everything was audible, and nothing was hidden, sort of an exhibitionist kind of texture.

Now, I'm not going to speak much about how these pieces were written, in the technical sense of the word, partly because I have forgotten most of it. But there's kind of a story behind every piece, except *No. 2*, which is completely empty as far as expression goes. *No. 1* is about communication and frustration in communication. One might imagine (this doesn't have to be the case) but one might imagine that this person, this imaginary person, comes in and uses a language that nobody understands, but it's clearly a language. It has its syntax and its idioms and everything. He or she becomes really frustrated because there is no communication, no sense of understanding. Then he gets stuck in certain syllables, certain sentences. We all know this situation when one has to speak publicly perhaps. Then, the language, the unknown, alien language starts to deteriorate. So, finally there are only onomatopoetic sounds left, all sort of dirty noises. Then, the language, which is music in this case, starts to come back. All of the sudden in the middle of the mess we would hear a note, like this, and then the music stops. Then, gradually the language comes back, but it doesn't help. The end is very certain hopeless. There's nothing more to say.

[Performance of *Yta I*]

The next piece is a piano piece, which is completely opposite aesthetics to this piece because I was very interested in all of the obvious possible things you can imagine, being able to make on an alto flute. Then, I felt when I wrote the second piece, something like a year and a half after the first one, that now it would be nice to do something beautiful instead, whatever it means. The piano piece is very static, although everything goes rapidly and there's a lot of notes played in a very short space of time. But my idea was like a little diamond, or a jewel of some kind which is not completely regular but reflects light. Then, you just take this jewel, and you just look at it from different positions. That's the piece.

There are some elements that are common in all these solo pieces. One of those is that every piece gets stuck on a c natural at some point. I don't know why, but it just happens. That happens in this piece as well. Now, from this piece, apart from the original piano version, there is a harpsichord realization. Now, we're going to hear a computer realization, which is interesting because I haven't heard it before. The nice thing about computers is that you can speed it up limitlessly. So, one is able to hear a real *prestissimo* for once.

[Computer realization of *Yta II*]

In a way, the cello piece can be seen as an extension to a piano piece by Scriabin that is called *Vers la flamme*. There is a story, I guess most of you know the piece, but it's a story about a butterfly or a moth or something, a little flying object, flying around a candle and gradually getting closer and closer until it burns itself in the flame, and that's the end of the piece. But my piece starts from that very moment, when it touches the flame for the first time because I felt that, what is there within this relatively short space of time, from the first contact to death? That is something that must be frightening and unpleasant, but also terribly interesting. So, what I did was I wrote a piece that sort of describes those events, but in a slightly larger scale; it's like slow motion in many ways. So, it starts off from the first touchdown, so to speak, and the rest is spastic movements. So, I hope you'll enjoy it.

[Performance of *Yta III*]

So, the next piece I wrote after this was for chamber ensemble and coloratura soprano. That was based on poems by Stanislaw Lem, who is a Polish science fiction writer, and a very interesting one as well. He wrote a book—I think it's called *The Cyberiad* in English—which tells about a posthuman era where all the living creatures are cybernetic systems, i.e., robots. There are two robots that decide to build a machine that writes poetry. It's meant to replace all the living poets because of cheaper expenses and much faster production and all this. I mean, we have heard it before, haven't we?

The machine is brilliant as such, but it has some initial problems. The first verses it produces are simply nonsense. The very first line includes elements that we usually don't use in conversation. You'll hear. The second verse is much more like language. There's less farting, less burping, but still nonsense. Then gradually the machine shapes itself up and ends up being the best poet [that] ever lived on this planet. My music tries to follow this kind of development. So, the musical language in the beginning is very simple, primitive. And, when the machine develops, the music tries to develop. When the machine finally reaches its artistic climax, that is a sonnet in the classic sense. So, my musical style has reached the peak of Western music, which is funk in this case. Unfortunately, I didn't have the text here with me. The singer is very good, but it's sort of difficult to understand what she's saying because she's very busy with notes. But I think you can get an idea.

[Recording played of *Floof*]

Alan:

Are you working on anything now?

Salonen:

I'm not writing anything at the moment, but I'm thinking of a few things. The next thing I have to complete is a commission for the London Sinfonietta. That piece was supposed to be performed three years ago in February, so I'm sort of behind schedule.[16]

Audience Member:

What is your instrument?

Salonen:

I play the French horn. That was perhaps my main instrument. Then I play the piano and the cello I play a little bit. I was a lousy cello player, but French horn mainly.

---

16 Salonen's *Five Images after Sappho* finally got its premiere with the London Sinfonietta on June 4, 1999.

Alan:

Do you find that as your career increases as a conductor, as you have so much more music to deal with, that it's possible to turn all that off when you sit down to compose?

Salonen:

No, it isn't, but instead what I'm trying to do is to learn how to use that. My head is like a filter. I'll just pick up whatever happens to stay in the filter and try to make a musical language that makes sense for me at least. When I started to compose, my aesthetics were extremely rigid in the worst European avant-garde tradition. But the more I have conducted, the more I have communicated with musicians and audiences, the less rigidly I think of music. So, I think in a sense my career as a performer has helped me.

April 17, 1994

Alan:

So, I suppose one of the first things that one must ask is: Is it possible to be a composer and a conductor?

Salonen:

Yes.

Shall I develop this answer a little bit? Maybe I should. In fact, the very idea of having conductors only conduct other people's music rather than their own is very new in the history of music. I do think [Arthur] Nikisch was the first conductor who was a specialized conductor who didn't compose. [Arturo] Toscanini was the epitome of a noncomposing conductor. And of course, [Herbert von] Karajan cultivated this idea further.

I think one of the problems in our musical culture today is that composers and performers have quite often alienated themselves from the act of musical creation. And therefore, when you go to a supermarket and you want to buy a Beethoven cycle, you see the conductor's name first or the record company's name first, then the conductor, then Beethoven printed in a smaller print. This is partly the result of this kind of evolution.

Now, even if you think of conductors like Mahler or Strauss—they are not remembered for their conducting, although they happened to be the leading conductors of their day. People like [Otto] Klemperer and [Wilhelm] Furtwängler considered themselves primarily composers. Now, this was an inaccurate analysis of the situation, of course, because generations after them have somehow valued things differently. But, if you would have asked Klemperer, for instance, he would have been quite adamant about composing coming first and conducting as number two.

I think we do have a lot of practical and technical problems about being a conductor and being a composer at the same time. One thing is marketability. In the eyes of record companies and the sort of standard classical music audiences, people who are strongly involved in contemporary music for any reason (but for instance being composers themselves) are slightly suspicious. I have seen this many times when a singer for instance who in the early days of his or her career sings quite a bit of contemporary music and then hits the big time, makes a debut in Salzburg or something—after that the agent starts pushing this person away from contemporary music because it's somehow dangerous for the reputation, dangerous for the image. You cannot be a matinée idol when you also deal with dirty things like Stockhausen and Boulez.

So, therefore, practically it's quite difficult to maintain a so-called ticket-selling power and a contact with creative musical minds at the same time. Obviously, we have to be quite clear about the priorities, what is most important. I think it is more important to be in touch with creative minds than to sell tickets. Both parts are necessary, however, but the priorities have to be clear. Then we have the typical problems such as lack of time and the peripatetic lifestyle and all that, but that's something one can overcome. So, the answer is still yes!

Alan:

If I can go on from that a little bit: what is the state of your mind after you've spent a couple of weeks or several weeks conducting music of other people? Is it possible for you when you sit down at your composer's table to wipe out everything that has entered your conscience and your subconscious during the weeks that you've been doing Beethoven, Brahms, and the guys?

Salonen:

That is very difficult. It's a question of temperament and character. For me, I find it almost impossible to do the two things at the same time, especially if I conduct music with which I identify very strongly. I remember when I was writing a woodwind quintet and at the same time, I was studying *Petrouchka* for the first time in my life for performances a month later. That just felt completely impossible because I felt very uncomfortable.

Alan:

How do you control that now? Do you set aside certain times of the year for composing? Do you shut yourself off from the repertoire?

Salonen:

Yes. That's the only possibility for me, to have a longer period of no conducting, no studying, no classical music. I do listen to folk music, ethnic music quite a bit. I do listen to rock and pop music sometimes, just out of curiosity mostly.

Alan:

You grew up mostly as a composer, as I understand it, in Finland—which is an unusually receptive country, it seems to me, considering its modest profile, let's say, in the cultural world—an unusually receptive country to the idea of composers. There's an enormous amount of support. There is an excellently functioning Finnish music information service that makes sure that people even as far west as California find out what goes on in that country. Does the receptivity of your own country, or for that matter of other countries in Europe, make a difference to you as a composer compared, say, to the climate for composers in this country?

Salonen:

I think I had a fantastic start in terms of teachers, colleagues, general atmosphere in the culture. The only criticism now that I can think of is maybe the certain greenhouse atmosphere that this sort of a culture creates. I never had to deal with reality in terms of ticket sales or funding or anything until I was about thirty years old. That came as quite a shock because in fact all my teachers tried to tell me to never think of anything else. Just think of the art. Complexity is all right. You don't have to communicate. You don't have to worry about the message that you're sending. You don't have to worry about the very quality of your thinking. This is not completely true, of course. I do think that new music suffered from this kind of attitude in the '60s and the '70s, especially in Europe. Composers lost contact with their audiences because of this completely hermetic thinking. But, even so, I'm grateful that I could spend my first fifteen active years as a musician in this kind of very supportive atmosphere.

An audience member chimes in:

I heard you on a radio program discussing the effect of cartoons and I think you mentioned Prince as somebody that you thought was very inventive as a composer. Could you amplify that a little bit?

Yes, *Salonen replies*. I think it would be only stupid not to react to what's going on in the world elsewhere. The existence of popular rock music is a fact, and also the success of pop and rock music is a fact. I don't think we win anything if we just ignore the existence of this particular area. I think instead what we should do is to learn everything that's there to be learned about.

Prince just came to my mind as one example of a composer/performer who has stretched the limits of his art and invented lots of new forms and new sounds and new kinds of expressions within his field. He's one of the few very well-known mainstream rock or pop musicians who really interests me from the artistic and compositorial point of view.

I can't quite remember what I said about cartoons, but everybody who has seen the classic *Tom and Jerry* cartoons from the '30s can remember the wild twelve-tone music, very sort of wild, vividly, gesticulating twelve-tone music that seems to go fantastically well hand in hand with the rather violent action in those cartoons. The sounds when the cat tries to jump over an abyss and realizes in the middle that the distance was too long, and the feet start going like this and then you hear this sort of tiny, tiny cluster. Somehow, it's quite brilliant music, very difficult to play as well.

I don't think of serious composers looking outside of just this small world, *another audience member speaks up*. It's important to me because, as a member of the audience, sometimes we divide ourselves and say, well you like jazz and you like rock and I don't like that and I don't want to hear chamber music but I'll go to the symphony. And if the composers can be that wide in their tastes then certainly we as audience should also expand.

Salonen:

You know it's not even a question of choice or taste. It's a fact, because we live in this kind of world, we live in this kind of culture. When I grew up, when I was five years old, the main influences were Donald Duck and Tom and Jerry and what have you. And that's the truth. To ignore this would be false.

Alan:

I think that anyone who's involved in so-called serious or so-called popular music these days who tries to maintain the idea that there's a barrier between them is making a terrible mistake. I notice that with some of my less fortunate colleagues in the critical world that they run up against that wall and they're not willing to look to see what's on the other side. I think that's especially [true] today with so much that is possible with electronics and with the circulation of musical ideas through the fact that you can produce a compact disc in two days, all of that really violates the whole idea of there being any kind of a wall. The wall is always a sociological rather than a musical phenomenon anyhow.

Salonen:

Also, if you think historically what in fact happened when Bach wrote his dance suites, for instance, he was basically using the musical forms that belonged to the realm of light music. This has been going on of course throughout the history of music until after the Second World War, when the isolation became a virtue in a way. Of course, it's very easy to understand why isolation became a virtue after the war because it was the trauma caused by the war itself, so the composers didn't want to have anything to do with the musical forms and expression before the war because that had led to disaster in a way. So, that was the reason behind the Darmstadt phenomenon. If you think of a composer like Chopin, how he took the form of a mazurka or a waltz and cultivated it into something which is beyond the very idea of a mazurka or a waltz. Stravinsky is a perfect example, what happened to ragtime in his hands, and so on. I think for those composers it was not a conscious action in order to break through a barrier of some sort because they didn't see the barrier in the same way as we do today.

The composers whom I admire are not all the composers who have been direct influences in my own work, but the ones I admire, you know, there are many of them. I grew up also under the very rigid serialist thinking, first in Finland and then when I went abroad to study in Italy and Germany. I went to Darmstadt in the summer of '80 when the Neue Schönheit (the "New Beauty") was just about to start. That was an interesting summer. I'm afraid I spent more time in the Bierstube than in the concert hall. It was an interesting summer, nevertheless. But then lately I've discovered a lot of things that I didn't care for earlier. I suppose that's progress.

Alan:

What do you do about influences from other conductors? What do you look for and what do you isolate yourself from when preparing your own concept of a performance?

Salonen:

We don't live in a vacuum, so whether you want or don't want to be influenced by the people that's not the point because you are influenced by other people anyway. If one starts preparing a Beethoven symphony or a Brahms symphony or a Schumann symphony or whatever, you cannot avoid the fact that somewhere in your subconscious or even your conscious mind there are models, performances even you have heard on the radio or on a record or in the concert hall or in a sort of funny Muzak tape in a department store or whatever. Very rarely is there a clean start. So, we are influenced by colleagues whether we want it to be or not.

I think when I was younger, I was more directly influenced by colleagues in terms of technique and things. Obviously, what happens when you're studying conducting, you sit in other people's rehearsals. Mainly that's where the learning happens mostly. You see people doing certain things with their hands and creating a certain kind of a result and either you like it or you don't, either you copy it or you don't. That's how it works. Now, lately when the technical apparatus has been more or less professional for some years already, so of course I still learn from my colleagues. It's more specific now. It's more little ideas and little nuances here and there. There are some conductors whose work I follow very closely, even on a personal level.

We are going to hear one piece twice, although in two very different versions. The first piece is called *Second Meeting*. It's written for oboe and piano. Then after

I'm going to play one track of a CD where the orchestral version of this piece is played. The orchestral version is more than just an arrangement of the piano and oboe piece. It's slightly enlarged and it's a little bit bigger.

Before, I might, if you're interested in hearing some little analysis, a little bit, I could give you some. Carolyn, do you mind coming up here? Carolyn Hove from the Los Angeles Philharmonic. She's usually the cor anglais player of the orchestra. Now, I'll explain the title first. It's called *Second Meeting*, therefore there has to be a first meeting. There *is* a first *Meeting*. The first *Meeting* is a piece for clarinet and harpsichord which I wrote in '82. I like to think in longer time spans than just one piece, so in '82 I also started a series for solo instruments called *Yta*, which is a Swedish word meaning "surface." Then I thought I would start a series of duos, for two instruments, and this series is called *Meetings*. So, this is the *Second Meeting* in that series.

After my very rigid serial training, I all of a sudden became interested in some old-fashioned musical phenomena that I quite missed sometimes when I listened to my own music. Variation is one of them, the technical idea of variation. Somehow, of course this is all semantics, but for me the kind of variation technique that composers in the Darmstadt school used after Webern was more metamorphosis than variation. You might disagree, but metamorphosis for me is something where the material, the code essentially remains the same, but the phenotype, i.e., the surface, the appearance of the thing, changes like a lifespan of a butterfly or something. You know, the genetic code is the same, but the various stages in the life of the butterfly are very, very different. Unless you knew the link between these various stages, you wouldn't actually know that they are the same thing. This is metamorphosis for me. Most of the serial variation is metamorphosis in the minds of the listener. So, therefore I got interested in the idea of variation where the basic material is always there so you can identify it throughout the piece and you can also follow the story as it were, what happens to this material and what is the result of a certain process.

In this piece, I did some very unholy things, like writing melodies. I wrote seven melodies which all contain a specific gesture that could be called a fanfare. There's a tiny fanfare in each of these seven melodies and also these seven melodies are interchangeable so they can be chopped up in smaller gestures and put together again and there will be a new melody that sounds roughly the same, but the fanfare sort of changes places. Compatible is the word, I think.

To Carolyn:

So, now do you think you could play just maybe this line? This is the first melody.

[Excerpt played from *Second Meeting*]

Salonen:

Thank you. A tiny fanfare, but a fanfare, nevertheless. Then, the second melody is here.

[Excerpt played from *Second Meeting*]

Salonen:

Thank you. An even tinier fanfare. Could you play from here? Now the fanfare is a bit more prominent.

[Excerpt played from *Second Meeting*]

Salonen:

Thank you. That was the first three of the melodies, so you got the picture I suppose. So, that's that. Then there's another thing which didn't strictly speaking have very much to do with the variation. I always admired the way Stravinsky builds up forms from *Petrouchka* onward. If you think of the opening scene of *Petrouchka*, you have a menu of gestures of a few bars each. The menu contains maybe six or seven elements. Then, he builds the form simply by building a puzzle, or as dominos. He can put them in any order and thus create unity, of course, because he uses the same material, but also formally very interesting things. This technique he developed much further in the *Rite of Spring*, of course. Most of the dances in the *Rite of Spring* are built of little blocks or bricks and used in this kind of way. What I did in this piece was that I wrote little musical identities, not themes or anything, not motives even, but identities, little animals as it were—*events* probably is the proper word—without actually defining the pitch or the rhythm terribly clearly, but [rather] the shape. I had them on little pieces of paper and then I threw them on the floor and started putting them in various orders. Then I picked up the ones I liked. So, the middle section of this piece is the result of manual work. Obviously, the material, where the pitches come from in this piece, where the actual notes come from, it all comes from the same source, the few chords I have been playing with since I was 20 years old, two chords in fact. I'll invent a third one soon.

Maybe I could describe these little events so you can follow the form better. One of these events is a sort of sea bird [*mimics the sound*]. That's one, quite simple. This is mostly followed by another animal [*mimics another animal sound*]. So, you have the combination. These are interchangeable though. Then, what else have we got here? There's another kind of bird.

To Carolyn again:

Can you play the double trill thing, one of them?

[Excerpt played from *Second Meeting*]

Yeah, it's a bit bird like, that too, *he continues*. She plays double trills using two keys at the same time instead of one, producing this slightly suspicious sound. So, it's the same pitch, but it comes out of different places at the same time. Hence the little wobble. There are a number of these little gestures than can be linked in various ways. I deal with the melodies a few times in various formations, then I leave out the melodic part and concentrate on the fanfares and take one fanfare and go through a sort of very meticulous compositorial process with it in the good tradition of masters. So, it's canons usually and the old-fashioned polyphonic things. Then, in the end the material is sort of all squeezed together, again in a very sort of noble tradition of classical music.

[Performance of *Second Meeting*]

It's a piece for Southern California. This is the sort of setting to present chamber music.

Judith Rosen, host:

But then we need one hundred rooms like this in Los Angeles, at least.

Salonen:

The reason why I wrote this for orchestra was that I always admired Ravel a lot. What I think is fantastic is his ability to transcribe his own piano pieces for small symphony orchestra without changing a note, really adding nothing, taking nothing away, and just writing it for orchestra and it sounds like orchestral music and not like piano music orchestrated. *Tombeau de Couperin* is maybe the best example, but also the *Mother Goose* ballet was originally conceived as a piano duet. There are other pieces, too. *Alborada del gracioso* I think is one. These are all masterpieces, real demonstration of professionalism in controlling the material, how to write for an orchestra.

Now, I thought it would be nice to try to write this piece for orchestra without changing a note. I didn't quite succeed, however. I realized that certain things needed thickening a little bit. The chords as you could hear in this piece are pretty much on both sides of the keyhole. That's how composers identify the middle "c" on the piano. Here, more or less like this. Eventually, the piano goes down here a couple of times, but mostly here because of the type of harmony that is identifiable in the middle, just in sort of close position, but if you spread out, the harmony loses its identity. Now, this doesn't work for an orchestra very well because you have lots of instruments who can't do anything and then some instruments who play all the time. Also, I realized that formally, because what happens when you write this kind of piece for orchestra the speeds drop slightly. It cannot go in this sort of rhythmic structure. It cannot go this fast. It's just humanly not possible and I knew that. Therefore, I added certain things to compensate the lack of speed. I added a little cadenza in the middle where the piece comes to a standstill, so I made the standstill a little longer and gave the oboe a little cadenza and then I carry on. But it's essentially the same harmony. The way I enlarge the harmony in the orchestral version is simply by duplicating things in octaves, which is also something I haven't done ever. You know, octaves used to be a taboo in my school and in everybody else's school as well. But now I simply did it and I even wrote my first c major chord in this orchestral version. It's very high up in the piccolo and two solo violins, so it's hardly recognizable, but it's there.

[Recording played of *Mimo II*]

Betty:

Does this piece have anything to do with the birth of your daughter? It's so alive!

Salonen:

Well, actually there was an incident when the material produced this little, very simple, Ravel-like figure. I was playing it on the piano for Jane, my wife. I said, "Can I write this kind of stuff?" She said, "Look, you're a father. You're a changed man. You don't have to be so bloody hyper all the time." The answer is yes.

Instead of themes, in my recent pieces I more thought about entities, identities, whatever you call them. They became like little persons or animals. So, they develop certain ways of behavior. This little animal usually does this kind of thing, and this little animal does this kind of thing. I'm working basically on the same material still and somehow, I hope that in a few years' time I know these animals so well that I can just let them do what they want to do and they make my music for me.

Roger Reynolds, composer and faculty member at UCSD:

You began with this notion of a duality between ticket sales and sort of following one's creative need. That suggested to me the idea that the materials involved in those two possible lives would be different, but as a result of what you presented today and what you just said, it seems as though a more likely thing is to consider the way in which the same idea can be restated or recast or rethought about or represented. I think back to some of Alan's questions earlier. If you think of the progress through their careers of two other composer-conductors, Boulez and Lutoslawski, it's very clear that their musical ideas didn't change radically, but the way in which they've decided to present them, at least in orchestral contexts, changed radically. How does your interaction with this monster change the form of the idea?

Salonen:

Boulez is a very, very good example because of the fact that he's constantly rewriting his old music. Now, the piece he's conducting at the [Los Angeles] Philharmonic, for instance, is an old piece which he wrote in the '40s—'47 or early '50s, somewhere there.[17] It was practically unplayable and the demands on the singers and the orchestra were just enormous. Even with an enormous amount of rehearsal time it just wasn't satisfactory. It didn't sound good. Then he sort of forgot about the piece for almost forty years. Then, after having been dealing with musical material every day of other composers and his own, he rewrote the piece, now keeping the same goal in mind, but having found the shortcut to present the idea. Now it's a perfectly functioning piece and very beautifully sounding piece of music.[18] I think we are talking about exactly the same process. The goal is the same, but how you get there varies. It varies depending on your personal orientation, from what angle you look at music.

I'm not terribly interested in what I seem to be, seen from outside. For me, it doesn't really matter whether I'm considered to be important as a composer or not because it's a need. I have to compose. I like to compose. I think it's fun. Having to be recognized as a composer is of course nice when it happens. It's not my problem ultimately. So, here I am, a conductor, music director of the Los Angeles Philharmonic, and I have the responsibility of symphonic music in Los Angeles more or less, completely. Of course, there are some other symphony orchestras in the area, but we are the only one who gives regular concerts and covers a wide variety of repertoire and so on and so forth. So, it's a very complex field because the responsibilities are very complex and toward many different directions. Primarily, I think I'm trying to keep classical music alive in southern California. To keep classical music alive is again a complex issue.

Audience member:

What is keeping classical music alive?

Salonen:

Well, making sure that it's not seen as something that has reached its peak long ago and now it's in decline, or to make sure that we are developing something, we are developing a tradition, we are questioning certain conventions, we

17 By this time, Boulez was a regular guest conductor with the Los Angeles Philharmonic. The piece Salonen is referring to is Boulez's *Le Visage Nuptial*, an enormous song cycle for soloists, chorus, and orchestra that Boulez continually revised for the next several decades. Boulez conducted the work with the Los Angeles Philharmonic several nights in a row the week after Salonen's salon appearance.

18 Boulez would continue to revise the piece. The final revisions of the work were performed in 2014.

are presenting old works in new light, new works in new contexts, and basically serving the dualistic function of a symphony orchestra, taking care of the tradition, of course, because we need it, but also taking care of the talent of today, both performing talent and composing talent. The complexity is enormous of course. But of course, since I am a composer—recognized or not, but I am a composer—my sympathies lie very much in the music that is composed today because it interests me and it excites me. And for me, it's the most natural way of communicating with the rest of the world, to deal with composers who reflect the world in their music now.

Rosen:

I think that's a wonderful place to stop. You obviously realize we could go on for about six more hours, I think, with this audience.

The End

"IT WAS GOOD while it lasted."

With those words, Alan Rich ended his introduction to his and Betty's *Salotto* book. By the time he was compiling their book there was little certainty this story of their salons would ever see the light of day. The series was long over, and so was their relationship. Alan and Betty had tried but failed time and again to get the transcripts into the hands of a public. What they wanted was what Betty's house never made possible: an endlessly expansive room with an impressively long guest list. We are all invited now. It almost feels too late.

The ending of Betty and Alan's salon series also feels like a poetic conclusion to traditional salon culture. It was already an odd pairing, salons in the age of MTV. Gatherings of this sort run perpendicular to the spirit of the times. After all, salon culture was built to host Enlightenment values and to spread awareness of an aesthetic style built for an audience, warts and thorns and all. Betty's home was instead the nexus of a musical culture that had long given up on audiences, on master narratives, on tradition in a most casual sense. Why salons?

Salons are about constraint and they are about mobility, to borrow a phrase from Stephen Greenblatt.[1] The fuel running salon culture's engine is siphoned from a constrained outside world. Unsovereign women on the outside became magically powerful and autonomous hosts inside their home. Closeted men at a salon can sit together on a piano bench and play duets, knees knocking and fingers

1 Stephen Greenblatt, "Culture," in *Critical Terms for Literary Study*, ed. Frank Lentricchia and Thomas McLaughlin (Chicago: University of Chicago Press, 1995), 225–232.

The Music Room. Jake Johnson, Oxford University Press. © Oxford University Press 2025.
DOI: 10.1093/9780197775752.003.0008

intimately crossing with a musical excuse for what is otherwise inexcusable proximity. Part of what makes salons powerful sites is how those interior moments of possibility eventually spill into and stain the everyday world with change. But that also means that once constraint is subtracted, the salon suddenly empties of magic and becomes simply another gathering—the wardrobe is just a wardrobe; the gate to Narnia has to be discovered somewhere new.[2]

One obvious constraint facing much of the music featured in Betty's home is the demand it places on the audience. This was an art that so often did not ask to be loved or understood. And to make matter worse, Los Angeles is uniquely a city that lives and breathes the plentiful and uncomplicated oxygen of entertainment. It was in 1941 when Theodor Adorno and Max Horkheimer, practically still unpacking boxes as political refugees from the Third Reich, got to work critiquing what they called the "culture industry" surrounding them in Hollywood.[3] Mass culture and amusement was for them an existential threat on par with the fascist ideology they had fled in Europe. Both represented thoughtless behavior. Both saw simple solutions to a complex world. Both were totalizing machines that could not so easily be unplugged. Only avant-garde music capable of withstanding mass commodification could yank on the cord hard enough to stop the machine's ceaseless roll. Within the thorniest of music lay a spark of hope for us all.

If Adorno and Horkheimer's *Dialectic of Enlightenment* failed to see a way around Hollywood's encroachment on American thought at mid-century, then West Coast elites were by the Reagan era shrugging their shoulders at the resultant depravity of California culture. The promise of radical futures and countercultural experiments eventually flaked off the surface of what Robert Fink calls the "resort archipelago" of the American southwest, showing that beneath its Endless Summer surface the birthright of the desert region belonged as much to the visions of Richard Nixon and Ronald Reagan.[4]

It was out of this sense of emptiness, vacancy, and rot that Betty and Alan formed their salons. These salons were, in fact, designed in some ways as remedies against what they and others saw as a fast rush toward insincere and disempowered

2 For more on the role of women in salons, see Rebecca Cypess, *Women and Musical Salons in the Enlightenment* (Chicago: University of Chicago Press, 2022), and Ralph P. Locke, "Paradoxes of a Woman Music Patron in America," *Musical Quarterly* 78 (1994): 798–825; for context on queer identities in salon gatherings, see Philip Brett, "Piano Four-Hands: Schubert and the Performance of Gay Male Desire," *19th-Century Music* 21, no. 2 (1997): 149–176, and Gavin Butt, *Between You and Me: Queer Disclosures in the New York Art World, 1948–1963* (Durham, NC: Duke University Press, 2005).

3 Max Horkheimer and Theodor W. Adorno, "The Culture Industry: Enlightenment as Mass Deception," in *Dialectic of Enlightenment* (Palo Alto, CA: Stanford University Press, 2002), 94–136.

4 Robert Fink, "On the Edge of the Desert," in *The Possibility Machine: Music and Myth in Las Vegas*, ed. Jake Johnson (Urbana: University of Illinois Press, 2023), 13–19.

art forms. Betty and Alan wanted California—home and host to so many musical visionaries from Charles Seeger to Harry Partch to Frank Zappa to Pauline Oliveros—to lean hard into its possible role in contemporary art and politics. Salon gatherings had invigorated Europe's Enlightenment and New York's modernism, so the two set up shop building a care center for the edgiest of music. They plugged in their avant-garde machine just five miles down the road from Hollywood's happiness machine and for fourteen years yanked as hard as they could.

It worked for a while. It was good while it lasted.

But even if these Beverly Hills salons popped up unannounced, tinged with nostalgia for gatherings of the past, and that they now recede further into a murky past where contemporary music was believed to be capable of defeating the powers that be, there may be reason to see Betty and Alan's work as increasingly prescient. Decades later and now with the isolation of a pandemic fresh in mind, Betty and Alan's salons feel perhaps even more cut from an irretrievable age. I wonder sometimes if salons are possible any longer or, if they are, what odd shape they are taking in their afterlives. Small rooms and intimate gatherings feel simultaneously triggering and idyllic to me now, and I'm sure to many others as well. I mentioned in the introduction that the simple act of gathering around food weighs awkwardly against the importance of these events. Now, it would take a good deal for me to leave my own small room and engage with others. I doubt our collective malaise and atrophied social muscles are helping build new pathways either aesthetically or politically.

To say nothing, also, of the overabundance of noise in the world since the advent of social media. Conversations such as those in this book are evidence that people once sought out and relished intimate gatherings. They sought knowledge, inspiration, ideas. They needed one another; they were not overly saturated with one another. Gatherings in this time were special, if not because of their everyday banality. Can we say the same for our virtual boxes and swipes and double-taps and scrolling?

The greatest constraint we place on one another today may be an inability to withhold. We know too much silliness about one another that the significance of one another often fails to hold our attention. Great ideas are too easily available. So too are bad ideas. If this book of stories about intimate gatherings serves as any kind of morality lesson for us today, then it may be as a reminder of a moment when ideas were important enough and valuable enough to be shared only in private. In good company. In a room to gather. With an invitation in one hand and a bowl of pasta balanced on the other. "What an honor to have this room and that music in our lifetime," as Alan put it so well.

This was how it was once done. It was good then. Maybe it could happen again.

Appendix

MUSIC ROOM PROGRAMS, 1981–1994

AT BETTY FREEMAN'S HOME

Beverly Hills, California

25 October 1981	David Hush, Earle Brown
6 December 1981	Pia Gilbert, Charles Amirkhanian, Virgil Thomson, Earle Brown
3 January 1982	Robert Erickson, David Raksin
31 January 1982	Philip Glass
8 March 1982	John Cage, Nicolas Slonimsky
4 April 1982	Joan LaBarbara, Morton Subotnick, David Hockney
7 November 1982	William Kraft, John Adams
5 December 1982	Janis Mattox, Loren Rush, Robert Wilson
16 January 1983	Steve Reich
13 February 1983	Rhonda Kess, Marta Feuchtwanger, Harry Partch film
6 March 1983	Dorrance Stalvey, Lou Harrison
13 November 1983	Mel Powell, Carl Stone
11 December 1983	Henri Lazarof, Rand Steiger
8 January 1984	Paul Dresher, Halsey Stevens

29 January 1984	Conlon Nancarrow, Nicolas Slonimsky, Eva Soltes
4 March 1984	Bernard Rands, Daniel Lentz
11 November 1984	Luciano Berio, Jack Larson
9 December 1984	Roger Reynolds, Harold Budd
6 January 1985	Terry Riley, Barry Schrader
10 February 1985	Morton Subotnick, Leonard Rosenman
3 March 1985	Andrew Imbrie, Louis Andriessen
3 November 1985	John Adams, Conlon Nancarrow
1 December 1985	Ingram Marshall, Henry Brant
12 January 1986	Morton Feldman, George Heussenstam
9 February 1986	Peter Garland, Charles Shere
2 March 1986	Milton Babbitt, Charles Dodge
27 April 1986	Frederic Rzewski, Ted Peterson
9 November 1986	Pauline Oliveros, Steven Mosko
7 December 1986	Steve Reich
11 January 1987	Gordon Getty, Fred Myrow
8 February 1987	John Harbison, Richard Felciano
3 March 1987	Pierre Boulez
5 April 1987	James Tenney, Brian Ferneyhough
15 November 1987	Ned Rorem, David Rosenboom
6 December 1987	Gerhard Samuel, Paul Lansky
10 January 1988	John Adams, John King
7 February 1988	Ed Applebaum, Rand Steiger
6 March 1988	Mauricio Kagel, Kraig Grady
24 April 1988	David Behrman, Mark McGurty
6 November 1988	Charles Amirkhanian, Malcolm Goldstein
4 December 1988	Frederick Lesemann, Daniel Lentz
8 January 1989	Tod Machover, Paul Dresher
5 February 1989	David Cope, Will Ogden
5 March 1989	Gregg Wager, Poul Ruders
9 April 1989	Laura Karpman, Kaija Saariaho
22 October 1989	Philip Glass
12 November 1989	Oliver Knussen, Janice Giteck
3 December 1989	Aaron Jay Kernis, Esa-Pekka Salonen
23 January 1990	Steven Stucky, Michael McNabb

11 February 1990	John Bergamo, John Naples
4 March 1990	Jacob Druckman, Sheila Silver
1 April 1990	Charles Wuorinen, Donald Crockett
9 September 1990	John Adams and Peter Sellars
14 October 1990	Anthony Davis, Frank Royon Le Mée
16 December 1990	Mel Powell
6 January 1991	Witold Lutoslawski, Joji Yuasa
10 February 1991	John Harbison, Chinary Ung
3 March 1991	George Perle, David Ocker
31 March 1991	Brian Kehlenbach, Gordon Mumma

AT JUDITH ROSEN'S HOME

Sherman Oaks, California

10 October 1991	Stephen Hartke, Carlos Rodriguez
1 December 1991	Silvano Bussotti, William Kraft
2 February 1992	Christopher Rouse, Olly Wilson
23 February 1992	Aulis Sallinen
17 May 1992	Pierre Boulez and John Chowning
4 October 1992	Anthony Braxton, Libby Larsen
25 October 1992	Mel Powell, Joan Huang
6 December 1992	Alexander Goehr, Joanna Bruzdowicz
28 February 1993	György Ligeti
21 March 1993	Voyager Co., Morton Subotnick, Alan Rich
25 April 1993	Roger Reynolds, Leonard Rosenman
16 May 1993	Shulamith Ran (in absentia), Steven Stucky
12 January 1994	Elliott Carter
27 February 1994	Bernard Rands, Augusta Read Thomas
17 April 1994	Esa-Pekka Salonen

BIBLIOGRAPHY

ARCHIVES

Alan Rich Papers, University of California, Los Angeles Special Collections
Betty Freeman Papers, University of California, San Diego Mandeville Special Collections
Judith Rosen Collection, Stanford University Archive of Recorded Sound
Los Angeles Philharmonic Archive

SECONDARY SOURCES

Agee, James. 1941. *Let Us Now Praise Famous Men: Three Tenant Families*. Boston: Houghton Mifflin.

Bachelard, Gaston. 1958. *The Poetics of Space: The Classic Look at How We Experience Intimate Places*. Boston: Beacon Press.

Barr, Cyrilla. 1998. *Elizabeth Sprague Coolidge: American Patron of Music*. New York: Schirmer.

Barr, Cyrilla, and Ralph P. Locke. 1997. *Cultivating Music in America: Women Patrons and Activists since 1860*. Berkeley: University of California Press.

Beal, Amy. 2007. "An Interview with Earle Brown." *Contemporary Music Review* 26, nos. 3/4 (June/August): 341–356.

Becker, Howard S. 1982. *Art Worlds*. Berkeley: University of California Press.

Bernheimer, Martin. 1986. "Boulez in a Basketball Stadium: Electronic Avant-Garde at UCLA." *Los Angeles Times*, February 13.

Bernstein, David W., ed. 2008. *The San Francisco Tape Music Center: 1960s Counterculture and the Avant-Garde*. Berkeley: University of California Press.

Boulez, Pierre. 1991. "Schoenberg Is Dead." In *Stocktakings from an Apprenticeship*, 268–275. New York: Clarendon Press.

Breatnach, Mary. 1996. *Boulez and Mallarmé: A Study in Poetic Influence.* Farnham, UK: Ashgate.

Brett, Philip. 1997. "Piano Four-Hands: Schubert and the Performance of Gay Male Desire." *19th-Century Music* 21, no. 2: 149–176.

Brody, Martin, ed. 2014. *Music and Musical Composition at the American Academy in Rome.* Rochester, NY: University of Rochester Press.

Brooks, Jeanice. 1993. "Nadia Boulanger and the Salon of the Princess de Polignac." *Journal of the American Musicological Society* 46, no. 3 (Autumn): 415–468.

Bunzel, Anja, and Natasha Loges, eds. 2019. *Musical Salon Culture in the Long Nineteenth Century.* Rochester, NY: Boydell Press.

Butt, Gavin. 2005. *Between You and Me: Queer Disclosures in the New York Art World, 1948–1963.* Durham, NC: Duke University Press.

Cage, John. 1969. *Notations.* New York: Something Else Press.

Cage, John. 1982. *John Cage: Etchings 1978–1982.* San Francisco: Crown Point Press.

Calvino, Italo. 1988. *Six Memos for the Next Millennium.* New York: Vintage.

Carter, Elliott. 1977. "The Rhythmic Basis of American Music." In *The Writings of Elliott Carter*, edited by Else Stone and Kurt Stone, 160–165. Bloomington: Indiana University Press.

Collins, Randall. 1998. *The Sociology of Philosophies: A Global Theory of Intellectual Change.* Cambridge, MA: Harvard University Press.

Crawford, Dorothy L. 1995. *Evenings on and off the Roof: Pioneering Concerts in Los Angeles, 1939–1971.* Berkeley: University of California Press.

Curry, Vicki. 2006. *Life and Times.* Segment 3: "A Patron of Composers." Aired July 14, 2006 on KCET.

Cypess, Rebecca. 2022. *Women and Musical Salons in the Enlightenment.* Chicago: University of Chicago Press.

Daughtry, J. Martin. 2015. *Listening to War: Sound, Music, Trauma, and Survival in Wartime Iraq.* New York: Oxford University Press.

DeNora, Tia. 1997. *Beethoven and the Construction of Genius: Musical Politics in Vienna, 1792–1803.* Berkeley: University of California Press.

Desantos, Sandra. 1997. "Acousmatic Morphology: An Interview with Francois Bayle." *Computer Music Journal* 21, no. 3 (Autumn): 11–19.

Dohoney, Ryan. 2022. *Morton Feldman: Friendship and Mourning in the New York Avant- Garde.* London: Bloomsbury.

Dolan, Emily. 2013. *The Orchestral Revolution: Haydn and the Technologies of Timbre.* Cambridge: Cambridge University Press.

Drinkler, Sophie. 1948. *Music and Women: The Story of Women in Their Relation to Music.* New York: The Feminist Press at The City University of New York.

Duchamp, Marcel. 1973. "The Creative Act." In *Salt Seller: The Writings of Marcel Duchamp*, edited by Michel Sanouillet and Elmer Peterson, 138–140. New York: Oxford University Press.

Eidsheim, Nina Sun. 2015. *Sensing Sound: Singing and Listening as Vibrational Practice.* Durham, NC: Duke University Press.

Fauser, Annegret. 2005. *Musical Encounters at the 1889 Paris World's Fair.* Rochester, NY: University of Rochester Press.

Feldman, Martha, ed. 2019. *The Voice as Something More: Essays toward Materiality.* Chicago: University of Chicago Press.

Fink, Robert. 2023. "On the Edge of the Desert." In *The Possibility Machine: Music and Myth in Las Vegas*, edited by Jake Johnson, 13–19. Urbana: University of Illinois Press.

Ford, Andrew. 2011. *Illegal Harmonies: Music in the Modern Age*. Collingwood, Victoria: Black.

Frisch, Walter. 1990. *Brahms and the Principle of Developing Variation*. Berkeley: University of California Press.

Gagne, Cole, and Tracy Caras. 1982. *Soundpieces: Interviews with American Composers*. Metuchen, NJ: Scarecrow Press.

Gann, Kyle. 1995. *The Music of Conlon Nancarrow*. Cambridge: Cambridge University Press.

Gann, Kyle. 2002. "No Escape from Heaven: John Cage as Father Figure." In *The Cambridge Companion to John Cage*, edited by David Nicholls, 242–260. Cambridge: Cambridge University Press.

Gann, Kyle. 2014. "Outside the Feedback Loop: A Nancarrow Keynote Address." *Music Theory Online* 20, no. 1 (March).

Garber, Marjorie. 2008. *Patronizing the Arts*. Princeton, NJ: Princeton University Press.

Glick, Wendell, ed. 2004. *The Higher Law: Thoreau on Civil Disobedience and Reform*. Princeton, NJ: Princeton University Press.

Glueck, Grace. 1977. "'Once Established,' Says Jasper Johns, 'Ideas Can Be Discarded.'" *New York Times*, October 16.

Goodman, Dena. 1994. *The Republic of Letters: A Cultural History of the French Enlightenment*. Ithaca, NY: Cornell University Press.

Greenblatt, Stephen. 1995. "Culture." In *Critical Terms for Literary Study*, edited by Frank Lentricchia and Thomas McLaughlin, 225–232. Chicago: University of Chicago Press.

Heller, Michael C. 2016. *Loft Jazz: Improvising New York in the 1970s*. Berkeley: University of California Press.

Henderson, W. J. 1912. *The Soul of a Tenor: A Romance*. New York: Henry Holt.

Herzogenrath, Wulf, and Andreas Kreul, eds. 2002. *Sounds of the Inner Eye: John Cage, Mark Tobey, Morris Graves*. Seattle: University of Washington Press.

Hicks, Michael. 1991. "The Imprisonment of Henry Cowell." *Journal of the American Musicological Society* 44, no. 1 (Spring): 92–119.

Hodder, Ian. 2012. *Entangled: An Archaeology of the Relationship between Humans and Things*. Hoboken, NJ: John Wiley and Sons.

Horkheimer, Max, and Theodor W. Adorno. 2002. "The Culture Industry: Enlightenment as Mass Deception." In *Dialectic of Enlightenment*, 41–72. Palo Alto, CA: Stanford University Press.

Iverson, Jennifer. 2018. *Electronic Inspirations: Technologies of the Cold War Musical Avant-Garde*. New York: Oxford University Press.

Jepson, Barbara. 1987. "A Cultivated Ear: Betty Freeman's Living Room Is the West Coast's Center for New Music." *Connoisseur* (February).

Johnson, Jake. 2014. "Two Studies of Harry Partch: Conversations with Danlee Mitchell and Betty Freeman." *Echo: A Music-Centered Journal* 12, no. 1. https://echo.humspace.ucla.edu/issues/two-studies-of-harry-partch-conversations-with-danlee-mitchell-and-betty-freeman/.

Lasar, Michael. 2000. *Pacifica Radio: The Rise of an Alternative Network*. Philadelphia, PA: Temple University Press.

Levy, Beth. 2001. "'The White Hope of American Music'; or, How Roy Harris Became Western." *American Music* 19, no. 2 (Summer): 131–167.

Lewis, George E. 2008. *A Power Stronger than Itself: The AACM and American Experimental Music*. Chicago: University of Chicago Press.

Locke, Ralph P. 1994. "Paradoxes of a Woman Music Patron in America." *Musical Quarterly* 78:798–825.

Matthews, M. V. 1963. "The Digital Computer as a Musical Instrument." *Science* 142, no. 3592 (November 1): 553–557.

McLuhan, Marshall. 1964. *Understanding Media: The Extensions of Man*. Cambridge, MA: MIT Press.

Nyman, Michael, and Wim Mertens. 1983. *American Minimal Music*. London: Kahn & Averill.

O'Brien, Kerry, and William Robin. 2023. *On Minimalism: Documenting a Musical Movement*. Berkeley: University of California Press.

Patteson, Thomas. 2015. *Instruments for New Music: Sound, Technology, and Modernism*. Berkeley: University of California Press.

Reidy, Brent. 2010. "Our Memory of What Happened Is Not What Happened: Cage, Metaphor, and Myth." *American Music* 28, no. 2 (Summer): 211–227.

Risset, Jean-Claude. 1991. "Some Comments about Future Music Machines." *Computer Music Journal* 15, no. 4 (Winter): 32–36.

Robin, William. 2021. *Industry: Bang on a Can and New Music in the Marketplace*. New York: Oxford University Press.

Rondeau, James, and Sheena Wagstaff. 2012. *Roy Lichtenstein: A Retrospective*. Chicago: Art Institute of Chicago.

Rousseau, Jean-Jacques. 1968. *Politics and the Arts: Letter to M.d' Alembert on the Theatre*. Edited and translated by Allan Bloom. Ithaca, NY: Cornell University Press.

Shaw-Miller, Simon. 2002. "'Out of Tune': Hauer's Legacy and the Aesthetics of Minimalism in Art and Music." In *Visible Deeds of Music: Art and Music from Wagner to Cage*, 163–207. New Haven, CT: Yale University Press.

Slonimsky, Nicolas. 1951. "Complicated Problem—Drastic Solution." *Christian Science Monitor*, November 10.

Smith, Catherine Parsons. 2007. *Making Music in Los Angeles: Transforming the Popular*. Berkeley: University of California Press.

Smith, Richard Langham, trans. 1977. *Debussy on Music: The Critical Writings of the Great French Composer Claude Debussy*. New York: Alfred A. Knopf.

Stojanovic-Novicic, Dragana. 2011. "The Carter-Nancarrow Correspondence." *American Music* 29, no. 1 (Spring): 64–84.

Taub, Robert. 1992. *Milton Babbitt: Piano Works*. Arles, France: Harmonia Mundi.

Torrey, Bradford, ed. 1906. *The Writings of Henry David Thoreau*. New York: Houghton Mifflin.

Uy, Michael. 2020. *Ask the Experts: How Ford, Rockefeller, and the NEA Changed American Music*. New York: Oxford University Press.

Varwig, Bettina. 2023. *Music in the Flesh: An EARLY Modern Musical Physiology*. Chicago: University of Chicago Press.

Wolff, Christoph. 2005. "A Bach Cult in Late Eighteenth-Century Berlin: Sara Levy's Musical Salon." *Bulletin of the American Academy of Arts and Sciences* 58, no. 3 (Spring): 26–31.

Yang, Mina. 2008. *California Polyphony: Ethnic Voices, Musical Crossroads*. Urbana: University of Illinois Press.

INDEX

For the benefit of digital users, indexed terms that span two pages (e.g., 52–53) may, on occasion, appear on only one of those pages.

*Figures are indicated by an italic *f* following the page numbers*

www.ingramcontent.com/pod-product-compliance
Lightning Source LLC
Chambersburg PA
CBHW030022300825
31867CB00021B/673
* 9 7 8 0 1 9 7 7 7 5 7 2 1 *